AF712248

The *Lochner* Court, Myth and Reality

The *Lochner* Court, Myth and Reality

Substantive Due Process from the 1890s to the 1930s

MICHAEL J. PHILLIPS

PRAEGER

Westport, Connecticut
London

Library of Congress Cataloging-in-Publication Data

Phillips, Michael J.
The Lochner court, myth and reality : substantive due process from the 1890s to the 1930s / by Michael J. Phillips.
p. cm.
Includes bibliographical references and index.
ISBN 0–275–96930–4 (alk. paper)
1. Due process of law—United States—History. I. Title.
KF4765.P48 2001
347.73'5—dc21 00–029848

British Library Cataloguing in Publication Data is available.

Copyright © 2001 by Michael J. Phillips

All rights reserved. No portion of this book may be reproduced, by any process or technique, without the express written consent of the publisher.

Library of Congress Catalog Card Number: 00–029848
ISBN: 0–275–96930–4

First published in 2001

Praeger Publishers, 88 Post Road West, Westport, CT 06881
An imprint of Greenwood Publishing Group, Inc.
www.praeger.com

Printed in the United States of America

The paper used in this book complies with the Permanent Paper Standard issued by the National Information Standards Organization (Z39.48–1984).

10 9 8 7 6 5 4 3 2 1

Contents

Preface

Late in the 1980s, I wrote a fairly conventional article on the substantive due process decisions of the so-called *Lochner* Court. The reference, of course, is to the U.S. Supreme Court's 1905 decision in *Lochner v. New York*,[1] in which it struck down a New York maximum hours law on due process grounds. For the most part, the article focused on *Lochner* itself and on the twenty or so other decisions that are widely thought to exemplify the old Court of the 1890s through the mid-1930s. The experience left me with some lingering questions. What else was back there? That is, what were the *Lochner* Court's other substantive due process decisions like? How many of them were there? How many times did the Court *uphold* government action that was challenged on substantive due process grounds?

For some time, there has been a rough consensus on the answers to these questions. The old Court, says the consensus, used due process to strike down substantive government action on about 200 occasions. Central to these cases was freedom of contract's insertion within the "liberty" protected by the Fifth and Fourteenth Amendments' due process clauses. Although it is not explicit on the point, the consensus suggests that, like the twenty or so exemplary decisions it does discuss, most of these 200 cases involved Progressive social legislation intended to protect economically powerless people against the vicissitudes of industrialization and the depredations of big business. However, the consensus concedes that the old Court rejected more substantive due process challenges than it granted, although the degree to which that was true is unclear.

Accompanying this standard descriptive picture of *Lochner*-era substantive due process is a normative critique. Today, few people embrace all of its components. The first strand in the critique, one now enunciated primarily by conservatives, is the familiar charge that because due process is procedural alone, the old Court usurped powers that properly reside with legislatures. The critique's second and third strands each depend on a common perception. This is the belief that the social legislation the old Court struck down was necessary to correct for inequalities in bargaining power between corporations and isolated, relatively powerless individuals. Because such laws restricted freedom of contract, they were vulnerable to a substantive due process attack, and all too often such attacks succeeded. When that happened, the Court effectively ratified a preexisting inequality in the private sphere. By doing so, it aided business. On one view of the matter, this unfortunate result was due to the justices' sincere, if unintelligent, nostalgia for a laissez-faire world that no longer existed. According to the critique's third strand, however, the justices knew exactly what they were doing when they concocted economic substantive due process. Almost always exempted from all these charges, finally, are certain justices who saw *Lochner*-era substantive due process for what it was and invariably dissented from the cases in which it was applied. The main examples, of course, are Holmes and Brandeis.

Some time in the mid-1990s, I began to scratch the itch described earlier. The result was a series of law journal articles on the *Lochner* Court and ultimately this book. Chapter 1 states in much more detail the standard descriptive picture and normative critique that I have just sketched. Chapter 2 lays out the results of my investigations, which as far as I know are more complete than any attempted to date.[2] My findings depart significantly from the standard picture. The old Court struck down nothing like 200 laws on substantive due process grounds; it rejected far more substantive due process claims than it granted; many of the measures it did strike down cannot be described as social legislation; and Holmes and Brandeis joined many of the cases in which their conservative brethren used substantive due process to overturn government action. Last, but not least, freedom of contract's insertion within Fifth and Fourteenth Amendment liberty was only one application of *Lochner*-era substantive due process—and not its most important application either.

These findings obviously have implications for the normative critique of *Lochner*-era substantive due process, and the remainder of the book explores those implications while critiquing the critique on other grounds as well. Chapter 3 debunks the idea that the old Court acted as business's agent when it used substantive due process to scrutinize government action. Chapter 4 addresses the question of unequal bargaining power. Turning from the old Court's liberal critics to its modern conservative foes, Chapter 5 examines the charge that *Lochner*-era substantive due process was an illegitimate assertion of judicial power. Chapter 6 summarizes what has gone before, briefly speculates about the reasons why the old Court has been so misrepresented, and attacks the modern Court's differential treatment of economic rights and "personal" rights. Finally, Chapter 6 speculates about the future of a little-recognized development first introduced in Chapter 2: the slow contemporary revival of economic substantive due process. Owing to that revival, *Lochner*-era substantive due process obviously has more than historical interest.

This book's conclusions naturally depend for their validity on its definition of substantive due process, its research methods and criteria, the time periods it examines, and the like. I hope that these matters are adequately discussed in Chapters 1 and 2, and I will not address them here. But maybe I should say something about the perspective from which this book is written. First, while I believe that the old Court has been unfairly maligned, I do not wish to deify its conservative justices or endorse all their substantive due process decisions. But neither do I implicitly employ liberal criteria to evaluate the *Lochner* Court. One of Chapter 2's major findings is that the Supreme Court of the 1890s through the 1930s was rather more Progressive than most people imagine. In making this point, I might be thought to accept Progressive standards of evaluation—to pat the old Court's conservatives on the head for dimly glimpsing the Light. But nothing could be further from my mind. To be sure, most of the cases in which the Court rejected a substantive due process challenge probably were justified on one of the many valid bases for trumping an economic rights claim. But I suspect that the real "liberal criteria" and "Progressive standards of evaluation" used to judge the *Lochner* Court are something rather different. As Chapters 3 and 6 suggest, they seem instead to resemble a creed of regulation for regulation's sake. Some of this is concretely exemplified in Chapter 3's long discussion of Brandeis's dissent in *New State Ice Co. v. Liebmann*,[3] which liberals still find inspirational and which I find confused and in places almost hallucinatory. As that discussion makes clear, the old Court had some things to teach its critics.

This book, then, has two main messages. First, taken as a whole, the old Court's substantive due process decisions were much more Progressive than is commonly imagined. Second, some of the cases in which it did strike down government action were more justified than is generally believed. If nothing else, these two conclusions ought to blunt the cries of *Lochnerism* that are almost certain to emerge if economic substantive due process continues its slow revival. The old Court was considerably less reactionary than most people think. And its occasional exercises of economic activism were not entirely, or even mainly, bad things. As we will see at various points, this may even be true of *Lochner* itself.

NOTES

1. 198 U.S. 45 (1905).
2. Note 1 to Chapter 2 addresses this subject.
3. 285 U.S. 262, 280–311 (1932).

The *Lochner* Court, Myth and Reality

Chapter 1

The Conventional Wisdom

Until the mid-1980s, New York City encouraged the demolition and redevelopment of single-room occupancy (SRO) properties because it considered them substandard housing. However, that attitude changed dramatically as homelessness became a national concern by the 1980s. Beginning in 1985, therefore, the city enacted a series of ordinances whose aim was to preserve its stock of low-rent SRO housing. The last of these measures (Local Law No. 9) imposed a five-year moratorium on the demolition, conversion, and alteration of SRO multiple dwellings. It also required that owners of SRO property rehabilitate every SRO unit in their buildings, make each of these units habitable, and lease them to bona fide tenants at controlled rents. The law did not compensate owners for these burdens.

Real estate developers with SRO properties naturally attacked Local Law No. 9 in the courts. By 1989, one of these suits had reached the state's highest court, the New York Court of Appeals. In *Seawall Associates v. City of New York,*[1] the Court of Appeals declared Local Law No. 9 an unconstitutional taking of private property without just compensation. The Fifth Amendment's takings clause, which applies to the states through its incorporation within Fourteenth Amendment due process, basically says that governmental takings of private property are unconstitutional unless they are for a public use and the property owner receives just compensation. Because today the public use requirement is very easily met, the *Seawall* court spent most of its time on the "taking" issue. One way that a taking might occur is through the physical occupation of the owner's property. Here, the court said, the city "occupied" the realtors' property by making them admit third parties to it. Another way that a taking might occur is through government regulation that either denies the owner an economically viable use of his property or fails to substantially advance a legitimate government interest. Under each test, the Court of Appeals concluded, there was a "regulatory taking." The court thought that Local Law No. 9's strictures obviously denied New York City realtors economically viable uses of their SRO properties. It also determined that while the law may have had some tendency to alleviate homelessness, it did not *substantially* advance that goal.

Whatever one might think about *Seawall* overall, two things about the case are obvious. The first is that New York's highest court was more than willing to second-guess a democratically elected lawmaking body's judgment on a social policy issue. The second is that it did so in the service of economic rights. Both stances trigger collective memories within the legal profession—memories *Seawall*'s dissenting opinion was quick to invoke. As the dissent put it: "In 1904, Justice Holmes wrote the quintessential dissenting opinion in *Lochner v. New York* . . . which presciently warned against his own court declaring unconstitutional an act of the New York State Legislature attempting to limit the working hours of children. The historical, economic, social, legal, policy and constitutional parallels to the facial jettisoning of New York City's SRO law suggest that it would be far better to harken to that history instead of being condemned to relive it."[2] "Eighty-five years after *Lochner*," the dissent continued, "we observe property rights, like the contract rights of that bygone era, being exalted over the Legislature's assessment of social policy. Like the economic theories underlying *Lochner* we, as Judges, should not inquire into the wisdom or wholesomeness of SRO's as shelter for potentially 52,000 new, displaced homeless persons—that policy choice belongs to the elected officials who enacted the law."[3]

The *Seawall* dissent was a bit loose with the facts—*Lochner* involved a maximum-hours law for bakery employees, not for children. And the case appeared in 1905, not 1904. Perhaps more important, *Lochner* was a due process case rather than a takings case. In fact, the same Oliver Wendell Holmes, Jr. who dissented in *Lochner* wrote for the Court in the decision establishing the concept of a regulatory taking.[4] Still, most lawyers would say that the dissent's perception of *Lochner* and the era that bears its name generally was correct and that its heart was in the right place. Within the profession, it remains a commonplace that during the first third of the century the Supreme Court frequently used due process to strike down Progressive social legislation, that this was an illegitimate exercise of judicial power, and the Court's conservative justices exercised such power either in the conscious service of business or in simple-minded thralldom to laissez-faire ideas that had outlived their time. This chapter elaborates these familiar beliefs about the Court's substantive due process decisions of the 1890s through the 1930s. The remainder of the book evaluates those beliefs. For the most part, it finds them wide of the mark. The old *Lochner*-era Supreme Court rejected far more substantive due process challenges than it granted, it used due process to strike down government action much less often than is commonly believed, it was more justified than many would allow when it did strike down state or federal laws, and it almost certainly did not act as the witting agent of business in those decisions.

These conclusions may be of some interest to historians, but why should anyone else care about them? The main reason is that they bear upon the legitimacy and desirability of constitutional restrictions on government regulation of business. As the *Seawall* case suggests, this issue is far from academic. And as this book notes in Chapter 2, successful substantive due process challenges to economic regulations have become more common over the past ten to fifteen years.[5] How one evaluates this phenomenon depends to a considerable degree on how one evaluates the original product. This question is widely regarded as having been settled long ago by the Progressive critiques of *Lochnerism*. Upon reexamination, however, those critiques look less compelling—and their main proponents less sagacious and less honest—than most people believe.

A final reason for revisiting *Lochner*-era substantive due process is that the old Court's conservatives knew things about business and government that their Progressive opponents were unable to understand or unwilling to admit. For example, most of these justices would have regarded Local Law No. 9 as something other than, or at least more than, a simple expression of concern for the homeless. As the *Seawall* majority suggested, for instance, although New York City's concern for the homeless no doubt was genuine, that concern had distinct limits. While the city was willing to burden realtors with the costs of sheltering the unfortunate, it evidently lacked the commitment to impose those costs on all its citizens.[6] Unless the realtors could pass those costs on to other tenants, that is, New York City made that relatively unpopular minority bear them alone. And Local Law No. 9's supporters may also have picked up a few votes in the process.

As *Seawall* also suggests, the Fifth and Fourteenth Amendments' due process clauses hardly are the only constitutional restrictions on government regulation of the economy. Nonetheless, this book limits itself to substantive due process. As the term "*Lochner* era" implies, substantive due process probably was the most important of the laissez-faire doctrines employed by the Supreme Court during the first third of this century. In addition, the cases employing substantive due process can be fairly exhaustively examined in a relatively short space. But what differentiates those cases from cases involving other constitutional checks on social and economic regulation? In other words, just what is *substantive due process*?

SUBSTANTIVE DUE PROCESS

The U.S. Constitution's Fifth Amendment (which applies to the federal government) and its Fourteenth Amendment (which limits the states) both say that the government cannot deprive people of life, liberty, or property "without due process of law." The core definition of due process—one exemplified in such basic notions as fair notice and a fair trial or hearing—is procedural. This "procedural due process" is concerned not with fairness in the tangible burdens and benefits the law creates but with fairness in the legal machinery through which they are enforced. But due process often has had a substantive dimension as well. In substantive due process cases, courts consider whether the benefits and burdens created by the challenged law are sufficiently fair to pass constitutional muster. To take an absurd example, suppose that State X imposes a $50,000 fine for picking one's nose in public and imposes this penalty without anything resembling a trial or hearing. Objections involving the wrongfulness of criminalizing such behavior or the excessiveness of the penalty are substantive; objections involving the absence of a fair trial or hearing are procedural.

How do courts determine the substantive fairness of government action? The tests employed for this purpose are many and varied. Perhaps the most common kind of substantive review, however, is some form of "means-ends analysis." Here, the challenged law is constitutional if it promotes some appropriate goal (the end) in a sufficiently direct or effective way (the means). Means-ends tests vary considerably in their stringency. Under the toughest test of constitutionality, often called "strict scrutiny" or "full strict scrutiny," the challenged law might have to be *necessary* to the fulfillment of a *compelling* governmental objective. In *Roe v. Wade*, for example, the Court asserted that the right of privacy contained in Fourteenth Amendment liberty includes the right to an abortion and that laws limiting this fundamental right are justified only if they are narrowly drawn to advance a compelling government interest.[7] Under the weak review imposed by the "rational basis test," on the other hand, some *reasonable* relationship to a *legitimate* government purpose might suffice. In fact, this was exactly the test the Court used in a 1978 case rejecting a substantive due process attack on an economic regulation.[8] Various forms of intermediate scrutiny exist as well.

Modern substantive due process is consistent with this broad definition of the term. Consider Chief Justice Rehnquist's survey of the doctrine in a 1997 right-to-die case. "The Due Process Clause," Rehnquist began, "guarantees more than fair process, and the 'liberty' it protects includes more than the absence of physical restraint."[9] "The Clause," he continued, "provides heightened protection against government interference with certain fundamental rights and liberty interests," including the rights to marry, have children, direct the education and upbringing of those children, enjoy marital privacy, use contraception, and have an abortion.[10] No matter what process is provided, he later observed, the government cannot infringe these fundamental liberty interests to any degree, "unless the infringement is narrowly tailored to serve a compelling state interest."[11] One paragraph down, he strongly suggested that government action that does not implicate a fundamental right need only have "a reasonable relation to a legitimate state interest."[12] Later on, having found the right to assistance in committing suicide nonfundamental, he applied that weak standard to the state ban on assisted suicides at issue in the case. A similar test usually applies in what are called economic substantive due process cases—cases that involve due process challenges to general social and economic regulations.[13] In addition, the Court has applied various weak substantive due process tests to certain actions by public institutions such as schools, universities, mental institutions, and police departments.[14] Substantive due process also forbids miscellaneous government actions that "shock the conscience."[15]

The kinds of rights receiving substantive due process protection—or receiving the most such protection—have varied considerably over time. Today, certain familial, procreational, and sexual rights get considerable protection, and economic rights get relatively little. Although this pattern may slowly be changing, substantive due process review of social and economic regulations has been very lenient over the last sixty years, and such attacks have had little or no chance of success. But things were different during the first third of this century. At that time, substantive due process mostly protected economic rights. It is widely believed that freedom of contract was the most important such right, but as Chapter 2 makes clear, this is simply untrue. Most traditional substantive due process cases involved deprivations of property, with relatively fewer involving freedom of contract and other liberties such as freedom of occupation. Rather than being central to *Lochner*-era substantive due process, or applying a doctrine distinct from it,[16] freedom-of-contract cases were simply one category of substantive due process decision—and not the numerically most significant category either.

Although the old Court never applied anything like modern strict scrutiny in due process challenges to social and economic regulations restricting such rights, those laws often got tougher review than they receive today. This review assumed many forms, perhaps the most common of which was means-ends analysis. For example, *Lochner* itself combined a fairly easy "ends" test with a relatively strict "means" test. In that case, as we will see, a law restricting freedom of contract had to have a "direct" relation to an "appropriate and legitimate" end.[17] The maximum-hours statute at issue in *Lochner* fell primarily because it did not advance the concededly legitimate goal of worker health with sufficient directness.

The *Lochner*-era cases that are the subject of this book, then, share two general features. First, they almost always self-identify as due process cases. (In fact, most of these decisions were unearthed through a plodding year-by-year LEXIS search using only the words "due process.") Of course, this includes cases in which due process was conjoined or intertwined with some other basis of decision, such as equal protection. Also included are a few decisions that do not expressly proceed under any provision of the Constitution but that descend from obvious due process cases, as well as a few cases decided under "the Fourteenth Amendment." Secondly, the cases discussed in this book involve due process challenges to substantive government action. With only a very few exceptions (cases involving presumptions come to mind), this criterion gave me few problems. The substantive government action in question almost invariably was a social or economic regulation of some kind—but only sometimes something fairly described as social legislation.

By way of conclusion, one significant additional criterion deserves mention. In this book, genuine substantive due process cases apply values native to the due process clauses—or at least values that do not derive from some other constitutional provision. What values are native to due process? In a 1998 substantive due process case, the Court said that the "touchstone of due process" and the "core of the concept" are "protection of the individual against arbitrary action of government."[18] This aim obviously is advanced by, among other standards, the rational basis text discussed earlier. Maybe the values advanced by the various fundamental rights should also be regarded as native to due process, but that is a question this book need not consider.

Why restrict substantive due process to governmental arbitrariness? The reason is to avoid treating so-called incorporation cases as substantive due process cases. During this century, the Supreme Court has applied most Bill of Rights provisions to the states by incorporating them within Fourteenth Amendment due process. In such cases, the values advanced via due process really originate elsewhere. The Bill of Rights' incorporation within the Fourteenth Amendment began during the *Lochner* era.[19] In addition to making First and Sixth Amendment provisions applicable to the states, the old Court included the Fifth Amendment's takings clause within Fourteenth Amendment due process. As Chapter 2 explains, this book generally does not treat such cases as substantive due process decisions. However, for one sizable subset of that group—the many cases involving rate rulings and other orders directed at regulated industries—things are not so simple.

THE STANDARD PICTURE OF *LOCHNER*-ERA SUBSTANTIVE DUE PROCESS

The *Lochner* Court's approach to substantive due process was rejected late in the 1930s and has been almost universally condemned ever since. The reasons for that condemnation vary, but it extends across the political spectrum. According to Aviam Soifer, *Lochner* "is still shorthand in constitutional law for the worst sins of subjective judicial activism."[20] Robert Bork once remarked that to be accused of *Lochnerism* is to suffer "the ultimate malediction of legal debate" and that were his court guilty of this enormity, "we would of course deserve the anathema pronounced upon us."[21] Such condemnations depend upon certain factual beliefs about *Lochner*-era substantive due process, and taken together these beliefs comprise a standard picture of the doctrine. Of course, not everyone adheres to each of these beliefs, but most observers affirm most of them. In other words, descriptions of the old Court's substantive due process cases have family resemblances: Taken collectively, these descriptions have many features in common, even though no two of them may affirm exactly the same beliefs about the old Court. This section outlines the standard picture of *Lochner*-era substantive due process; the next section describes the normative critique that usually accompanies this descriptive account.

The Exemplary Cases

Mainstream accounts of *Lochner*-era substantive due process almost invariably emphasize the same twenty or so cases.[22] Heading the list, of course, is *Lochner* itself,[23] which involved a due process attack on a New York statute limiting employment in bakeries to sixty hours a week and ten hours a day. Justice Rufus Peckham's opinion for the Court majority striking down the law began by observing that it restricted a freedom of contract contained within the liberty protected by Fourteenth Amendment due process. But that freedom, he continued, is subject to reasonable exercises of the states' police power: their power to advance the public health, safety, morals, and welfare. After discussing some of the Court's earlier freedom-of-contract cases, Peckham first inquired whether New York's maximum-hours law "is valid as a labor law, pure and simple."[24] By a "labor law, pure and simple," he apparently meant a measure that regarded shorter working hours for bakery employees as an intrinsic good and not as something good because it promoted more general, public aims.[25] After rejecting this justification as insufficiently "public," Peckham concluded that "[t]he law must be upheld, if at all, as a law pertaining to the health of the individual engaged in the occupation of a baker."[26] But some remote relationship to this goal would not suffice; instead "[t]he act must have a more direct relation, as a means to an end, and the end itself must be appropriate and legitimate."[27] Although worker health evidently was a legitimate state end, New York's law did not advance it with sufficient directness. The main reason was that, in the Court's view, there was nothing especially or unusually unhealthy about the bakery business. So tenuous did Peckham find the law's health rationale, in fact, that he could not believe it was the true inspiration for that measure. Rather, "[i]t seems to us that the real object and purpose were simply to regulate the hours of labor between the master and his employes [*sic*] . . . in a private business."[28] Or, as Peckham had put the matter earlier, laws like the New York measure "are mere meddlesome interferences with the rights of the individual."[29]

Like *Lochner*, many of the other most-emphasized cases in the standard picture involve employment. Almost invariably mentioned in connection with *Lochner* is *Adair v. United States*,[30] which struck down a federal law forbidding the discharge of railroad workers due to their union affiliation. The same is true of *Coppage v. Kansas*,[31] which overturned a state measure banning "yellow-dog" contracts: agreements conditioning employment on the employee's not joining a union or remaining a union member. Almost as notorious as *Lochner* is *Adkins v. Children's Hospital*,[32] which invalidated a District of Columbia minimum-wage law for women. Also typically included in the standard picture are three maximum-hours cases in which the old Court *upheld* the challenged law. These include *Holden v. Hardy*[33] (where the measure in question covered workers in underground mines), *Muller v. Oregon*[34] (involving a maximum-hours law for women), and *Bunting v. Oregon*[35] (concerning a similar law for factory workers).

Standard accounts of *Lochner*-era substantive due process also emphasize certain cases involving economic regulations. High on the list is the 1897 decision often said to unmistakably signal the doctrine's emergence, *Allgeyer v. Louisiana*.[36] In *Allgeyer*, the Court struck down a Louisiana law that forbade the obtaining of marine insurance on in-state property from any insurer that had not qualified to do business within the state. Also prominent in most accounts are three late-1920s cases striking down state statutes regulating the price of gasoline, employment agency fees, and the resale price of theater tickets.[37] Usually getting some mention are two other 1920s decisions overturning state laws that regulated the weights at which bread loaves could be sold[38] and prohibited the use of "shoddy" in beds, pillows, furniture, and the like.[39] Usually mentioned but not emphasized, finally, are two cases overturning state laws that restricted entry to the pharmacy business and the ice business.[40]

The standard picture also emphasizes two 1930s cases that marked the end of *Lochner*-era substantive due process. In the first of these decisions, *Nebbia v. New York*,[41] the Court upheld New York's system for the fixing of milk prices, effectively negating the three price-fixing cases just mentioned. The second, the Court's 1937 decision in *West Coast Hotel Co. v. Parrish*,[42] upheld a Washington minimum-wage law for women. In the process, it overruled the *Adkins* case noted earlier. *West Coast Hotel v. Parrish* is widely regarded as the watershed decision signaling the demise of *Lochner*-era substantive due process.[43] After that, the standard account concludes, government action challenged on substantive due process grounds usually has gotten only weak rational basis review.[44] As a result, substantive due process has done little or nothing to check government regulation of the economy.

Still, two *Lochner*-era substantive due process cases did survive the doctrine's general post-1937 demise. Each usually appears in the standard picture. *Meyer v. Nebraska*[45] and *Pierce v. Society of Sisters*[46] struck down state laws restricting the teaching of foreign languages in public and private schools and requiring that all children between the ages of eight and sixteen attend a public school. Each is commonly read as establishing and protecting parents' substantive due process right to direct the upbringing and education of their children. Due largely to their "familial" nature, these two cases helped legitimize the modern substantive due process decisions creating the constitutional right of privacy.[47]

The Centrality of Freedom of Contract

As noted earlier, a central feature of the *Lochner* case was the Court's conclusion that New York's maximum-hours law violated freedom of contract. Several of the prominent decisions just discussed, especially the employment decisions, also proceeded on the theory that the challenged measure restricted contractual liberty. A few others, such as the price-fixing cases, involved laws that obviously limited freedom of contract in substance. Consistent with all this, it has long been believed that one of the most important features—maybe *the* defining feature—of old-time economic substantive due process was freedom of contract's inclusion within the liberty protected by due process.[48] This belief apparently was common during the *Lochner* era itself,[49] and it remains common today. For example, the chapter on substantive due process in the second edition of Laurence Tribe's constitutional law treatise is entitled: "The Model of Implied Limitations on Government: The Rise and Fall of Contractual Liberty."[50] This "Pre-Modernist period in constitutional history," Herbert Hovenkamp has remarked, is "often called the age of 'liberty of contract.' "[51]

Freedom of contract's centrality to the standard picture also is evident in the way it develops the history of substantive due process's emergence and demise. In such accounts, the Court's 1897 decision in *Allgeyer v. Louisiana* often is identified as the first case using substantive due process to strike down a state law,[52] and *Allgeyer* plainly was a freedom-of-contract case.[53] *West Coast Hotel Co. v. Parrish,* the 1937 decision usually regarded as having ended the *Lochner* era, overruled *Adkins v. Children's Hospital,* another freedom-of-contract decision.[54]

Chief Justice Hughes's opinion in *West Coast Hotel v. Parrish* is significant in other ways as well. For one thing, the case marks a decisive break with the old Court's conception of due process. Comparing *Adkins* with the case before him, Hughes remarked:

> In each case the violation alleged by those attacking minimum wage regulation for women is deprivation of freedom of contract. What is this freedom? The Constitution does not speak of freedom of contract. It speaks of liberty and prohibits the deprivation of liberty without due process of law. In prohibiting that deprivation, the Constitution does not recognize an absolute and uncontrollable liberty. Liberty in each of its phases has its history and connotation. But the liberty safeguarded is liberty in a social organization which requires the protection of law against the evils which menace the health, safety, morals, and welfare of the people. Liberty under the Constitution is thus necessarily subject to the restraints of due process, and regulation which is reasonable in relation to its subject and is adopted in the interests of the community is due process.[55]

As Arthur Selwyn Miller observed on several occasions,[56] this means that due process, which previously had been a negative check on government, now required positive government regulation. And, Hughes added, "[t]his essential limitation of liberty in general governs freedom of contract in particular."[57] Of course, this radical transmutation of due process liberty is interesting in its own right. But maybe it also testifies to freedom of contract's significance. That is, if freedom of contract was *not* central to *Lochner*-era substantive due process, why did Hughes go out of his way to transform it?

The Impact of *Lochner*-Era Substantive Due Process

If *Lochner*-era substantive due process was without significant consequences, it is difficult to see why the doctrine has suffered so much obloquy over the years. And in fact it seems to be agreed that the doctrine was an important limitation on government. According to Justice David Souter, "It is most familiar history" that during the first third of this century "the Court routinely invalidated state social and economic legislation under an expansive conception of Fourteenth Amendment substantive due process."[58] To Chief Justice William Rehnquist, this period was one "in which it was common practice for this Court to strike down economic regulations adopted by a State."[59] For these reasons and others, Justice William Brennan believed that economic substantive due process "operated as a potent limitation on government's ability to interfere with economic expectations."[60]

But just how much effect did substantive due process have? As we have seen, most descriptions of the old Court's substantive due process cases focus on the same twenty-odd decisions. Exactly how many more substantive due process cases were there? What kinds of laws did they strike down? Perhaps more important, how often did laws challenged on substantive due process grounds survive the attack? To be sure, these measures are imperfect gauges of substantive due process's impact. For example, a single Supreme Court decision might generate numerous imitators in the states and the lower federal courts while remaining quantitatively insignificant in itself. A single decision might also deter Congress and the states from regulating certain subjects. Still, the number and nature of the Supreme Court's substantive due process decisions from the 1890s through the 1930s ought to tell us something about the doctrine's consequences.

The standard picture has more or less definite answers to all three questions just posed. As for the frequency with which the old Court used substantive due process to strike down government action, there is a remarkable consensus: This happened on about 200 occasions.[61] The sources comprising this consensus do not explicitly address the second question, but they do nothing to dispel the impression that the other 180-odd cases resemble the twenty or so they explicitly discuss. As for the third question, it seems to be generally conceded that the number of laws surviving a substantive due process challenge exceeded the number struck down during the *Lochner* era.[62] But no one is clear about the degree to which this was true.

THE INDICTMENT OF *LOCHNER*-ERA SUBSTANTIVE DUE PROCESS

The standard picture of *Lochner*-era substantive due process is easy to summarize. In all, it asserts, the old Court struck down about 200 laws on this basis from the 1890s through the 1930s. Most, if not all, of these laws involved government regulation of social and economic matters in general and the employment relation in particular. Many of the relevant cases proceeded on the theory that the challenged measure unjustifiably restricted freedom of contract. These cases striking down government regulation, however, were outnumbered by decisions in which the Court rejected a substantive due process challenge.

I suppose that some libertarians or laissez-faire conservatives might accept the standard picture and then applaud the old Court for its good work. The dominant reaction to the picture, however, has been negative in the extreme. One line of criticism maintains that by using substantive due process to strike down government action, the Court exceeded the proper judicial function and in effect became a kind of superlegislature. To some who think in this way, freedom of contract simply is not part of the liberty protected by due process. To many others of this mind, the conception of due process embraced by the Fifth and Fourteenth Amendments' drafters—a conception courts are bound to follow—is entirely procedural. Thus, substantive due process is simply an illegitimate usurpation of power that properly belongs to the legislature.

This traditional attack on substantive due process obviously is difficult for modern liberals to make. The reason is their embrace of modern substantive due process, with its various fundamental rights that get enhanced constitutional protection. But past and present liberals and progressives have other axes to grind with the old Court. Previously I suggested that economic libertarians might accept the standard picture of *Lochner*-era substantive due process and regard it as a good thing. Most liberals, however, would say that this view ignores twentieth-century social reality. In the words of a 1992 Supreme Court plurality opinion, the *Lochner* Court's interpretation of due process "rested on fundamentally false factual assumptions about the capacity of a relatively unregulated market to satisfy minimal levels of human welfare."[63] The main reason is that the emergence of large corporations late in the nineteenth century rendered traditional freedom of contract obsolete by creating profound inequalities in bargaining power between those firms and smaller entities of all kinds. Where such inequalities prevail, the argument continues, formal liberty of contract merely ratifies the stronger party's dictation of terms to the weaker. The classic example is employment, where isolated, powerless workers cannot bargain on equal terms with their vastly larger corporate employers and therefore have to accept whatever the latter offer. In response to this situation, the liberals continue, Progressive legislatures have passed endless varieties of social legislation to protect weaker parties. Because such laws almost inevitably violate freedom of contract, however, they were vulnerable to a substantive due process attack during the *Lochner* era. And all too often the attack succeeded.

Why did the old Court behave in this unfortunate fashion? On this question, liberal or leftish critics of *Lochner*-era substantive due process have traditionally divided into two more or less distinct, but overlapping, camps. According to one group, the old Court's justices acted as they did partly out of sheer ignorance and stupidity and partly out of their nostalgic attachment to a simpler nineteenth-century world whose time had passed. According to the other group, the justices knew very well that they were acting in the interests of the rich and powerful when they used substantive due process to strike down social legislation and did so because they *wanted* to aid the rich and powerful. In either version, among the main villains were the "Four Horsemen"—George Sutherland, James B. McReynolds, Willis Van Devanter, and Pierce Butler—who spearheaded substantive due process's greatest triumphs during the 1920s and fought the New Deal tooth and nail a decade later.[64] A 1972 article ranking Supreme Court justices gave McReynolds, Van Devanter, and Butler a grade of "Failure" for their performance on the Court.[65] The earlier justices who comprised the *Lochner* majority scarcely have fared better. Souter, for example, has noted the "nadir of competence" with which that case has long been identified.[66] He also has bemoaned the "disastrous mistakes" that characterized the whole *Lochner* era.[67]

This section fleshes out these three standard attacks on the old Court's substantive due process cases. I begin with the contention that inequalities in bargaining power have rendered traditional freedom of contract largely irrelevant in the modern world. Then, after developing the innocent and not-so-innocent explanations for the old Court's failure to recognize this reality, I consider the quite different argument that its substantive due process cases were illegitimate usurpations of legislative power.

Unequal Bargaining Power

Chief Justice Hughes's opinion in *West Coast Hotel v. Parrish* claimed that due process requires government regulation and that freedom of contract is subject to such regulation. Most likely, he made these remarks because he accepted the very familiar liberal beliefs sketched earlier. In *West Coast Hotel v. Parrish*, according to Miller, "[t]he Supreme Court recognized that liberty could be infringed by forces other than public government . . . and that its protection at times would require affirmative intervention of government to counteract those other forces."[68] "In the context of the *Parrish* case," Miller continued, "these forces could only be the corporations, which by 1937 had become giant in size and which had effective control over the terms and conditions under which most people worked."[69]

Of course, much of the inspiration for social legislation in its various forms is, broadly speaking, humanitarian. To many people, for instance, it simply is inhumane that workers should toil for more than eight, ten, or twelve hours a day and (the *Lochner* majority notwithstanding) almost certainly unhealthy as well. But such justifications for social legislation can easily be attacked as paternalistic. What, our economic libertarian might say, about the worker who for whatever reason simply *wants* to work ten or twelve hours a day or sixty hours a week? By what right does the state dictate terms of employment to such people? The frankly paternalistic response is that such people must, in effect, be protected from themselves.[70] Such we-know-better arguments, however, usually are a tough sell in the United States. But this problem can be surmounted if employers have considerable bargaining power and employees very little. In that event, workers "choose" to work for ten or twelve hours a day because in reality they have no other choice. Thus, as Justice John Paul Stevens once argued, when making the law struck down in *Lochner* the New York legislature acted not from paternalistic motives but in "response to the assumed disparity in the bargaining power of employers and employees."[71]

Of course, the perception that modern economic conditions have made unequal bargaining power the norm predates *West Coast Hotel v. Parrish.* "Since the adoption of the federal constitution, and notably within the last fifty years," Louis D. Brandeis wrote in a 1916 article, "we have passed through an economic and social revolution which affected the life of the people more fundamentally than any political revolution known to history."[72] Improvements in productivity, transportation, and communication, he continued, created the possibility "of emancipating women and of liberating men called free from the excessive toil theretofore required to secure food, clothing, and shelter." But then Brandeis warned that the introduction of the factory system and the development of the business corporation also had created new dangers to liberty. "Large publicly owned corporations replaced small privately owned concerns. Ownership of the instruments of production passed from the workman to the employer. Individual personal relations between the proprietor and his help ceased." Most important for present purposes, "[t]he individual contract of service lost its character, because of the inequality in position between employer and employee." "To anyone acquainted at first hand with actual industrial conditions," Roscoe Pound had written seven years earlier, statements like Brandeis's last remark go without saying.[73] And courts that assume otherwise—"as if the parties . . . were farmers haggling over the sale of a horse"—are entertaining a fallacy.

Views like these reached across the political spectrum. While dissenting in *Adkins v. Children's Hospital,* for example, Chief Justice William Howard Taft declared:

> Legislatures in limiting freedom of contract between employee and employer by a minimum wage proceed on the assumption that employees, in the class receiving least pay, are not upon a full level of equality of choice with their employer and in their necessitous circumstances are prone to accept pretty much anything that is offered. They are peculiarly subject to the overreaching of the harsh and greedy employer. The evils of the sweating system and of the long hours and low wages which are characteristic of it are well known.[74]

As Taft's language suggests, the view he attributed to legislatures almost certainly was his own, too. Immediately after the preceding quotation, he called the working conditions he had described "evils" and described the affected employees as "oppressed."[75]

Contemporary discussions of *Lochner*-era substantive due process often express the same perceptions. According to Archibald Cox, "The imbalance of economic bargaining power that led the farmers to seek legislative regulation of railroad and grain elevator rates found parallels in large-scale industry. Industrialization created an ever-growing class of urban wage earners dependent for survival on factory employment and rates of pay."[76] "Not only was the factory or railroad worker dependent upon his job," Cox continued, "but he had no power alone to affect his wages, hours, or other conditions of employment." Howard Gillman sounds the same notes in a recent book on the *Lochner* era, continually using the term "dependency" to describe the position of laborers and other weaker parties.[77] According to Tribe, this (and not their intrinsic inferiority) is why economic rights deserve much less constitutional protection than "personal" rights. As he put the matter, "*Lochner*'s downfall did not represent a denigration of economic liberties but a recognition that such liberties were not meaningfully protected by the 'free' market, at least for those who were more its victims than its masters."[78] To the theme of dependency, critics of the old Court sometimes add that workers' necessitousness prevented them from dealing on equal terms with their employers. While dissenting in a 1936 substantive due process case, for example, Justice Stone observed that "[t]here is grim irony in speaking of the freedom of contract of those who, because of their economic necessities, give their service for less than is needful to keep body and soul together."[79]

Innocent Explanations for the Old Court's Behavior

According to the standard critique of *Lochner*-era substantive due process, the inequalities just described required government intervention to protect the weaker contracting party. In Theodore Roosevelt's words:

> The only way in which our people can increase their power over the big corporation that does wrong, the only way in which they can protect the working man in his conditions of work and life, the only way in which the people can prevent children working in industry or secure women an eight-hour day in industry, or secure compensation for men killed or crippled in industry, is by extending, instead of limiting, the power of government. There once was a time in history when the limitation of governmental power meant increasing liberty for the people. In the present day the limitation of governmental power,

of governmental action, means the enslavement of the people by the great corporations who can only be held in check through the extension of governmental power.[80]

Under economic substantive due process, however, many such exercises of government power would restrict freedom of contract, some of these would encounter a constitutional attack, and some would not survive the challenge. As a result, business's dominance of individuals and smaller groups would continue. Why did the old Court bring about such an unfortunate result? Relatively innocent explanations for the old Court's behavior usually stress one or more of three interrelated tendencies in its thinking. Common to all three, perhaps, is the Court's excessive preoccupation with abstractions, and its failure to see their tangible implications.

Occupying center stage in Cox's appraisal of *Lochnerism* is Justice John Marshall Harlan. In a 1908 case striking down a federal law that forbade the firing of employees for their union membership, Cox notes, Harlan wrote that "the employer and the employee have equality of right."[81] Yet to Cox "Justice Harlan was not a conscious defender of wealth and privilege." Instead, he was a prisoner of the social conditions that had formed him.

The first Justice Harlan was born in 1833 in Boyle County, Kentucky, where he grew up to practice law. It was a time and place of small business units. Skilled labor was in short supply. The individual laborer was not without bargaining power in relation to his employer. I suspect that in 1908, when Justice Harlan was seventy-five years old, his statement that "the employer and the employee have equality of right" was drawn from the memory of the Kentucky of his youth without sufficient knowledge of the slums of industrial cities or the mines, mills, and factories of the giant corporations.

"Similar threads," Cox concludes, "probably ran through the thinking of the other Justices at the turn of the century." "All the Supreme Court Justices who participated in the consideration of *Lochner v. New York* were born in the 1830s and 1840s. They grew up in an America ignorant of large-scale industrial organization, urban squalor, and the helplessness of the individual in dealing with organized wealth."[82]

In the same section of his book, Cox also remarked that "nineteenth- and early-twentieth-century law was extraordinarily rigid."[83] It was applied, furthermore, "with logical consistency but little eye for the underlying facts." Here Cox echoes Felix Frankfurter, who seventy years earlier had complained that in maximum-hours cases "[t]he courts decided . . . on *a priori* theories, on abstract assumptions, because scientific data were not available or at least had not been made available for the use of courts."[84] Echoing this criticism is a biographer's remark about Justice George Sutherland:

> Paradoxically, Sutherland's concern with theory was the source of his greatest weakness as a judge. So addicted was he to speculative thinking that he came to depend upon it too much. There were vast areas in the world of fact with which he was almost totally unfamiliar. In a day when knowledge of sociology and economics was required of statesmen as never before, Sutherland knew little of either. Thus he could not know that when he talked of [one *Adkins* plaintiff's] freedom of contract, he was speaking of something that did not exist.[85]

The counterpoint to all of this—the rational, scientific way to approach the problems the Court faced—was exemplified by the fact-laden "Brandeis brief" employed by Brandeis and Frankfurter in a number of cases.[86] In Chapter 3, we consider a famous Brandeis dissent exemplifying this approach.

Besides nostalgia and abstractionism, *Lochner*-era substantive due process has a third relatively innocent explanation: the sincere but misguided reading of certain political and economic philosophies into the Constitution. In other words, the abstract, rigid ideas of which Cox and Frankfurter complained had definite content. That content, of course, was a mixture of antigovernment individualism, laissez-faire economics, and Social Darwinism. Thus we see Frankfurter complaining that even when the courts sustained social legislation, they did so only "as part of the prevailing philosophy of individualism" and not "as a recognition of a general social interest."[87] To Brandeis, courts "applied complacently 18th century conceptions of the liberty of the individual and of the sacredness of private property."[88] Worse yet, "[e]arly 19th century scientific half-truths like 'The survival of the fittest,' which translated into practice meant 'The devil take the hindmost,' were erected by judicial sanction into a moral law." A possible example is Sutherland, whose biographer traces his politics and his Court decisions to his youthful exposure to Herbert Spencer's ideas.[89] Due to the "relentless spirit of individualism" resulting from all these forces, Brandeis concluded, clearly constitutional statutes were construed narrowly, and those with any arguable defect were struck down.

By now, it is a commonplace that while the old Court's economic and political views may once have had some validity, that time is long past us. In 1992, for example, Justices Kennedy, O'Connor, and Souter considered the Court's 1937 decision in *West Coast Hotel v. Parrish,*[90] which while upholding a state minimum-wage law for women overruled *Adkins v. Children's Hospital*[91] and signaled the end of the *Lochner* era. In their view, *West Coast Hotel* was justified because "the Depression had come and, with it, the lesson that seemed unmistakable to most people by 1937, that the interpretation of contractual freedom protected in *Adkins* rested on fundamentally false assumptions about the capacity of a relatively unregulated market to satisfy minimal levels of human welfare."[92] By 1937, in other words, it was clear that "the facts of economic life were different from those previously assumed." Thus, "the thoughtful part of the Nation" recognized that it was the Court's "constitutional duty" to overrule *Adkins*.[93]

In contrast to its predecessor, all agree, the modern Court refuses to read any political or economic philosophy into the Constitution. As Justice Black declared in *Ferguson v. Skrupa*: "Under the system of government created by our Constitution, it is up to legislatures, not courts, to decide on the wisdom and utility of legislation."[94] "There was a time," he conceded, "when the Due Process Clause was used by this Court to strike down laws which were thought unreasonable, that is, unwise or incompatible with some particular economic or social philosophy." After mentioning a few examples from the standard list of twenty, however, Black pronounced this tendency "long since . . . discarded."[95] Instead, "[w]e have returned to the original constitutional proposition that courts do not substitute their social and economic beliefs for the judgment of legislative bodies, who are elected to pass laws." Thus, "[w]e refuse to sit as a superlegislature to weigh the wisdom of legislation, and we emphatically refuse to go back to the time when courts used the Due Process Clause to strike down state laws, regulatory of business and industrial conditions, because they may be unwise, improvident, or out of harmony with a particular school of thought."[96] "Whether the legislature takes for its textbook Adam Smith, Herbert Spencer, Lord Keynes, or some other is no concern of ours."

The Agent-of-Business Explanation

Earlier I asked how the old Court could ignore the tangible consequences of its substantive due process decisions, and then proffered some more or less innocent explanations for this phenomenon. But some readers probably have found these explanations unpersuasive. "How could they not have known?" such people may ask. A sizable body of commentary on *Lochner*-era substantive due process is of much this mind. To these observers, the old Court's justices knew that they were ratifying private power when they used substantive due process to strike down social legislation and did so for exactly that reason.[97] In other words, they were conscious agents of the business class.

People who make this particular indictment of the *Lochner* Court usually articulate one or more of the innocent explanations as well. Due to the complexity of human motivation and the diversity of the Court's personnel over the *Lochner* era, they hardly could do otherwise. Their accounts also state the indictment with varying degrees of severity. At the relatively mild end of the spectrum is Alpheus Thomas Mason's statement that during the 1920s the Court "could be counted on to save the businessmen from the folly of legislators."[98] Robert McCloskey stated the indictment more strongly when he characterized the old Court's decisions as "an unadorned endorsement of the strong and wealthy at the expense of the weak and poor."[99] Cox went even further by saying that, along with the innocent reasons stated earlier, "the Lochnerian decisions flowed partly from the willful defense of wealth and power."[100] Miller was the most emphatic. In his view, "one would have to be naive indeed if he supposed that the Justices did not know what they were doing. Of course they did. . . . The point is that they did not care."[101]

How did the Court become a tool of the rich and powerful? To some, this was almost inevitable, given the kinds of people the justices were. In some much-quoted lines from Justice Samuel Miller: "It is vain to contend with judges who have been at the bar the advocates for forty years of railroad companies, and all the forms of associated capital, when they are called upon to decide cases where such interests are in contest."[102] Two detailed scholarly renditions of the agent-of-business position, however, put more emphasis on the efforts of the organized bar. A 1960 book by Arnold Paul stated part of its main thesis early on. "As popular discontents grew more menacing in the 1890's, and conservative alarm for the security of property increased accordingly, the role of the courts assumed a new importance. Gradually at first, and then with rapid strides, the judiciary emerged in the mid-1890's as the principal bulwark of conservative defense."[103] One example was "[t]he transformation of due process into a substantive check upon legislative regulation." The remainder of Paul's thesis came toward the end of the book, where he laid out the consequences of the judiciary's new role. "[T]he delimitation of the police power in the name of due process of law and freedom of contract circumscribed the legislative discretion at the very time when the increasing complexities of the economy and the growing problems of the city with its masses of urban poor made imperative a greater flexibility in the regulation of business and the protection of social standards."[104]

To my mind, Paul was less than clear about the processes through which the judiciary emerged as capitalism's defender. Like many observers, he mentioned the influential laissez-faire writings of Thomas M. Cooley and Christopher G. Tiedeman, as well as the arrival of conservatives such as Chief Justice Melville W. Fuller and Justice David J. Brewer during the 1880s and 1890s.[105] However, Paul put most emphasis on the efforts of the organized bar.[106] In this, Paul was joined by an earlier book: Benjamin Twiss's *Lawyers and the Constitution: How Laissez-Faire Came to the Supreme Court*. Like Paul, Twiss stated his main thesis early on. The problem, he said, is to explicate the processes through which laissez-faire sentiment influenced judicial decisions early in the century. "The link," he continued,

> is to be found in the role of leading lawyers who, by propagating and defending laissez-faire before the courts, their colleagues, and the public, secured its adoption into the law of the land. They did this in the interest both of clients in cases and of protecting a philosophy and a way of life which they shared with their clients. . . . Some members of the bar merely assumed or expressed prevalent ideology; the shrewdest . . . made the necessary translation of philosophy into legal terms and constitutional devices for their special purposes, thus converting the "rule of law" into a rule of lawyers. As a group they sought to insulate the judges from any theories or facts but those consistent with their own outlook.[107]

Unlike Paul, who mainly limited himself to bar association speeches, Twiss provided numerous other examples of the bar's influence to bolster his assertions.[108] Probably the most important was the propagation of laissez-faire ideas in cases argued before the courts. Twiss also made some interesting remarks about the motivations of bench and bar.

> A question may have arisen in the reader's mind as to how far lawyers as well as judges considered laissez-faire to be an intrinsically valuable doctrine, and how far they consciously employed it as a tool to protect business interests in the courts. There is no clear dividing line. . . . [W]hile some lawyers argued the principle as one in which they sincerely believed, others made use of it merely for the purpose of the case at hand, as is shown by the fact that they could argue on both sides of the question when necessary.[109]

His earlier description of the bar, however, suggests that many lawyers were sincere believers in limited government, economic individualism, and natural rights.[110]

The Usurpation of Legislative Power

Few, if any, of the preceding arguments reject substantive due process as such. Instead, they only argue against its *economic* variant. Until at least the 1960s, however, liberals habitually condemned the old Court's substantive due process cases not only because they thwarted Progressive social legislation but because they involved an illegitimate exercise of judicial power. Felix Frankfurter's writings provide a relatively early example and Black's opinion in *Ferguson v. Skrupa* a later one.[111] This argument usually makes one or more of two basic assertions. The first, which obviously regards freedom of contract as central to *Lochner*-era substantive due process, says that this freedom simply is not contained within Fifth and Fourteenth Amendment liberty. While dissenting in a

1992 case, for example, Chief Justice Rehnquist claimed that the old Court did not assume that an unregulated market was fundamental to a stable economy. Instead, "it simply believed, erroneously, that 'liberty' under the Due Process Clause protected the right to make a contract."[112]

The second, and more important, reason why *Lochner*-era substantive due process was an illegitimate assertion of judicial power amounts to an attack on substantive due process itself. Today this argument usually begins by asserting that judges deciding constitutional cases should follow the original intent of that document's framers. Because the original definition of *due process* was procedural,[113] this means that *substantive due process* is an illegitimate oxymoron—like " 'green pastel redness.' "[114] Besides rejecting original intent, this illegitimate exercise of judicial power also offends against majority rule. Any time a court exercises judicial review to strike down a statute, John Hart Ely once remarked, "a body that is not elected or otherwise politically responsible in any significant way is telling the people's elected representatives that they cannot govern as they'd like."[115] This is permissible when, in exercising such power, the court follows clear constitutional language. Here, because "[t]he people have chosen the principle" under which a court acts when it strikes down a popular statute, "it may always reply to the resulting public outcry: 'We didn't do it—you did.' "[116] But this cannot be true for a judicially concocted "principle" like substantive due process.

In "the strangest turnabout in jurisprudence," Hadley Arkes has observed, most of today's conservatives embrace this second attack on the *Lochner* Court, whereas most liberals no longer can maintain it.[117] The fundamental rights branch of modern substantive due process, Arkes maintains, actually *requires* the natural rights jurisprudence of Sutherland, McReynolds, Van Devanter, and Butler. Today's most conservative judges, on the other hand, "have absorbed the jurisprudence of the New Deal and the jural reflexes of Hugo Black." For just one of several possible examples, consider Robert Bork's *The Tempting of America*.

In Chapter 7 of *The Tempting*, Bork sets out the method judges ought to follow in constitutional cases.[118] Central to that method is the claim that the Constitution is *law* that binds judges. Furthermore, its meaning is independent of the judge's desires. It is the meaning publicly understood at the time the relevant constitutional provision was enacted. That meaning is expressed in principles of greater or lesser generality. In order for courts to behave legitimately, those principles must be *neutrally derived* (based on the genuine original intent), *neutrally defined* (stated at the level of generality dictated by the text and the historical evidence), and *neutrally applied* (applied equally to different parties). The main justification for this method, I think, is democracy.[119] Bork evidently believes that judges who follow his approach will strike down legislation only when the Constitution clearly demands this and will defer to the majority in other cases. Presumably, this is just what the people want courts to do.

Of course, Bork's majoritarian justification for judicial restraint might collide with other important values on occasion. For example, the desire for stability underlying the doctrine of *stare decisis* might counsel that judges follow past decisions that fail to meet Bork's standards of legitimacy because they are inconsistent with the Constitution's original intent. Bork recognizes the problem, but his efforts to accommodate *stare decisis* cannot be succinctly summarized here.[120] For present purposes, suffice it to say that Bork cannot and does not absolutize his approach by always requiring that decisions inconsistent with it be overruled.

Needless to say, Bork believes that the publicly understood meaning of due process was entirely procedural at the times the Fifth and Fourteenth Amendments were enacted.[121] For that reason, he condemns both *Lochner*-era substantive due process and its modern counterpart.[122] So strong are his views on this subject that he even attacks Justice Holmes's famous *Lochner* dissent (on which there is more below) for allowing that due process has a substantive meaning.[123] Even though he finds their substantive views more congenial than those of the liberals, he also parts company with the minority of conservatives who desire an economically activist judiciary.[124]

THE DISSENTERS

At times, this chapter has made the old Court's justices look like a monolithic bloc, but of course this was far from the case. For one thing, the conservatives had their internal disagreements.[125] More important, as standard accounts of the *Lochner* era often emphasize, a few justices regularly dissented from the decisions using substantive due process to strike down government regulation. Although several names might be mentioned, the two that stand out are Holmes and Brandeis. As Black observed in *Ferguson v. Skrupa*, while the old Court's intrusion into the realm of legislative value judgments was strongly attacked at the time, these two justices were its strongest opponents.[126]

In Brandeis's case, it may suffice to make three observations, two of which have already been stated. As we saw, Brandeis rejected abstract, rigid, *a priori* principles in favor of the scientific facts presented in his famous "briefs." He also rejected the excessively individualistic content of the principles the old Court's conservative justices espoused. The first emphasis in Brandeis's thinking undermined economic substantive due process by revealing the tangible impact of the conservative justices' abstractions; the second attacked those abstractions themselves. Today, however, Brandeis may be best known for his belief that state legislatures should be "laboratories of democracy" free to experiment with different means of advancing the public good. He enunciated this view in his dissenting opinion in *New State Ice Co. v. Liebmann*,[127] a depression-era substantive due process case in which the Court struck down an Oklahoma law restricting entry into the ice business. Brandeis began the relevant portion of his dissent by observing that advances in science and technology have been due largely to experimentation. And "[i]t is one of the happy incidents of the federal system that a single courageous state may, if its citizens choose, serve as a laboratory; and try novel social and economic experiments without risk to the rest of the country." For this to occur, however, the courts must restrain themselves from using the Fourteenth Amendment to strike down state regulations. In fact, "some people assert that our present plight is due, in part, to the limitations set by courts upon experimentation in the fields of social and economic science."

Brandeis's reputation as a foe of *Lochner*-era substantive due process, however, pales beside that of the Great Dissenter, Oliver Wendell Holmes, Jr. According to Justice William J. Brennan, for instance, "Holmes adhered through the years to his view about the evils of substantive due process."[128] Indeed, he dissented from most of the well-known decisions in which the doctrine was used to strike down social legislation.[129] Once upon a time, people may have thought that Holmes dissented because he was a Progressive.[130] Today, though, those dissents are explained by his commitment to judicial restraint.[131] Indeed, Judge Richard Posner asserts that Holmes's dissents *created* the theory of judicial self-restraint.[132] This restraint, in turn, is often said to reflect Holmes's devotion to democracy.[133]

Of the three major criticisms of *Lochner*-era substantive due process, Holmes's views most resemble the third (or Borkian) group. These views were prominently on display in his famous *Lochner* dissent, which Chapter 5 examines in more detail. According to Max Lerner, that dissent made Holmes "almost overnight . . . the leader of liberal jurisprudence in America."[134] This opinion contains some of Holmes's most-recalled aphorisms: For example, "The Fourteenth Amendment does not embody Mr. Herbert Spencer's Social Statics"[135] and "General propositions do not decide concrete cases."[136] Also on display were Holmes's majoritarianism and his refusal to read his own values into the Constitution.

> This case is decided upon an economic theory which a large part of the country does not entertain. If it were a question whether I agreed with that theory I should desire to study it further and long before making up my mind. But I do not conceive that to be my duty, because I strongly believe that my agreement or disagreement has nothing to do with the right of a majority to embody their opinions in law.[137]

In fact, Holmes later claimed that the Constitution does not recognize *any* economic theory.

> [A] constitution is not intended to embody a particular economic theory, whether of paternalism and the organic relation of the citizen to the State or of *laissez-faire*. It is made for people of fundamentally differing views, and the accident of our finding certain opinions natural and familiar or novel and even shocking ought not to conclude our judgment upon the question whether statutes embodying them conflict with the Constitution of the United States.[138]

If the Constitution does not embody any economic theory, of course, judges are acting illegitimately if they apply one. This negative prescription has been influential. Recall, for example, Justice Black's assertion that the legislature may take for its model Adam Smith, Herbert Spencer, John Maynard Keynes, or anyone else.

THE PLAN OF THIS BOOK

This book examines and evaluates the very familiar description and critique of *Lochner*-era substantive due process just presented. Chapter 2 assesses the description by trying to systematically lay out all of the Supreme Court's substantive due process cases during the years 1897 to 1937 inclusive. Included here are some contemporary substantive due process cases that resemble the old Court's decisions. Chapters 3 through 5 concern the three major criticisms of the old Court's substantive due process decisions. Chapter 3 considers various explanations for the Court's behavior, among them the idea that it acted as a conscious agent of business. Chapter 4 examines the claim that, due to their failure to understand the nature of modern life, the old Court's conservative justices effectively were unwitting servants of the rich and powerful. Chapter 5 looks at the assertion that substantive due process amounts to the judiciary's assertion of powers properly reserved to legislatures and other law making bodies. After summarizing the chapters that precede it, Chapter 6 tries to explain why the old Court has been so misrepresented and then attacks the well-known double standard under which economic rights get relatively little constitutional protection while some "personal" rights receive a great deal. Chapter 6 concludes by inquiring how the nascent and little-known revival of economic substantive due process might best proceed.

NOTES

1. 542 N.E.2d 1059 (N.Y. 1989).
2. *Id.* at 1072 (Bellacosa, J., dissenting) (citation omitted), discussing Lochner v. New York, 198 U.S. 45 (1905).

3. *Id.*

4. *See* Pennsylvania Coal Co. v. Mahon, 260 U.S. 393, 415–16 (1922).

5. *See* Michael J. Phillips, *The Slow Return of Economic Substantive Due Process*, 49 SYRACUSE L. REV. 917 (1999).

6. *E.g.*, 542 N.E.2d at 1062, 1069, 1071–72.

7. Roe v. Wade, 410 U.S. 113, 152–56 (1973).

8. Exxon Corp. v. Maryland, 437 U.S. 117, 124–25 (1978).

9. Washington v. Glucksberg, 521 U.S. 702, 719 (1997).

10. *Id.* at 719–20.

11. *Id.* at 721.

12. *Id.* at 722.

13. *E.g.*, Exxon Corp. v. Maryland, 437 U.S. 117, 124–25 (1978).

14. For a somewhat dated account of these decisions, see Michael J. Phillips, *The Nonprivacy Applications of Substantive Due Process*, 21 RUTGERS L.J. 537, 549–75 (1990).

15. County of Sacramento v. Lewis, 523 U.S. 833, 846–47 (1998). This "test" originated with Rochin v. California, 342 U.S. 165, 172 (1952).

16. *E.g.*, Paul Kens, *The Source of a Myth: Police Powers of the States and Laissez Faire Constitutionalism 1900–1937*, 35 AM. J. LEGAL HIST. 70, 72 (1991) (apparently treating substantive due process and freedom of contract as distinct doctrines).

17. Lochner v. New York, 198 U.S. 45, 57–58 (1905).

18. County of Sacramento v. Lewis, 523 U.S. 833, 845 (1998).

19. *See* Michael J. Phillips, *How Many Times Was* Lochner-*Era Substantive Due Process Effective?* 48 MERCER L. REV. 1049, 1064–66 (1997).

20. Aviam Soifer, *The Paradox of Paternalism and Laissez-Faire Constitutionalism: United States Supreme Court 1888–1921*, 5 LAW & HIST. REV. 249, 250 (1987).

21. Jersey Central Power & Light Co. v. Federal Energy Regulatory Comm'n, 768 F.2d 1500, 1504 (D.C. Cir. 1985).

22. *See, e.g.*, GERALD GUNTHER & KATHLEEN M. SULLIVAN, CONSTITUTIONAL LAW 454–74 (13th ed. 1997); ROBERT G. MCCLOSKEY, THE AMERICAN SUPREME COURT 100–108 (2d rev'd ed. 1994); JOHN E. NOWAK ET AL., CONSTITUTIONAL LAW 340–50 (3d ed. 1986); BERNARD H. SIEGAN, ECONOMIC LIBERTIES AND THE CONSTITUTION 110–55 (1980); LAURENCE H. TRIBE, AMERICAN CONSTITUTIONAL LAW 567–86 (2d ed. 1988); MELVIN I. UROFSKY, A MARCH OF LIBERTY: A CONSTITUTIONAL HISTORY OF THE UNITED STATES 500–505, 542–66 (1988). *See also* Michael J. Phillips, *Another Look at Economic Substantive Due Process*, 1987 WIS. L. REV. 265, 270–82 (where I did much the same).

23. Lochner v. New York, 198 U.S. 45, 52–65 (1905).

24. *Id.* at 57.

25. "[T]he Court concluded that one objective the law was meant to secure—fewer hours of work for bakery employees, understood not merely as conducive to an employee's well-being but indeed as a constituent of it, and of his family's well-being as well—was not a 'public' benefit." MICHAEL J. PERRY, THE CONSTITUTION IN THE COURTS: LAW OR POLITICS? 163 (1994).

26. 198 U.S. at 57.

27. *Id.*

28. *Id.* at 64.

29. *Id.* at 61.

30. 208 U.S. 161 (1908).

31. 236 U.S. 1 (1915).

32. 261 U.S. 525 (1923).

33. 169 U.S. 366 (1898).

34. 208 U.S. 412 (1908).

35. 243 U.S. 426 (1917).

36. 165 U.S. 578 (1897).

37. Williams v. Standard Oil Co., 278 U.S. 235 (1928) (gasoline); Ribnik v. McBride, 277 U.S. 350 (1928) (employment agency fees); Tyson & Bro. v. Banton, 273 U.S. 418 (1927) (resale price of theater tickets).

38. Jay Burns Baking Co. v. Bryan, 264 U.S. 504 (1924).

39. Weaver v. Palmer Bros. Co., 270 U.S. 402 (1926). Shoddy consists of various torn or cut-up fabrics.

40. Louis K. Liggett Co. v. Baldridge, 278 U.S. 105 (1928) (state law requiring that drug stores be owned by a licensed pharmacist or pharmacists); New State Ice Co. v. Liebmann, 285 U.S. 262 (1932) (state law restricting entry into the ice business).

41. 291 U.S. 502 (1934).

42. 300 U.S. 379 (1937).

43. *E.g.*, Robert G. McCloskey, *Economic Due Process and the Supreme Court: An Exhumation and Reburial*, 1962 SUP. CT. REV. 34, 36–37.

44. *See, e.g.*, TRIBE, *supra* note 22, at 581–86.

45. 262 U.S. 390 (1923).

46. 268 U.S. 510 (1925).

47. *E.g.*, GUNTHER & SULLIVAN, *supra* note 22, at 516–18.

48. *See, e.g.*, BERNARD SCHWARTZ, THE NEW RIGHT AND THE CONSTITUTION: TURNING BACK THE LEGAL CLOCK 85–88 (1990).

49. *Cf.* Roscoe Pound, *Liberty of Contract*, 18 YALE L.J. 454 (1909).

50. TRIBE, *supra* note 22, at 560. The third edition reads: "The Model of Implied Limits on Government: The Rise and Fall of Contractual Freedom and of Substantive Due Process in the 'Natural Law' Style." 1 LAURENCE H. TRIBE, AMERICAN CONSTITUTIONAL LAW 1332 (3d ed. 2000).

51. Herbert Hovenkamp, *The Political Economy of Substantive Due Process*, 40 STAN. L. REV. 379, 380 (1988).

52. *E.g.*, GUNTHER & SULLIVAN, *supra* note 22, at 460.

53. Allgeyer v. Louisiana, 165 U.S. 578, 589–92 (1897).

54. West Coast Hotel Co. v. Parrish, 300 U.S. 379, 400 (1937) (overruling *Adkins*). On the freedom-of-contract element in the latter case, see Adkins v. Children's Hosp., 261 U.S. 525, 545–62 (1923).

55. *West Coast Hotel*, 300 U.S. at 391.

56. *See, e.g.*, ARTHUR SELWYN MILLER, THE MODERN CORPORATE STATE: PRIVATE GOVERNMENTS AND THE AMERICAN CONSTITUTION 94–97 (1976).

57. 300 U.S. at 392.

58. United States v. Lopez, 514 U.S. 549, 605 (1995) (Souter, J., dissenting).

59. Central Hudson Gas & Elec. Corp. v. Public Serv. Comm'n, 447 U.S. 557, 589 (1980) (Rehnquist, J., dissenting).

60. Allied Structural Steel Co. v. Spannaus, 438 U.S. 234, 259 (1978) (Brennan, J., dissenting).

61. McCloskey, *supra* note 22, at 101; Gunther & Sullivan, *supra* note 22, at 465–66; Richard J. Pierce, Jr. & Ernest Gellhorn, Regulated Industries in a Nutshell 80 (1994); Tribe, *supra* note 22, at 567 n.2. These sources do not explicitly say that the 200 or so invalidations they mention proceeded on substantive due process grounds. Since the relevant statements occur during discussions of the old Court's substantive due process cases, however, it is difficult to see how else they could be read.

62. *E.g.*, Gunther & Sullivan, *supra* note 22, at 465–66; Pierce & Gellhorn, *supra* note 61, at 80 & n.4; Tribe, *supra* note 22, at 567 n.2.

63. Planned Parenthood v. Casey, 505 U.S. 833, 861 (1992) (plurality opinion of Justices O'Connor, Kennedy, and Souter).

64. On the Four Horsemen, *see* G. Edward White, The American Judicial Tradition: Profiles of Leading American Judges ch. 9 (1976).

65. *Id.* at 178, citing Blaustein & Mersky, *Rating Supreme Court Justices*, 58 A.B.A.J. 1183, 1186 (1972).

66. Seminole Tribe of Florida v. Florida, 517 U.S. 44, 166 (1996) (Souter, J., dissenting).

67. Washington v. Glucksberg, 521 U.S. 702, 764 (1997) (Souter, J., concurring).

68. Miller, *supra* note 56, at 95.

69. *Id.*

70. I read Learned Hand, *Due Process of Law and the Eight-Hour Day*, 21 Harv. L. Rev. 495 (1908) as tending toward this position.

71. Watters v. National Ass'n of Radiation Survivors, 473 U.S. 305, 367 (1985) (Stevens, J., dissenting).

72. Louis D. Brandeis, *The Living Law*, 10 Ill. L. Rev. 461, 463 (1916). All the quotations in this paragraph come from the page just cited.

73. Pound, *supra* note 49, at 454. The following quotation appears on the same page.

74. Adkins v. Children's Hosp., 261 U.S. 525, 562 (1923) (Taft, C.J., dissenting).

75. *Id.*

76. Archibald Cox, The Court and the Constitution 129 (1987). The following quotation appears on the same page.

77. *See* Howard Gillman, The Constitution Besieged: The Rise and Demise of *Lochner* Era Police Powers Jurisprudence 11, 13, 21–22, 63–64, 76–86, 114–18, 147–59 (paperback ed. 1993).

78. Tribe, *supra* note 22, at 1374.

79. Morehead v. New York *ex rel.* Tipaldo, 298 U.S. 587, 632 (1936) (Stone, J., dissenting).

80. Gillman, *supra* note 77, at 151, quoting William H. Harbaugh (ed.), The Writings of Theodore Roosevelt 288–91 (1967).

81. All the quotations in this paragraph come from Cox, *supra* note 76, at 135–36. The Harlan quotation is from Adair v. United States, 208 U.S. 161, 175 (1908). Cox's rendering of the quotation departs slightly from my copy of *Adair*, and I use my version both here and in the quoted paragraph below.

82. Expressing similar ideas is Urofsky, *supra* note 22, at 502.

83. COX, *supra* note 76, at 136. The following quotation is from the same page.

84. Felix Frankfurter, *Hours of Labor and Realism in Constitutional Law*, 29 HARV. L. REV. 353, 364 (1916).

85. JOEL FRANCIS PASCHAL, MR. JUSTICE SUTHERLAND: A MAN AGAINST THE STATE 241 (1951).

86. *See generally* David P. Bryden, *Brandeis's Facts*, 1 CONSTITUTIONAL COMMENTARY 281 (1984).

87. Frankfurter, *supra* note 84, at 363.

88. Brandeis, *supra* note 72, at 464. The following quotation comes from this page.

89. *See* PASCHAL, *supra* note 85, at 6–20, 28–31, 126–27, 242.

90. 300 U.S. 379 (1937).

91. 261 U.S. 525 (1923).

92. Planned Parenthood of Southeast Pennsylvania v. Casey, 505 U.S. 833, 861 (1992) (plurality opinion).

93. *Id.* at 862.

94. Ferguson v. Skrupa, 372 U.S. 726, 729 (1963). The following quotations come from *id.* at 729–32.

95. *Id.* at 730.

96. *Id.* at 731–32.

97. For some examples, see the sources collected in GILLMAN, *supra* note 77, at 4, 207–8 n.8; Michael Les Benedict, *Laissez-Faire and Liberty: A Re-evaluation of the Meaning and Origins of Laissez-Faire Constitutionalism*, 3 LAW & HIST. REV. 293, 293–94 (1985); Mary Cornelia Porter, *That Commerce Shall Be Free: A New Look at the Old Laissez-Faire Court*, 1976 SUP. CT. REV. 135, 138–39.

98. ALPHEUS THOMAS MASON, THE SUPREME COURT FROM TAFT TO WARREN 40–41 (1968).

99. ROBERT G. MCCLOSKEY, AMERICAN CONSERVATISM IN THE AGE OF ENTERPRISE, 1865–1910, at 84 (1951).

100. COX, *supra* note 76, at 135.

101. MILLER, *supra* note 56, at 45–46.

102. *Id.* at 46, quoting CHARLES FAIRMAN, MR. JUSTICE MILLER AND THE SUPREME COURT 374 (1939).

103. ARNOLD M. PAUL, CONSERVATIVE CRISIS AND THE RULE OF LAW: ATTITUDES OF BAR AND BENCH, 1887–1895 2 (1960).

104. *Id.* at 227; *see id.* at 227–37.

105. *See, e.g., id.* at 12–13, 16–18, 23–27, 42, 142–43.

106. *See, e.g., id.* at 21–29, 35–38, 61–72, 76–81.

107. BENJAMIN R. TWISS, LAWYERS AND THE CONSTITUTION: HOW LAISSEZ-FAIRE CAME TO THE SUPREME COURT 3 (1942).

108. *See generally id.*, chs. 2–7.

109. *Id.* at 148.

110. *Id.* at 12–13.

111. *See, e.g.*, FELIX FRANKFURTER, MR. JUSTICE HOLMES AND THE SUPREME COURT (1938). On Black's opinion in *Ferguson v. Skrupa*, see *supra* notes 94–96 and accompanying text.

112. Planned Parenthood v. Casey, 505 U.S. 833, 961 (1992) (Rehnquist, C.J., dissenting) (some quotations omitted).

113. *E.g.*, JOHN HART ELY, DEMOCRACY AND DISTRUST: A THEORY OF JUDICIAL REVIEW 14–21 (1980).

114. *Id.* at 18.

115. *Id.* at 4–5.

116. Thomas C. Grey, *Do We Have an Unwritten Constitution?*, 27 STAN. L. REV. 703, 705 (1975) (stating this familiar view but not necessarily endorsing it).

117. HADLEY ARKES, THE RETURN OF GEORGE SUTHERLAND: RESTORING A JURISPRUDENCE OF NATURAL RIGHTS 28 (1994).

118. Unless otherwise indicated, support for the text in the next two paragraphs comes from ROBERT H. BORK, THE TEMPTING OF AMERICA: THE POLITICAL SEDUCTION OF THE LAW ch. 7 (1990).

119. *See* Michael J. Phillips, *Review and Commentary*, 28 AM. BUS. L.J. 499, 507–11 (1990) (reviewing BORK, *supra* note 118).

120. For the details, see BORK, *supra* note 118, at 155–59.

121. *E.g.*, *id.* at 43.

122. *See id.* at 36–49, 57–58, 95–100, 110–26.

123. *Id.* at 45.

124. *See id.* ch. 10.

125. *See, e.g.*, Stephen A. Siegel, Lochner *Era Jurisprudence and the American Constitutional Tradition*, 70 N.C. L. REV. 1, 8–12 (1991).

126. Ferguson v. Skrupa, 372 U.S. 726, 729 (1963).

127. 285 U.S. 262 (1932). The remainder of this paragraph comes from *id.* at 310–11 (Brandeis, J., dissenting). Chapter 3 discusses Brandeis's *Liebmann* dissent in some detail.

128. William J. Brennan, Jr., *In Defense of Dissents*, 37 HASTINGS L.J. 427, 436 (1986).

129. *See* Michael J. Phillips, *The Substantive Due Process Decisions of Mr. Justice Holmes*, 36 AM. BUS. L.J. 437, 442, 450 (1999). As both this article and Chapter 2 reveal, however, Holmes joined a great many of the old Court's other substantive due process decisions.

130. *See* G. Edward White, *The Rise and Fall of Justice Holmes*, 39 U. CHI. L. REV. 51, 56–61 (1971) (asserting that Holmes often was viewed as a Progressive during the years 1903–1931).

131. *E.g.*, Thomas C. Grey, *Molecular Motions: The Holmesian Judge in Theory and Practice*, 37 WM. & MARY L. REV. 19, 27 (1995).

132. RICHARD A. POSNER, THE ESSENTIAL HOLMES xii (1992).

133. *E.g.*, WILLIAM E. LEUCHTENBURG, THE SUPREME COURT REBORN: THE CONSTITUTIONAL REVOLUTION IN THE AGE OF ROOSEVELT 18 (1995).

134. MAX LERNER, THE MIND AND FAITH OF JUSTICE HOLMES 143 (1943).

135. Lochner v. New York, 198 U.S. 45, 75 (1905) (Holmes, J., dissenting).

136. *Id.* at 76.

137. *Id.* at 75.

138. *Id.* at 75–76.

Chapter 2

An Overview of *Lochner*-Era Substantive Due Process

Chapter 1 tried to state the conventional wisdom about *Lochner*-era substantive due process from the viewpoint that wisdom represents. How well it succeeded is for readers to judge. But if I failed to convey complete conviction, this is because I lack it. In my view, the conventional wisdom about old-time economic substantive due process is misleading at best and a caricature at worst. To be more precise, some of that wisdom is true and significant, some is technically accurate but misleading, some is debatable, and some is just plain false. Overall, I think, the standard views about *Lochner*-era substantive due process mislead more than they instruct.

This book tries to detail these charges. In order for that to occur, we first need an overview of *Lochner*-era substantive due process that sketches the number of times the doctrine was used successfully, the number of times it failed, and the kinds of government action at issue in these cases. This chapter provides such an overview—one that so far as I know has not appeared until now.[1] In the process, the chapter critiques the standard descriptive picture of *Lochner*-era substantive due process developed in Chapter 1. It begins by seeking the origins of the belief that the Supreme Court struck down some 200 laws on substantive due process grounds. Then the chapter whittles that list down by eliminating or downplaying two classes of cases contained within our list of approximately 200: (1) those that simply do not involve substantive due process and (2) those that are peripheral or penumbral applications of substantive due process because they incorporate values native to other constitutional provisions. After that, the chapter lays out substantive due process's central, core applications during the first third of the twentieth century. At this point, it also begins to consider the many cases in which the Court rejected substantive due process challenges to government regulation. Interspersed with this discussion are various modern applications of substantive due process that mirror some of its traditional applications. After summarizing the results of its endeavors, the chapter concludes with a look at the substantive due process cases involving freedom of contract and at Justice Holmes's substantive due process decisions.

THE MYTH OF THE 200 INVALIDATIONS

Among other things, this chapter will demonstrate that *Lochner*-era substantive due process was a considerably more variegated phenomenon than Chapter 1's standard picture allows. In the process, it will cram a sizable number of cases into a relatively short space. For this reason, the chapter makes demands on its readers. Mostly this is an unavoidable consequence of its subject matter. But a gradual introduction to that subject matter may render the problem less severe. To ease our way into the thicket, therefore, I begin by examining the consensus view that the old Court struck down some 200 laws on substantive due process grounds.

Articulations of the Standard View

What do the standard sources articulating this view actually say? According to a prominent constitutional law textbook, "From the *Lochner* decision in 1905 to the mid-1930s, the Court invalidated a considerable number of laws on substantive due process grounds."[2] During that era, this text continues two sentences later, "while nearly 200 regulations were struck down, most challenged laws withstood attack."[3] The latest edition of Laurence Tribe's constitutional law treatise puts things this way: "The standard estimate is that the Supreme Court invalidated state or federal regulations pursuant to the Due Process Clause, usually coupled with another provision such as the Equal Protection Clause, in 197 cases between 1899 and 1937, while an even larger number of regulations survived scrutiny."[4] Citing an earlier edition of Tribe's book, a West *Nutshell* says that during the fifty years preceding the 1930s "almost 200 state and federal regulations were invalidated by the High Court."[5] Although none of these sources explicitly say that the Court struck down 200 laws on *substantive due process grounds,* because the quoted remarks occur during discussions of *Lochner*-era substantive due process, that is virtually the only way to read them.

Where did these authorities get the 200 figure? The answer is revealed by yet another member of the 200 Club, Robert G. McCloskey, who stated that "B. F. Wright has counted some 184 decisions between 1899 and 1937 which invalidated state laws on the basis of either the due process or equal protection clause. . . . Those involving federal laws were far fewer."[6] (Within the ellipsis, McCloskey claimed that during the period named the judiciary often used due process and equal protection in tandem and that denials of equal protection frequently are regarded as denials of due process too.) McCloskey did not provide a citation to Wright's work, but two of the other standard sources do.[7] The ultimate source of the 200 figure is Wright's *The Growth of American Constitutional Law*, first published in 1942 and reissued as a 1967 paperback.

Wright's Figures

What did Wright say? Early in his book's eighth chapter, entitled "The Rights of Persons," he stated: "Between 1899 and 1937 there were 212 cases in which state legislation was held to be unconstitutional for failure to preserve the guarantees of the Constitution regarding the rights of persons. There were 18 such cases involving Congressional acts."[8] In a footnote, Wright added that "[t]his figure does not include 17 cases in which the Court relied upon the commerce and either the due process or the equal protection clause."[9] This gives us a base of 247 cases. Of this 247 total, however, some were "civil rights" decisions involving race, voting, criminal procedure, education, free speech, and freedom of the press.[10] A few pages later, therefore, Wright provided figures for decisions involving "the rights of property." "Excluding the civil liberties cases, there were 159 decisions under the due process and equal protection clauses in which state statutes were held to be unconstitutional, plus 16 in which both the due process and commerce clauses were involved, plus 9 more involving due process and some other clause or clauses."[11] This gives us McCloskey's figure of 184.

Readers, however, may have noticed a problem with both Wright's statement and McCloskey's rendition of it: Each leaves it unclear whether all 184 cases involved due process. Specifically, it seems possible that some of the 184 involved equal protection alone. Indeed, some of the cases Wright discusses look like equal protection decisions, and a Fourteenth Amendment privileges and immunities case appears as well.[12] Another problem emerges upon reading Wright's extended account of the "property rights" cases: their imperfect resemblance to the twenty or so archetypal *Lochner*-era substantive due process cases discussed in Chapter 1. For example, he observed that nearly one-third of the 184 cases involved public utilities.[13] Later, while emphasizing the importance of the cases concerning employment regulations, he conceded that the number of such decisions "has not been large."[14]

A final difficulty with Wright's account is the number of cases he cites. Although he provides a reasonably good summary of the old Court's decisions striking down government action on Fourteenth Amendment grounds, that summary's footnotes contain nothing like 184 cases.[15] And the total declines further if one eliminates decisions made on grounds other than due process and decisions occurring outside the 1897–1937 period. Clearly it would be useful to have a complete list, and fortunately Wright suggests one. "In the appendix to Felix Frankfurter, *Mr. Justice Holmes and the Supreme Court* (1938)," he wrote, "will be found a comprehensive list of cases in which state action was held contrary to the Fourteenth Amendment through 1938."[16]

The Frankfurter List

Frankfurter's appendix is entitled "Cases Holding State Action Invalid under the Fourteenth Amendment."[17] It cites and briefly describes cases decided during the years 1877 to 1938.[18] Of these, 220 were decided between the years 1897 and 1937 inclusive. These 220 cases, however, do not support the claim that the old Court struck down some 200 laws on substantive due process grounds.[19] For one thing, some of the 220 cases did not involve due process at all. One such decision proceeded mainly under the privileges and immunities clause of the Fourteenth Amendment,[20] and thirty-three others involved equal protection. Worse yet, some of the thirty-three equal protection cases are Progressive decisions by today's standards. Examples include *Nixon v. Herndon,*[21] which struck down a state law preventing blacks from voting in a Democratic Party primary, and *Nixon v. Condon,*[22] which made the white primary unconstitutional. Four more race cases involved the exclusion of blacks from service on juries or grand juries.[23] Another of Frankfurter's equal protection decisions involved discrimination against aliens.[24] Of the remaining twenty-six equal protection cases, fifteen struck down state taxes. Although these fifteen decisions might seem easy to stereotype as probusiness, about half of them involved state laws favoring local interests over their out-of-state competitors and thus tended to promote competition.[25] The other half, which involved state taxes deemed discriminatory for various other reasons, are difficult to stereotype.[26] The remaining eleven equal protection cases, however, involve general economic regulations rather than tax laws.[27]

Obviously the 200-laws-struck-down-under-substantive-due-process argument is in deep trouble if it has to rely on cases attacking discrimination on the bases of race and alienage. Even if such decisions somehow count toward the total, moreover, they make the old Court look rather good by today's lights. Still, some of the other equal protection cases might be thought to support standard views about the *Lochner* Court. Actually, though, more of them appear to involve laws favoring domestic over out-of-state businesses, or firms of one kind over firms of another. I would detail the point, were it not irrelevant here. These are *equal protection* decisions, and the contention we are considering is that the old Court struck down some 200 laws on *substantive due process* grounds. With only a very few possible exceptions,[28] our thirty-three equal protection decisions simply do not involve substantive due process.

After these equal protection and privileges and immunities deletions, something like 186 of the original 220 cases on Frankfurter's list remain. Nearly thirty of these cases, however, involve what today would be called procedural due process, or closely related subjects. I say "what today would be called procedural due process" because the Supreme Court did not use this term until the 1930s and did not use the term "substantive due process" until over a decade later.[29] Nonetheless, on about twenty-two occasions between 1897 and 1937, the Court struck down government action because it was not accompanied by adequate notice, a fair trial or hearing, or some requirement fairly closely derived from either.[30] Also applying procedural due process's fair-notice requirement were six cases striking down state laws as unconstitutionally vague.[31] These twenty-eight decisions apply notions of due process that have long been accepted and remain so today. They do not scrutinize the substance of legislation.

All this brings us down to perhaps 158 potential substantive due process cases from Frankfurter's list. Of these, approximately thirty more must be discarded as irrelevant here because their main concern is state power over out-of-state matters rather than the substantive fairness of government regulation. One subset consists of four cases involving a standard subject in first-year law school civil procedure courses: the constitutional reach of state in personam jurisdiction.[32] Another, much larger group of about twenty-three cases mainly concern state power to tax out-of-state property, income, and activities.[33] These decisions do not resemble anyone's idea of *Lochner*-era substantive due process. As Wright remarked of the group, they involve "the relationship between state and state, or, perhaps it would be more accurate to say, between state and property located in other states."[34] "It is one of the surprising characteristics of modern American constitutional law," he also observed, "that an elaborate set of rules and precedents concerning what is essentially one phase of federalism should have been built up under protection of the clauses of the Fourteenth Amendment which were expected to give protection to certain civil liberties."[35] As if to underscore their irrelevance to his inquiry, Wright cited only a very few of these tax cases, which is one reason why his total fell well short of 200. A final group of three cases involving the relations between state and state essentially concern one state's ability to declare rules of law governing contracts made in other states.[36] With this paragraph's thirty cases deleted, our list of potential *Lochner*-era substantive due process decisions falls to about 128.

THE INCORPORATION CASES

It is widely believed that the old Court struck down some 200 laws on substantive due process grounds. But the sources from which this claim evidently arose plainly do not support it. As they make clear, getting to 200 cases requires that we class equal protection cases, procedural due process decisions and cases involving interstate power relations as *Lochner*-era substantive due process cases. But these decisions are either doctrinally distinct from the twenty or so archetypal substantive due process cases discussed in Chapter 1, remote from them in a practical sense, or both. If such decisions count as examples of *Lochner*-era substantive due process, it is unclear what cases would not qualify. To put the dilemma in another way, the cost of making the old Court's substantive due process cases number 200 is to render the doctrine considerably less ferocious than advertised. For example, there must be something good about *Lochner*-era substantive due process if it includes a decision knocking out the all-white primary.

All this being the case, why have so many standard sources repeated the 200-cases myth? The apparent reason is a confusion between Fourteenth Amendment or personal rights cases and substantive due process cases. Wright's compilation covered "the guarantees of the Constitution regarding the rights of persons," and Frankfurter's list covered the Fourteenth Amendment. Each category, of course, embraces considerably more than substantive due process. Still, defenders of the standard picture might reply that approximately 128 cases remain, and 128 is no small number. As things finally turn out, however, the number of true *Lochner*-era substantive due process cases is substantially lower than 128. Before beginning to say why, I must adjust the 128 figure. The primary research behind this chapter was a plodding LEXIS search using the term due process for the years 1897–1937 inclusive. That research jibed reasonably well with the due process cases on Frankfurter's list, but I would delete a few of his cases and add some of my own. The additions are seven decisions striking down actions of the federal government on substantive due process grounds,[37] plus two cases involving Philippine laws,[38] two utility rate cases,[39] and two miscellaneous decisions.[40] By my reckoning, on the other hand, four cases on Frankfurter's list deserve to be removed.[41] This boosts our total to approximately 137 cases.

Some Incorporation Decisions

Chapter 1 basically defined substantive due process as the courts' use of the Fifth and Fourteenth Amendments' due process clauses to impose substantive review on government action. But it added a restriction: that while doing so the court apply values native to due process and not to some other provision of the Constitution. The aim of this restriction was to avoid classing so-called incorporation cases as substantive due process cases. During the course of this century, of course, most Bill of Rights provisions have been made applicable to the states through their incorporation within the liberty protected by the Fourteenth Amendment. This process began during the *Lochner* era, and our modified Frankfurter list contains many examples. It also contains some decisions in which a due process invalidation is conjoined with some other basis of decision, that other basis seems to capture the Court's objection to the challenged law, and the due process holding therefore looks gratuitous. None of these cases deserve to be classed as true *Lochner*-era substantive due process decisions.

In addition to applying values that originate outside due process, our first set of incorporation cases do not involve economic rights and thus do not inspire the standard attacks on *Lochner*-era substantive due process. Indeed, these are decisions that almost all of *Lochner*'s critics would applaud. Six of the seven cases in question were early applications of the First Amendment to the states,[42] and the other made the Sixth Amendment's right to counsel applicable to them.[43]

Another, less well-known, set of *Lochner*-era incorporation cases involved a provision that already applies to the states. Article I, section 10 of the Constitution prevents the states from passing any law impairing the obligation of contracts. This contract clause has long been held to apply only retrospectively—to contracts made before passage of the law that impairs their obligations and not to those made after. Therefore, it has less potential to disrupt social legislation than substantive due process. Even within its sphere, the contract clause was becoming a less potent check on government as the twentieth century opened.[44] Nonetheless, in seven cases the Court struck down state laws on what amounted to combined contract clause and due process grounds.[45] These cases involved a private agreement or a government grant that had been wrongly impaired by subsequent state action. They did not contain separate due process and contract clause discussions. In these decisions, therefore, the gratuitous due process clause basically was replicating the contract clause.

Article I, section 8 of the Constitution gives Congress the power to regulate interstate commerce. Despite that section's failure to expressly say so, it is well established that Article I, section 8 also forbids state laws that unduly restrict, hinder, or burden interstate commerce. Many of the laws struck down on this basis over the years have been protectionist measures designed to benefit in-state firms and disadvantage their out-of-state competitors. Eight cases from our modified Frankfurter list, seven of which involved state taxation of foreign corporations, invalidated state laws on the basis that they unduly burdened interstate commerce.[46] Without a separate discussion, each of these cases also said that the challenged law violated due process. As with the contract clause decisions just described, this last ruling is gratuitous. These are burden-on-commerce cases in substance.

The Fifth Amendment's takings clause says that takings of property by the federal government are unconstitutional unless they are for a public use and the property owner receives just compensation for the taking. In 1897, the Supreme Court stated (but did not hold) that a state court judgment taking private property for public use without just compensation violates Fourteenth Amendment due process.[47] Although it is unclear whether the Court meant to incorporate the takings clause within Fourteenth Amendment due process, the clause applied to the states thereafter. On as many as five occasions during the *Lochner* era, state action involving an apparent taking without compensation was declared unconstitutional on due process grounds.[48] The best-known example is Justice Holmes's decision in *Pennsylvania Coal Co. v. Mahon*, which held that regulation that goes "too far" constitutes a taking.[49] Today, *Mahon* is almost universally regarded as a takings case,[50] and it is just as widely believed that the clause has been incorporated within Fourteenth Amendment due process.[51] All things considered, therefore, we probably should treat the five decisions just mentioned as takings cases. As James W. Ely, Jr. has observed, the turn-of-the-century Court "analyzed some cases under the due process framework that today would likely be treated as a takings problem."[52]

The Utility Regulation Cases

Not all of the previous section's twenty-seven decisions are standard examples of incorporation, but they generally share at least two features. First, they apply values that originate outside due process.[53] Today, secondly, these decisions most likely would be regarded either as incorporation cases or as cases applying something other than due process. Specifically, the First Amendment, Sixth Amendment, and takings decisions probably would be viewed as incorporation cases, and the contract clause and burden-on-commerce decisions probably would proceed under the contract and commerce clauses, respectively. For these reasons, it is difficult to see why the twenty-seven cases just discussed should be regarded as *Lochner*-era substantive due process decisions.

Subtracting these twenty-seven cases from the earlier running total of 137 brings us down to about 110 cases that supposedly used substantive due process to invalidate government action during the years 1897 to

1937 inclusive. Now we turn to a sizable group of decisions that are difficult to classify. Conceptually, they closely resemble the cases incorporating the takings clause within Fourteenth Amendment due process and thus seem not to be true substantive due process decisions. But their practical importance and their apparent pro-business bias make them difficult to ignore. The cases in question involve rates and other regulations for various public utilities or regulated industries.

The place to begin in discussing these cases is the Supreme Court's well-known 1877 decision in *Munn v. Illinois*,[54] which upheld state regulation of the rates charged by grain elevators. *Munn* established the doctrine that businesses "affected with a public interest" are subject to extensive state regulation.[55] Among the businesses so characterized were railroads, electric utilities, gas companies, street railways, telephone companies, and water companies.[56] During the latter part of the nineteenth century, the Court began to impose substantive restrictions on the states' power to regulate the rates such industries charged.[57] It did so through due process tests that were replete with takings themes. For example, three 1890s due process rate cases quoted with approval an 1886 case in which the Court declared that the states could not "do that which in law amounts to a taking of private property for public use without just compensation, or without due process of law."[58] And as we have seen, in 1897 the justices strongly suggested that the Fourteenth Amendment makes Fifth Amendment takings standards applicable to the states.

The process just described reached full fruition with the Supreme Court's 1898 decision in *Smyth v. Ames*,[59] which reaffirmed the courts' power to review the reasonableness of rate regulations while striking down the challenged railroad rates under tests that melded due process and takings themes. At one point, for example, the Court inquired whether the challenged rates were "so unreasonably low as to deprive the carrier of its property without such compensation as the Constitution secures, and therefore without due process of law."[60] The basic idea was that rate regulation takes private property for public use because it restricts the owner's use of the property and that such a taking requires just compensation if it is to be constitutional.[61] Just compensation, in turn, was a rate that permitted the regulated business a reasonable return on its property. This required that the courts both value the claimant's property and determine a reasonable rate of return on that property.

According to Stephen Siegel, *Smyth v. Ames* was "a landmark in constitutional law" because it "enunciated the test that for the next forty years distinguished rate regulations from confiscations."[62] The details of that test and the disputes about its proper operation fortunately need not concern us.[63] What does concern us is the test's practical impact. By my count, the Court struck down state or federal rate regulation of railroads, utilities, and other businesses affected with a public interest on some thirty-nine occasions between the years 1897 and 1937 inclusive.[64] This compares with at least twenty-eight instances in which the Court rejected due process attacks on state or federal rate-setting during the same period.[65]

If we deduct the thirty-nine decisions striking down rate regulations from our earlier figure of 110 cases invalidating government action on substantive due process grounds, we are left with about seventy-one such decisions. But should we make this deduction? Several considerations argue that we should not and instead should treat the rate cases as examples of *Lochner*-era substantive due process. These cases seem to reinforce the standard picture of the *Lochner* Court. At first glance, they appear to have pitted monopoly business interests, their shareholders, and their bondholders against all the smaller businesses and ordinary citizens who had to pay the rates necessary to ensure the regulated industries a reasonable return. In particular, the rate cases often involved the railroads, whose various misdeeds prompted extensive state and federal regulation during the second half of the nineteenth century.[66] Other considerations, however, suggest that the rate cases should be discarded. Conceptually, they are difficult to distinguish from due process–takings cases such as *Mahon*, which I basically treated as incorporation cases rather than true substantive due process cases. Today, furthermore, the rate cases often are classed as takings decisions.[67] Due to this standoff, the proper classification of the rate cases is a major problem for this book. In the present chapter, I exclude the rate cases from my official list of true-blue *Lochner*-era substantive due process decisions but refer to them parenthetically from time to time. In subsequent chapters, I discuss the rate cases when they seem relevant.

Similar problems beset another group of *Lochner*-era decisions concerning businesses affected with a public interest. These cases involved due process challenges to government action commanding that a regulated industry perform some burdensome or costly action. They often proceeded on the theory that the challenged regulation unconstitutionally took private property without compensation either by compelling that the property be used in a particular way or by forcing the claimant to incur expenses for which it received no recompense. In *Missouri Pacific Railroad Co. v. Nebraska*,[68] for instance, the Court overturned a Nebraska statute under which a grain elevator could force a railroad to construct and maintain a side track to the elevator, at the railroad's expense. The Court struck down about fifteen such regulatory orders on due process grounds during the years 1897 to 1937.[69] But here, unlike the rate cases, the decisions upholding the challenged government action were considerably more numerous, totaling at least forty-two in all. Many such cases involved orders by regulatory commissions,[70] some concerned local ordinances,[71] and some presented challenges to statutes.[72]

THE CORE OF *LOCHNER*-ERA SUBSTANTIVE DUE PROCESS

If we delete the fifteen cases striking down public utility regulations from our previous running total of about seventy-one, approximately fifty-six decisions remain. However one might regard the thirty-nine rate cases and the fifteen cases involving other regulations, these remaining fifty-six decisions clearly constitute the core of *Lochner*-era substantive due process. These decisions, that is, clearly used due process to strike down substantive government action while applying values that either are native to due process or at least do not originate elsewhere. Although the following discussion includes the stereotypical substantive due process cases featured in Chapter 1, many of the decisions it highlights differ considerably from those cases. Within most of the categories comprising the core of *Lochner*-era substantive due process, furthermore, cases rejecting a substantive due process challenge considerably outnumber those striking down government action on that basis. Interestingly, some of these categories resemble the contexts in which substantive due process is again finding application today.[73] To add some color and relevance to the historical discussion, and to illustrate the slow return of economic substantive due process, I intersperse some modern cases from time to time. The first such addition is a lengthy and important one.

Liability and Damages

In its 1996 decision in *BMW of North America, Inc. v. Gore*,[74] the Supreme Court used due process to strike down a $2 million Alabama punitive damages award to the purchaser of a $41,000 BMW sedan that had been damaged and repainted by BMW prior to the sale. The damage evidently did not exceed three percent of the car's price. The Court's decision purported to be applying a criterion central to procedural due process: fair notice. "Three guideposts," the Court continued, "each of which indicates that BMW did not receive adequate notice of the magnitude of the sanction that Alabama might impose . . . lead us to the conclusion that the $2 million award against BMW is grossly excessive."[75] These were (1) the reprehensibility of BMW's nondisclosure, (2) the disparity between the harm the plaintiff suffered and the size of his punitive damages award, and (3) the difference between that award and the civil penalties applicable in comparable cases. In the Court's view, the $2 million award flunked all three criteria. Mainly because the plaintiff's only injuries were economic and these seemed minimal, the Court concluded that BMW's behavior was not especially reprehensible. As for the second factor, the justices regarded the 500-to-1 ratio between the plaintiff's actual damages and his punitive damages award as excessive. For this reason and others, the Court also found that the third factor pulled in BMW's favor.

However, it is difficult to believe that the *Gore* decision had much to do with fair notice. The Court did little or nothing to explain how its three criteria measured the adequacy of the notice Alabama provided. Except for the third factor's use of existing civil penalties, moreover, it is unclear what that connection might be. For example, the amount of punitive damages a state is willing to impose and the ratio between actual and punitive damages obviously are different things than the means used to notify potential litigants of those facts, and unfairness in the former is tested differently than unfairness in the latter. To approach the matter from another angle, suppose that Alabama had given BMW all the notice in the world and then had imposed the same $2 million punitive damages award. Under *Gore*'s three criteria, that award would still have been unconstitutional.

Besides having little to do with fair notice, the three *Gore* tests look substantive. If so, the case was a substantive due process decision. This is the way that the dissenting opinions of Justices Scalia and Ginsburg regarded it.[76] Several commentators[77] and a few courts[78] have done the same. To all of this, one might object that the *Gore* majority never used the phrase *substantive due process*. But neither did the *Lochner* Court; the term is of much later coinage.[79] And it is easy to see why the Court might be loathe to admit what it was doing in *Gore*. With one exception,[80] *Gore* probably is the first case since the late 1930s to strike down government action of an economic nature on pure substantive due process grounds, without incorporating some other provision of the Constitution.

Another reason for regarding *Gore* as a substantive due process case is its resemblance to an 1890 decision that historians regard as an important transition point in the emergence of *Lochner*-era substantive due process.[81] *Chicago, Milwaukee & St. Paul Railway v. Minnesota*[82] reversed a state court ruling that a railroad had violated a rate order issued by the state's railroad commission. The Supreme Court's main objection to the state court decision was that the state statute giving the commission power to set rates did not allow judicial review of its decisions and instead made the commission the final word. One page later, however, this procedural objection evolved into a substantive rule that the rates imposed by the state must be reasonable. Although the Court did virtually nothing to connect these two propositions, maybe the second is a practical outgrowth of the first. Suppose that procedural due process requires state courts to review the rate decisions made by state regulators. If so, what happens when those courts fail to properly perform their mission? In that event, the due process guarantee seems empty unless the U.S. Supreme Court corrects the error. And when it reviews a state court decision that passes on a commission's rate order, can the Court avoid deciding the substantive reasonableness of the challenged rates? Presumably, the purpose of the whole exercise is to ensure nonarbitrary state rate decisions. And if that purpose is to be fully achieved, the Supreme Court must look at substance.

Although they were a subsidiary theme in *Gore*, similar forces may have been at work there. Justice Breyer's concurrence stressed the importance of " 'appellate review [that] makes certain that the punitive damages are reasonable in their amount and rational in light of their purpose to punish what has occurred and to deter its repetition.' "[83] Breyer also joined the *Gore* majority, and it seems safe to say that the rest of that majority agreed with him about the importance of judicial review. As in *Chicago, Milwaukee*, however, what should the Supreme Court do when state appellate review fails to produce reasonable punitive damage awards? The Court might conceivably limit its inquiry to procedural defects in the state's system for determining and reviewing such awards. But the result at which this inquiry aims—reasonable punitive damage awards—probably is better achieved simply by reviewing the substance of those awards. And at the very end of his concurrence, Breyer did exactly that. After reemphasizing how Alabama's system for awarding punitive damages did not significantly constrain a court's or a jury's discretion, he turned to another factor: "the severe disproportionality between the award and the [state's] legitimate punitive damages objectives."[84] "[F]or these two reasons," he concluded, "the award in this unusual case violates the basic guarantee of nonarbitrary governmental behavior that the Due Process Clause provides."[85]

A final reason for treating *Gore* as a substantive due process case is that some of the Supreme Court's earlier punitive damages cases had described themselves in this way. In 1994, for example, Justice Stevens wrote that "[o]ur recent cases have recognized that the Constitution imposes a substantive limit on the size of punitive damages awards" and that a majority of the Court derived this limit from due process.[86] In one of those cases, a plurality opinion discussed or cited with apparent approval several *Lochner*-era decisions that assertedly used due process as a substantive attack on state civil penalties.[87] "While respondents 'unabashedly' denigrate those cases as '*Lochner*-era precedents,' " the Court continued, "they overlook the fact that the Justices who had dissented in the *Lochner* case itself joined those opinions."[88] "More importantly," it added, "respondents do not dispute the proposition that the Fourteenth Amendment imposes a substantive limit on the amount of a punitive damages award."[89] For some members of the modern Court, therefore, the *Lochner* era apparently contained good and bad applications of substantive due process, and the test for identifying cases of the former kind was whether the *Lochner* dissenters joined the majority. This criterion might relegitimize much of *Lochner*-era substantive due process. As we will see later, for example, the most prominent of those dissenters, Oliver Wendell Holmes, Jr., joined many of the old Court's core substantive due process cases.

More important for present purposes, the preceding remarks introduce us to one component of that core: the *Lochner*-era substantive due process cases involving measures that imposed civil liability and/or civil damages on railroads, other carriers, and certain businesses for injuries connected with the services they provided. The old Court struck down five such measures on due process grounds.[90] In *St Louis, Iron Mountain, & Southern Railway Co. v. Wynne,*[91] for instance, it rejected an Arkansas statute imposing double liability plus attorney's fees on railroads that refused a demand for compensation for the killing of livestock. In the Court's view, the law was an arbitrary exercise of government power and a denial of due process because, by imposing onerous penalties for a railroad's refusal to pay extravagant demands, it deprived the railroad of property merely for exercising a right it undoubtedly possessed. Two years later, however, the Court distinguished *Wynne* in a case involving the same Arkansas statute.[92] It also upheld at least fifteen other state laws imposing special liability and/or damages on railroads,[93] other businesses,[94] and even individuals.[95]

Somewhat related to the civil liability and civil damages cases are two *Lochner* Court decisions striking down evidentiary presumptions on due process grounds. This might be regarded as a procedural matter, but the cases in question did apply means-ends analysis to the challenged presumption. One of these cases struck down a presumption that a railroad is liable for injuries resulting from its operations absent a showing of reasonable care,[96] and another rejected a presumption that bank directors are criminally liable for fraud upon the bank's insolvency.[97]

The Tax Cases

So far as I am aware, the next group of *Lochner*-era substantive due process cases lacks a modern counterpart. These cases involve tax legislation broadly construed. They should be distinguished from the aforementioned due process cases involving state taxation of out-of-state property, income, and activities and from the due process tax cases essentially decided on burden-on-commerce grounds. (Some of the equal protection decisions noted earlier in the chapter also involved tax measures.) The tax cases considered here, by contrast, involve the basic due process requirement of nonarbitrariness. Some of them concerned conventional federal and state tax laws of various kinds. During the 1920s and 1930s, the old Court struck down seven such provisions on due process grounds. Three involved presumptions, and the other four involved other tax laws of various kinds.[98] But the Court upheld at least four federal tax provisions during that period,[99] plus perhaps thirteen state measures.[100]

The largest single group of *Lochner*-era "tax" cases, however, involved a less conventional set of revenue-raising measures. At issue in these cases were the assessments made by state laws that apportioned the costs of public improvements among the private landowners ostensibly most benefitted by those improvements. As the Court declared in a 1924 case, the states may require that the cost of a local public improvement be distributed over the lands especially benefitted thereby and may make this distribution according to the lands' value, their area, or the benefits they will receive. "Only where the legislative determination is palpably arbitrary, and therefore a plain abuse of power," the Justices continued, "can it be said to offend the due process of law clause of the Fourteenth Amendment."[101] The main abuse presented by the four cases in which the old Court struck down such assessments was the imposition of liability on landowners who either did not benefit from the improvement or did not benefit in proper proportion to their tax burden.[102] But the Court upheld about three times as many assessments as it struck down.[103]

Land Use

In *Village of Euclid v. Ambler Realty Co.*,[104] decided in 1926, the Supreme Court upheld a comprehensive zoning ordinance enacted by a Cleveland suburb. This landmark case is routinely cited with approval by the modern Court.[105] But *Euclid* was a *Lochner*-era substantive due process case whose test for determining zoning's constitutionality had some teeth. The suburb's ordinance was challenged on the basis that it took liberty and property without due process of law. And Justice Sutherland's majority opinion stated that, to be unconstitutional, zoning provisions "must be clearly arbitrary and unreasonable, having no *substantial* relation to the public health, safety, morals, or general welfare."[106] In 1928, the Court used that test while striking down a generally valid zoning scheme's application to a particular property owner.[107]

Euclid is routinely invoked in cases upholding land-use regulations. But that case's other side—its potential for upsetting such regulations—also is much in evidence today. The cases in question are too numerous to be discussed here.[108] Most often, they involve arbitrary and irrational local land-use decisions that are the product of local officials' politics, economic self-interest, or simple incompetence. Sometimes, however, the government behavior in question is best described as predatory. In *Parkway Garage, Inc. v. City of Philadelphia*,[109] for example, the Third Circuit Court of Appeals reinstated a $5 million jury award in favor of a developer on that party's substantive due process–based civil rights claim. The plaintiff asserted, and the jury found, that the city of Philadelphia had endeavored to maximize the net sale value of a municipally owned parking garage by closing the garage after declaring it structurally unsound. This enabled the city to break its sublease with the developer and thus to remove a significant charge against the proceeds to be realized from the garage's sale. Actually, however, the garage was in good shape, and the city was acting on a pretext. The decision to close the garage was made at a meeting attended by high City and Parking Authority officials.

Another example of government predation comes from a group of modern substantive due process cases involving water and sewer service.[110] Using tactics that resemble Philadelphia's phony garage closing in *Parkway,* local governments sometimes deny landowners water or sewer service in order to benefit local economic interests or to themselves acquire the property at a good price. The clearest example is *Walz v. Town of Smithton,*[111] in which the town refused to issue the excavation permit necessary for the plaintiff homeowners to obtain water service. Shortly after refusing to grant the permit, the town's Superintendent of Highways told the plaintiffs that they would not receive water service unless they conveyed the front fifteen feet of their land to the town so that the town could improve the road on which they lived. Plaintiffs' subsequent substantive due process suit against the town and the superintendent resulted in a jury verdict for $102,000 in compensatory damages, $9,500 in punitive damages, and $48,276 in attorney's fees; and the Second Circuit Court of Appeals affirmed that judgment.

Despite cases like *Parkway* and *Walz,* modern substantive due process litigation challenging land-use regulations usually results in a victory for the government. The same sometimes was true during the *Lochner* era. *Euclid* is one example. One year later, moreover, the Court upheld two other land-use regulations on *Euclid*'s authority.[112] Five years before *Euclid,* it also had upheld wartime rent regulations in two acrimonious 5–4 decisions.[113] In addition to these "pure" land-use decisions, the old Court rejected seven substantive due process challenges to laws that might be said to have regulated land for aesthetic or "quality-of-life" purposes. The laws in question restricted the locale of activities such as the erection or maintenance of stables, the herding and grazing of sheep, the manufacture of bricks, and the placement of billboards.[114]

In addition to the *Euclid* follow-up mentioned earlier, the *Lochner* Court also struck down a few other land-use regulations. The laws at issue in two of these cases involved an especially egregious kind of governmental arbitrariness: handing one set of landowners sovereign power over the use of others' land without standards to control that power's exercise. In *Eubank v. City of Richmond,*[115] the offending ordinance required that the city set a specified building line on a street once two-thirds of the property owners on the street requested such a line. And in *Washington* ex rel. *Seattle Title Trust Co. v. Roberge*[116] the ordinance in question conditioned construction of a home for the aged poor on the consent of two-thirds of the property owners living within 400 feet of the planned home. Involving similar themes, finally, was perhaps the most striking of the old Court's substantive due process land-use cases: *Buchanan v. Warley.*[117] There, the Court struck down an ordinance whose practical effect was to block the sale of a house to a black person if over half the property owners on the block were white.

General Police Measures

Some of the land-use laws just discussed are particular exercises of the states' police power: their power to regulate for the public health, safety, morality, and general welfare. The *Lochner* Court upheld many other kinds of police power measures. This section considers due process challenges to laws that claim justification under one of the listed police power desiderata and that do not fit within one of the specific applications of the police power discussed in other sections. We begin where the land-use laws upheld by the old Court left off: with statutes that might be termed regulations of the environment. Then we move through safety measures, to laws regulating personal morality. In these areas, *Lochner* Court substantive due process decisions striking down government action were few and far between.

The environmental decisions to which I just referred include three cases rejecting substantive due process attacks on laws that required particular methods for disposing of garbage and other waste, one upholding a measure that forbade the emission of dense smoke in certain areas of a city, and another upholding a law requiring that diseased trees be cut down.[118] Five somewhat distinguishable cases upheld provisions designed to conserve resources such as natural gas, oil, mineral waters containing carbonic gas, and the supply of game and fish.[119] These cases segue into a group of decisions in which health and safety concerns are more prominent. Two such cases upheld laws regulating the storage of flammable fluids.[120] Six other decisions of this kind rejected substantive due process challenges to measures requiring vaccination, indemnifying property owners for damages from mobs and riots, requiring that toll roads be kept in repair, requiring electric headlights on trains, and regulating the extraction and production of gas and oil.[121] Sometimes the Court upheld laws of this kind even when their health and safety rationale was weak. For instance, in *Laurel Hill Cemetery v. City & County of San Francisco*[122] it sustained an ordinance forbidding burial of the dead within a city and its surrounding county. The challenger's main argument was that the law's health rationale lacked scientific support and was based on superstition. Without ever challenging the substance of this argument, however, Justice Holmes's opinion for a unanimous Court upheld the ordinance. It did so partly out of deference to the legislature. Furthermore, Holmes opined, "[t]radition and the habits of the community count for more than logic."[123]

The same pattern of deference persists when we consider measures whose aim was to promote public morality. This is most evident in the Court's substantive due process decisions regarding the regulation of alcohol, where it bowed to the Prohibition-era *zeitgeist* on at least four occasions.[124] Displaying a similar spirit were four decisions that upheld state laws requiring able-bodied men to work on public roads, banning fraternities in state schools, prohibiting billiard halls, and attacking gambling.[125] Last but hardly least, we have *Buck v. Bell*,[126] in which all but one of the justices joined Holmes's opinion upholding a state statute that permitted the compulsory sterilization of certain mental defectives.

Today the law at issue in *Buck v. Bell* probably would collide with one or more of the fundamental substantive due process rights mentioned in Chapter 1. These rights arguably had their genesis in some well-known *Lochner*-era substantive due process cases involving "personal" rights.[127] These cases are significant exceptions to the old Court's pattern of deference toward laws purporting to advance public morality and communal solidarity. *Meyer v. Nebraska*[128] and a companion case,[129] along with *Pierce v. Society of Sisters*,[130] affirmed and protected parents' substantive due process right to control the upbringing and education of their children.[131] The law at issue in *Meyer* regulated the teaching of foreign languages in public and private schools, and *Pierce* involved a measure requiring that students of certain ages attend a public school.

Meyer and *Pierce* were authored by the man many regard as the worst of the *Lochner* Court's reactionaries, Justice James Clark McReynolds.[132] Although when McReynolds joined the Court as a Wilson appointee in 1914, some thought him a Progressive or a radical,[133] he soon enough proved otherwise. Indeed, until his retirement in 1941 he was almost certainly the New Deal's most implacable foe on the Supreme Court. By modern lights, at least, McReynolds qualified as a reactionary in other respects as well. In the words of a relatively friendly biographer, for example, "He discriminated against blacks, patronized women, and disliked Jews."[134] But for all that, McReynolds had a passion for freedom that ran strong and deep, and in *Meyer* that passion found expression in the following definition of due process liberty.

> Without doubt, it denotes not merely freedom from bodily restraint but also the right of the individual to contract, to engage in any of the common occupations of life, to acquire useful knowledge, to marry, establish a home and bring up children, to worship God according to the dictates of his own conscience, and

generally to enjoy those privileges long recognized at common law as essential to the orderly pursuit of happiness by free men.[135]

As I noted earlier, this passage helped justify some of the early cases that gave rise to the "fundamental rights" branch of modern substantive due process. The review the old Court gave laws restricting "personal" rights, however, was not nearly so rigorous as the full strict scrutiny typically applied to government action limiting today's fundamental substantive due process rights.

The Regulation of Business and Commerce

Although some of these measures defy ready categorization,[136] many of the *Lochner*-era police power regulations that survived a substantive due process attack seem best classed as laws aimed at the public *welfare* rather than the public health, safety, or morality. The biggest group of "public welfare" laws involved the regulation of business, trade, and other economic matters. To be sure, some of these laws could be classified in more than one way. Truck weight limits,[137] for example, can be regarded as regulations of business or as public safety measures. Furthermore, some public health laws might also be termed consumer protection regulations. During the period 1897–1937, the Court rejected at least five substantive due process attacks on laws intended to protect consumers against unsafe or unhealthy products.[138] In *Weaver v. Palmer Brothers*,[139] however, it struck down a state law banning the use of "shoddy" in mattresses, pillows, bolsters, feather beds, upholstered furniture, and so forth. It did so in part because the law could not be defended as a health measure.

However, some consumer protection laws mainly promote buyers' economic interests rather than their health and safety. The old Court also upheld at least four measures of this kind. These were substantive due process challenges to alleged antideception measures requiring that products be described (or not described) in certain ways.[140] (I say "alleged" because some measures of this kind may favor one competitor over another and indeed may have been enacted for precisely that reason.) However, the Court was less consistent in its treatment of laws regulating the packaging of consumer products. After upholding three such measures approximately a decade earlier,[141] in 1924 it struck down a state statute regulating the weights at which bread loaves could be sold.[142] But in 1934 the Court reversed course again, upholding a very similar law while distinguishing the 1924 precedent.[143]

Another way for government to protect consumers is to directly regulate the substantive terms of consumer contracts. Here, the *Lochner* Court was more apt to strike down the challenged regulation. The main examples are three well-known 1920s decisions invalidating laws that fixed the prices of consumer goods or services: *Tyson & Brother v. Banton,*[144] *Ribnik v. McBride,*[145] and *Williams v. Standard Oil Co.*[146] These cases all proceeded on the theory that the states lack the power to regulate prices for businesses *not* affected with a public interest. But this doctrine bit the dust in 1934, when *Nebbia v. New York* upheld that state's price-fixing scheme for milk.[147] Thereafter, state price-fixing laws encountered few due process problems.[148] Earlier, moreover, two federal price-fixing measures had survived due process attacks.[149] In 1932, finally, the Court also upheld a state law directly regulating a contract's nonprice terms.[150]

While the affected-with-a-public-interest doctrine still held sway, insurance was regarded as a business so affected.[151] In part for this reason, the old Court upheld several different regulations on the subject. These included a law regulating the impact of misrepresentations in life insurance applications, a measure penalizing insurers that collude to fix rates, a statute ensuring the insurer's continued liability despite the insured's insolvency, a provision compelling arbitration of policy disputes, and a law making insurance contracts for hail loss take effect twenty-four hours after the application.[152] The Court also upheld two statutes requiring that certain businesses insure.[153] Also involving insurance was the old Court's 1897 decision in *Allgeyer v. Louisiana,*[154] which is thought by some to be the first *Lochner*-era case to invalidate a state law on substantive due process grounds.[155] The law struck down in *Allgeyer* basically forbade any act to obtain marine insurance on in-state property from any insurer that had not complied with state law. Although not all of them self-identified as due process decisions or as decisions relying upon *Allgeyer,* four other *Lochner*-era insurance cases sufficiently resemble *Allgeyer* to deserve inclusion here. Like *Allgeyer,* three of these cases struck down state laws that arguably discriminated against foreign insurers,[156] and the other resembled *Allgeyer* because it is a freedom-of-contract case.[157]

Whether or not banking ever attained affected-with-a-public-interest status,[158] the old Court rejected substantive due process challenges to regulation of that industry. The main examples are *Noble State Bank v. Haskell* and two companion cases,[159] in which the justices upheld laws charging banks a fee to create guaranty funds for their customers. If it is unclear whether banking was a business affected with a public interest, one would not expect the securities industry to qualify. Still, three *Lochner*-era cases upheld regulations of the securities industry against substantive due process attacks.[160] These laws involved bans on practices—futures contracts and stock purchases on margin—that hardly any legislature would prohibit today. Advertising is another area in which the old Court's substantive due process cases were more deferential than one might expect. Today, government regulation of commercial speech is subjected to a fairly stringent form of intermediate First Amendment scrutiny.[161] During the *Lochner* era, however, the Court applied little more than rigorous rational basis review while upholding three laws restricting commercial advertising.[162] Even though the First Amendment had already been incorporated within Fourteenth Amendment due process by the time one of these cases was decided,[163] both were more or less normal *Lochner*-era substantive due process decisions that did not involve the free speech guarantee.

By now, we have moved away from consumer protection in the ordinary sense of the term and toward measures ordinarily regarded as government regulation of business. In one such case,[164] the Court sustained a due process attack by Chinese businesspeople on a Philippine statute making it illegal to keep business accounts in any language other than English, Spanish, or a local dialect. But it upheld many other general business regulations. Relatively clear examples include two cases involving lien laws,[165] two more concerning the regulation of bulk sales,[166] and about eight involving miscellaneous business matters.[167] A more common kind of business regulation, albeit one with its consumer protection aspects, was state antitrust law. In this area, as in many others, the old Court usually deferred to the legislature, rejecting due process attacks on seven of the eight measures it considered.[168] And the lone antitrust law that it struck down was decided on narrow grounds. In *Fairmont Creamery Co. v. Minnesota*,[169] the Court considered a state law forbidding price discrimination between localities in dairies' purchase of milk products. Because the measure forbade price discrimination irrespective of motive, the Court said, it lacked a reasonable relation to the prevention of predatory bidding and thus violated due process.[170] This leads one to believe that the Court would have upheld an earlier version of the statute that did require an anticompetitive purpose.

Entry Restrictions and Other Limitations on Occupational Freedom

As part of the doctrine's slow revival, modern courts have struck down several general economic regulations on substantive due process grounds. Some of these cases protect landowners against especially oppressive state and local regulations, sometimes through arguments that resemble those the old Court employed in the utility rate cases.[171] Others involve miscellaneous regulations of economic matters.[172] A few more modern decisions strike down a particular kind of "consumer protection" law that assumes considerable importance throughout this book. The measures in question purport to protect consumers by limiting entry to a business, trade, or profession or by otherwise restricting occupational freedom.[173]

As one might suspect, cases striking down such laws were more common during the *Lochner* era than they are today. Indeed, the freedom "to engage in any of the common occupations of life" was one of the due process liberties specifically listed by McReynolds in *Meyer v. Nebraska.* That freedom certainly is thwarted by laws that profess to protect the public by completely banning a particular business, trade, industry, or line of commerce. The old Court struck down one such prohibition in *Adams v. Tanner,*[174] which involved a Washington law that virtually banned employment agencies. Another way that states restrict the right to pursue an occupation is by forbidding the sale of particular products by particular parties. The old Court upheld at least one such law against a substantive due process challenge.[175]

The most common limitations on occupational freedom the old Court encountered, however, were not outright bans on the pursuit of some business or the sale of some product but restrictions on entry to a lawful profession, business, trade, or calling. Entry restrictions take several forms, but perhaps the most common is the familiar phenomenon of occupational licensing. The Court sustained a wide variety of licensing laws and their functional equivalents against several different constitutional attacks during the *Lochner* era.[176] In my judgment, only six of these cases clearly were substantive due process decisions.[177] Several more, however, might be characterized in that fashion.[178] The old Court also upheld a related restriction on occupational freedom, a license tax, in three substantive due process cases decided in 1916.[179]

But while the old Court almost always upheld occupational licensing laws that prevented individuals from pursuing some trade or profession, it was much tougher on other kinds of entry restrictions. The two best-known examples are *New State Ice Co. v. Liebmann*[180] (which struck down a state law limiting access to the ice business) and *Louis K. Liggett Co. v. Baldridge*[181] (which invalidated a state law essentially requiring that every pharmacy or drug store going into business after the law's passage be wholly owned by a licensed pharmacist or pharmacists). In addition, the old Court also struck down three state trucking laws converting private carriers into public carriers and thereby subjecting them to much more extensive requirements for doing business,[182] while upholding one such law.[183] In *Smith v. Texas,*[184] finally, the Court struck down a state statute making it a misdemeanor to serve as a freight train conductor without having previously served for two years as a brakeman on freight trains.

Employment

As Wright observed in 1942, "While the number of cases in which the Court has held unconstitutional statutes seeking to ameliorate the conditions of labor has not been large, these decisions have a significance out of all proportion to their quantity."[185] These are the cases that tend to dominate the standard picture of *Lochner*-era substantive due process set out in Chapter 1. The most prominent examples are *Lochner* itself (which struck down a state maximum-hours law for bakery employees), *Adair v. United States* (which invalidated a federal law that forbade firing workers for their union affiliation), *Coppage v. Kansas* (which overturned a state law banning yellow-dog contracts), and *Adkins v. Children's Hospital* (which struck down a D.C. minimum-wage law for women).[186]

These famous cases are supplemented by several other decisions—some fairly well known and some obscure—in which the old Court struck down employment regulations. Before the tide turned in 1937, the Court applied *Adkins* to wipe out three other minimum-wage laws.[187] In the same year that it decided *Adkins*, furthermore, the Court overturned portions of a state industrial relations act empowering a state body to set pay rates and other terms of employment in businesses the state deemed affected with a public interest.[188] Thereafter, it followed this decision in two other cases.[189] Furthermore, in *Truax v. Corrigan*,[190] the Court struck down one application of a state statute limiting the use of injunctions and restraining orders in labor disputes. In this 1921 case, the state statute in question was applied to permit union picketing and handbilling that, in the Court's view, libeled a restaurant owner and threatened injury to his customers. Finally, even though the case is commonly described involving Congress's legislative power under the commerce clause, much of the Court's opinion in *Railroad Retirement Board v. Alton Railway*[191] pretty clearly involves substantive due process. In that New Deal–era case, the Court struck down the compulsory retirement and pension provisions of the Railroad Retirement Act.

These twelve cases, however, are considerably outnumbered by those in which the Court rejected a substantive due process attack on an employment regulation. Three cases upholding maximum-hours laws, *Holden v. Hardy*, *Muller v. Oregon*, and *Bunting v. Oregon*, make regular appearances in standard accounts of *Lochner*-era substantive due process.[192] In addition to *Muller*, which involved a maximum-hours law for women, the old Court rejected due process attacks on at least four other state laws of this kind.[193] As we have seen, though, things were different when the question was the constitutionality of a minimum-wage law. In part, at least, this distinction reflected the old Court's view that the price paid for goods or services is central to any contract.[194] On at least four occasions, however, the old Court sustained laws prescribing the character, methods, and time for the payment of wages, because such laws were aimed at abuses such as fraud rather than at the substance of the deal.[195] The Court also upheld four statutes regulating wages and other matters in public works contracts, basing those rulings on "the right of the government to prescribe the conditions upon which it will permit work of a public character to be done for it."[196] Finally, in what probably can be characterized as a substantive due process case, the Court upheld a federal statute regulating the wages and hours of railroad employees.[197]

The *Lochner* Court also was willing to sustain employment regulations with some reasonable link to worker health and safety. Indeed, Hadley Arkes was not far off the mark when he remarked of the old Court's justices that "it is hard to find a case where they failed to sustain regulations of business that were aimed at the safety of workers and the health of the public."[198] Although *Lochner* might be cited as an example to the contrary, there the majority's argument was not the unimportance of worker health but rather the New York maximum-hours law's failure to promote it with sufficient directness. On the other hand, the justices' belief that women were especially susceptible to industrial labor helped justify maximum-hours laws for their protection.[199] Also upheld on health safety and general welfare grounds were state laws forbidding the employment of children below sixteen in certain hazardous occupations, prohibiting the nighttime employment of women in restaurants located in large cities, regulating the width of entries to coal mines, and requiring coal mines to maintain wash houses for their employees at the request of twenty or more workers.[200] Fitting roughly within this category, furthermore, are two decisions upholding state laws that required employers to grant requests by departing employees for a letter stating the particulars of their employment and the reasons for their leaving the job.[201] In 1937, finally, the Court rejected due process attacks on a state unemployment compensation act and on provisions of the federal Railway Labor Act that made employers "treat with" an authorized employee representative and that forbade company unions.[202]

The most important *Lochner* Court substantive due process cases regarding workers' health, safety, and welfare—cases virtually never noted in standard treatments of the subject[203]—are its many decisions upholding workers' compensation laws and other measures regulating employee recovery for on-the-job injuries. In 1911 and 1912 decisions, the Court upheld federal and state laws that prevented employer and employee from contracting out of the employer's statutorily created liability for on-the-job injuries.[204] Six years later, in *New York Central Railroad Co. v. White*[205] and *Mountain Timber Co. v. Washington*,[206] it rejected substantive due process challenges to workers' compensation laws for hazardous employments. These measures contained many of the features found in contemporary laws of this kind—for example, strict liability; the elimination of contributory negligence, assumption of risk, and the fellow-servant rule as employer defenses; and a statutory scheme of damage recoveries. Using rationales like those employed in *White* and *Mountain Timber*, the Court upheld another workers' compensation law in 1919 and sustained the federal Longshoreman's and Harbor Workers' Compensation Act in 1932.[207] Some eleven other decisions upholding workers' compensation provisions concerned matters such as employee recoveries, other parties eligible for recovery, the industries covered by the act, scope-of-employment questions, the operation of elective systems, and the fees attorneys could charge clients.[208] In all, the old Court probably rejected eighteen substantive due process attacks on workers' compensation provisions and kindred laws.

ASSESSING THE STANDARD PICTURE

This chapter's main aim is to evaluate the standard descriptive picture of *Lochner*-era substantive due process set out in Chapter 1. That picture had several components. Substantive due process from the 1890s through the 1930s, it asserts, was exemplified by twenty or so cases. Perhaps one-third of these cases involved laws regulating employment. Overall, the doctrine claimed some 200 victims in the Supreme Court over the years 1897–1937. Although the standard picture does not describe the additional 180 laws struck down on substantive due process grounds, it does nothing to dispel one's natural impression that these cases resemble the approximately twenty decisions it does discuss. This conventional wisdom also suggests that many or most of the 200 *Lochner*-era cases striking down government action did so because that action violated freedom of contract. Despite all this, however, the standard picture recognizes that substantive due process challenges were not invariably successful during the *Lochner* era. Indeed, it claims that more laws survived a substantive due process attack than succumbed. Furthermore, the standard picture concludes that after 1937 such attacks virtually never succeeded. This meant that the judicial restraint advocated by implacable foes of substantive due process such as Justices Holmes and Brandeis eventually became the dominant view.

If nothing else, the preceding discussion casts considerable doubt on one assertion in my recapitulation of the standard picture. Although the fact is not widely recognized, economic substantive due process is making a slow comeback, and the doctrine is once again being used to strike down economic regulation. More important for this book's purposes, the other elements of the standard picture are wrong or misleading to varying degrees. This is clear from Figure 2.1, which restates this chapter's conclusions thus far. In that figure, the numbers at the far right all involve cases striking down government action. The "claims rejected" numbers within the parentheticals under the bottom two headings are cases in which a substantive due process attack failed.

The first major conclusion illustrated by Figure 2.1 is that during the *Lochner* era substantive due process claimed nothing like 200 victims within the Supreme Court. Indeed, the figure is more like fifty-six if we limit ourselves to pure substantive due process cases, and about 110 if

Figure 2.1
Substantive Due Process, 1897–1937 (all figures are approximate)

1897–1937 Cases from Frankfurter's List		220
Nonsubstantive Due Process Cases		
Privileges and Immunities Cases		–1
Equal Protection Cases		–33
Cases Involving Procedural Due Process and Related Matters		–28
Cases Involving Reach of State Power		–30
		=128
Adjustments to Frankfurter's List		
Additions		+13
Deletions		–4
		=137
Peripheral Substantive Due Process Cases		
First Amendment Incorporation Cases		–1
Sixth Amendment Incorporation Cases		–6
Due Process/Contract Clause Cases		–7
Due Process/Burden-on-Commerce Cases		–8
Due Process/Takings Cases		–5
		=110
Borderline Substantive Due Process Cases		
The Rate Cases	[28 claims rejected]	–39
Regulatory Orders for Regulated Industries	[42 claims rejected]	–15
		=56
Core Substantive Due Process Cases		
Liability and Remedies Cases	[16 claims rejected]	–7
Tax Cases	[29 claims rejected]	–11
Land-Use Cases	[12 claims rejected]	–4
Cases Involving General Police Regulations	[28 claims rejected]	–3
Cases Involving Regulation of Business	[59 claims rejected]	–12
Occupational Freedom Cases	[12 claims rejected]	–7
Employment Cases	[43 claims rejected]	–12
		=0

we include rate decisions and regulatory orders for businesses affected with a public interest. The main reason for including the latter groups is their apparent conformity to certain stereotypes about *Lochner*-era substantive due process. Otherwise, these cases basically are takings decisions—that is, decisions incorporating the Fifth Amendment's takings clause within Fourteenth Amendment due process. Conceptually, therefore, they resemble the twenty-seven "peripheral" substantive due process cases in Figure 2.1, which apply values that originate outside due process. As their description suggests, finally, the ninety-two "nonsubstantive due process cases" in Figure 2.1 simply do not involve substantive due process in any accepted sense of the term. If by some alchemy these cases could be so described, it is difficult to see what individual-rights cases would not qualify. Worse yet, many decisions in the "nonsubstantive due process" and "peripheral" categories would find favor with most people today. Thus, to classify them as *Lochner*-era substantive due process cases is to render that doctrine much less fearsome. How can one totally excoriate a doctrine that includes the white primary cases and the early cases incorporating the First Amendment within Fourteenth Amendment due process?

Thus, we are left with the fifty-six "core" substantive due process cases—and perhaps their fifty-four "borderline" brethren—as plausible *Lochner*-era substantive due process cases. Once we do that, a second defect in the standard picture soon becomes apparent. At least implicitly, this picture suggests that the twenty-odd cases it highlights exemplify the rest. But plainly this is not so. Both quantitatively and in terms of emphasis, the standard picture stresses employment cases like *Lochner Adair, Coppage,* and *Adkins,* yet such decisions comprise only a small portion of the 110 "core" and "borderline" decisions. Worse yet, perhaps, the standard picture does not emphasize several quantitatively significant categories within that list of 110—the rate cases, the cases involving orders to regulated industries, the liability and remedies cases, the tax cases, and the land-use cases. These cases comprise seventy-six of the total of 110 "core" and "borderline" substantive due process decisions. Of course, these problems might be reduced by refusing to include the "borderline" decisions. But if these fifty-four decisions are eliminated, the number of *Lochner*-era substantive due process cases falls to fifty-six.

Although it provides no specific numbers, the standard picture also suggests that the number of unsuccessful substantive due process claims exceeded the number of successful claims during the *Lochner* era. This assertion is technically correct. But as Figure 2.1 makes clear, it fails to convey the degree to which unsuccessful claims exceeded successful ones. For the "core" and "borderline" categories together, the latter exceeded the former by about 269 to 110 (2.45 to 1). Exclude the borderline cases, and the margin becomes approximately 199 to 56 (3.55 to 1). Interestingly, the margins become even greater if we focus on the types of cases emphasized in the standard picture. For the employment cases, the edge is 43 to 12 (3.6 to 1), for the business regulation cases it is 59 to 12 (4.9 to 1), and for the general police cases it is 28 to 3 (9.3 to 1). For these three categories together, plus the occupational freedom cases, the total is 142 to 34 (4.2 to 1). In other words, *Lochner*-era substantive due process attacks had their lowest kill ratios in precisely those areas where the doctrine is supposed to have done the most damage. One might think that all these figures are biased by my inclusion of cases from the 1930s, when old-time substantive due process obviously was losing force. But the numbers for the years 1902–1932 tell much the same story.[209]

THE FREEDOM-OF-CONTRACT MYTH

What about the widespread belief that *Lochner*-era substantive due process emphasized freedom of contract? This chapter's discussion did not focus on that question, but it nonetheless casts some doubt on freedom of contract's centrality. As virtual takings decisions, one might expect the rate cases and the utility-order cases to have involved deprivations of property rather than liberty. Similarly, the liability and remedies cases, the tax cases, and the land-use cases are easier to imagine as "property" cases than as "liberty" cases. In fact, these surmises are almost entirely correct. Among the remaining cases, moreover, freedom-of-contract claims were the exception rather than the rule. In fact, only *fifteen* Supreme Court substantive due process cases striking down government action during the years 1897 to 1937 proceeded on the theory that the challenged law limited contractual liberty.[210] Furthermore, five of these decisions did not contain the words "freedom of contract," "liberty of contract," or the like; instead, they merely followed earlier freedom-of-contract cases. By contrast, a relatively informal search unearthed over forty cases in which the Court refused freedom-of-contract challenges to government regulation during the years 1902 to 1932 inclusive.[211] Rather than being central to *Lochner*-era substantive due process, freedom of contract was but one application of a much more general doctrine.

THE SUBSTANTIVE PROCESS DECISIONS OF MR. JUSTICE HOLMES

Another significant element in the standard picture of *Lochner*-era substantive due process is its choice of heroes and villains. Among the latter, of course, are Chapter 1's Four Horsemen: Justices Sutherland, McReynolds, Butler, and Van Devanter. Chief among the former were Justices Holmes and Brandeis. But while Holmes and Brandeis certainly had their differences with the Court's more laissez-faire members, neither had any objection to substantive due process as such. Each joined many of our fifty-six "core" and our fifty-four "borderline" substantive due process cases. In fact, each occasionally wrote for the Court in such cases. In the interest of brevity, I will limit my discussion to Holmes.[212] As G. Edward White has rightly remarked, commentators have overemphasized Holmes's dissents and "ignored the more numerous instances in which [he] joined Taft, Van Devanter, McReynolds, Sutherland, and Butler in extending and refining the categories of orthodox early-twentieth-century jurisprudence."[213]

Holmes's reputation as an enemy of substantive due process probably resulted from his frequent attacks on freedom of contract[214] and on that doctrine's identification with substantive due process. But in fact Holmes always allowed due process a substantive meaning. The first opinion he wrote for the Court involved a due process–based freedom-of-contract challenge to a California constitutional provision voiding contracts for margin sales of, or futures contracts on, corporate stock. Evidently regarding such a challenge as legitimate, Holmes declared that "neither a state legislature nor a state constitution can interfere arbitrarily with private business or transactions, and . . . the mere fact that an enactment purports to be for the protection of the public safety, health or morals, is not conclusive upon the courts."[215] But courts were to intervene only when that law violated "relatively fundamental rules of right, as generally understood by all English-speaking communities," or constituted " 'a clear, unmistakable infringement of rights secured by the fundamental law.' "[216] In *Lochner*, Holmes said that Fourteenth Amendment liberty "is perverted when it is held to prevent the natural outcome of a dominant opinion, unless it can be said that a rational and fair man necessarily would admit that the statute proposed would infringe fundamental principles as they have been understood by the traditions of our people and our law."[217] After *Lochner*, Holmes's well-known substantive due process dissents tended to use a "reasonable man" standard when they bothered to state a test.[218] But they almost always adduced some substantive justification for the challenged government action, no matter how weak or speculative.[219] In his dissent from a 1928 case striking down a state statute limiting the pharmacy business to firms owned by licensed pharmacists, for example, Holmes found a public health justification for this apparent restriction on competition. Shareholders who also are licensed pharmacists, he argued, are "more likely to observe the business with an intelligent eye than a casual investor who looked only to the standing of the stock in the market."[220]

By itself, Holmes's acceptance of substantive due process is not too significant. What counts is the uses to which he put the doctrine. And defenders of the conventional wisdom can maintain that Holmes consistently opposed a particularly important and vicious use of substantive due process: the invalidation of Progressive social legislation that limited freedom of contract. It is true that Holmes vociferously dissented in several cases of this kind. But as we have seen, decisions striking down government action on freedom-of-contract grounds were not especially numerous during the *Lochner* era. Worse yet, Holmes joined several of these decisions. Indeed, in 1922 he wrote one such opinion. *St. Louis Cotton Compress Co. v. Arkansas*[221] struck down an Arkansas statute that taxed premiums paid to insure in-state property with an insurer who was not authorized to do business in the state. Holmes's opinion for the Court did not use the words "freedom of contract," but he based the decision on *Allgeyer v. Louisiana,*[222] which clearly did. In *Allgeyer* the Court had invalidated a similar Louisiana law because it deprived the aggrieved firm of its due process liberty to contract for insurance outside the state. Holmes also wrote for the Court in an ambiguous later case that resembles *St. Louis Cotton Compress.*[223] In addition, he joined a freedom-of-contract decision that discussed *Allgeyer* but did not explicitly follow it.[224]

More important, during the same year that saw the Court strike down a minimum-wage law over Holmes's dissent in *Adkins v. Children's Hospital,*[225] Holmes joined a unanimous decision invalidating a different minimum-wage regulation. In *Chas. Wolff Packing Co. v. Court of Industrial Relations,*[226] the Court sustained a freedom-of-contract challenge to the schedule of wages imposed on a Kansas meatpacker by the state's industrial board. In 1924, the Court extended *Chas. Wolff*'s holding to include coal mining,[227] and one year later it struck down a maximum-hours provision contained in a writ of mandamus issued by the Kansas Supreme Court following the original *Chas. Wolff* case's return to that court.[228] Holmes joined both of these decisions.

So far, we have seen that Holmes certainly was willing to give due process substantive content and that he even wrote or joined several substantive due process decisions striking down government action because it limited freedom of contract. A more important indicator of the extent to which he embraced *Lochner*-era substantive due process, however, is the number of cases within our "borderline" and "core" categories in which he joined a majority voting to strike down government action. As we will see shortly, that number is sizable. In evaluating it, moreover, remember that Holmes served on the Court from 1902 until 1932 and that this chapter covers the period 1897 through 1937.

My account slights one important Holmes decision from this chapter's "peripheral" group—his 1922 opinion in *Pennsylvania Coal Co. v. Mahon,*[229] which established that regulation that goes "too far" "will be recognized as a taking."[230] The "borderline" substantive due process cases are conceptually similar to *Mahon* in their blending of due process and takings reasoning. Within that category, Holmes joined all but five of the cases striking down the rate orders directed at businesses affected with a public interest during the years 1902–1932.[231] Of the decisions striking down regulatory orders directed at such businesses over those same years, Holmes dissented from only one.[232] Indeed, he wrote for the Court in three of these cases.[233] Turning to my "core" substantive due process decisions, Holmes joined all seven of the cases striking down liability and remedies measures and evidentiary presumptions and all four of the cases knocking down land-use regulations. He also wrote for the Court in one of the former.[234] Although some of Holmes's substantive due process dissents came in tax cases,[235] he joined three of the decisions that struck down state laws apportioning the costs of public improvements among the private landowners benefitted by those improvements and assessing the landowners on that basis.[236]

However, things are different within the core group's other categories. Of the three "general police regulation" cases striking down government action, Holmes joined but one, and that most likely was due to *stare decisis*.[237] In the entry restriction and occupational freedom cases invalidating state laws during Holmes's tenure on the Court, he joined the majority only twice—in two trucking regulation decisions.[238] Within the "business regulation" category, Holmes joined a little-known case that was decided under the due process provision of the Philippine Bill of Rights and that cited many well-known substantive due process decisions of the time.[239] He also joined the three *Allgeyer* follow-ups discussed earlier.[240] As for the employment cases, we have seen that Holmes went along with the Court in *Chas. Wolff* and the two subsequent decisions applying it.[241] He also joined the Court in two *Adkins* follow-ups striking down minimum-wage laws, but those votes almost surely were attributable to *stare decisis* and nothing else.[242]

All told, Holmes joined something like seventy percent of the "core" and "borderline" cases striking down government action and slightly over fifty percent of the latter group alone.[243] Thus, his reputation as a foe of *Lochner*-era substantive due process is undeserved. Nonetheless, Holmes obviously had his differences with the old Court's conservatives. But rather than being disputes about the propriety of substantive due process in general, these were disputes *within* substantive due process. As the previous discussion also suggests, there was a rough pattern to Holmes's differences with the conservative majority. With some exceptions, Holmes tended to dissent in substantive due process cases involving Progressive social legislation and to join the majority where other kinds of laws were at issue. In other words, there was a Progressive tilt to Holmes's substantive due process decisions. For various reasons, not the least of them Holmes's extremely conservative politics, this tilt is not easy to explain.[244] But perhaps it accounts for the widespread belief that he rejected substantive due process. If (as the standard picture wrongly suggests) *Lochner*-era substantive due process's main victims were laws designed to protect the downtrodden, and if (as is actually the case) Holmes's dissents came disproportionately from among such cases, then it is natural to regard him as a foe of substantive due process. Then again, maybe Holmes's immense prestige helps explain the standard picture. On that view, the substantive due process cases in which he dissented would be the only decisions worth anyone's concern. The question, then, goes like this: Is Holmes regarded as the Great Dissenter because his dissents involved laws dear to liberals and progressives, or are these cases important simply because Holmes dissented in them?

NOTES

1. I am aware of only three possible exceptions to this generalization, the first two of which are discussed later in the chapter. An important standard source on the old Court's substantive due process cases, BENJAMIN F. WRIGHT, THE GROWTH OF AMERICAN CONSTITUTIONAL LAW 148–79 (Phoenix Book paperback 1967) (originally published in 1942), provides a reasonably good, if incomplete, rendition of the cases in which the Court struck down government action on substantive due process grounds. As we also shall see, most cases of this kind also appear in FELIX FRANKFURTER, MR. JUSTICE HOLMES AND THE SUPREME COURT 97–137 (1938). However, neither of these sources devotes significant attention to decisions in which the Court rejected a substantive due process claim. Many such cases *can* be found in U.S. GOVERNMENT PRINTING OFFICE, THE CONSTITUTION OF THE UNITED STATES OF AMERICA: ANALYSIS AND INTERPRETATION 1310–1406 (1973), but this source does not attempt a history of the *Lochner* era or total the cases it cites.

Also worth a mention are the estimates made by Charles Warren at various times during the first third of the century. *See* 2 CHARLES WARREN, THE SUPREME COURT IN AMERICAN HISTORY 741 (rev. ed. 1926); Charles Warren, *The Progressiveness of the United States Supreme Court*, 13 COLUM. L. REV. 294 (1913). As the dates of these sources make clear, they do not cover the full 1897–1937 period. Also, they are not limited to substantive due process cases. A final source, Ray A. Brown, *Due Process of Law, Police Power, and the Supreme Court*, 40 HARV. L. REV. 943 (1927), obviously does not cover the full period discussed in this book. In addition, it does not include the full spectrum of substantive due process cases examined here.

2. GERALD GUNTHER & KATHLEEN M. SULLIVAN, CONSTITUTIONAL LAW 465 (13th ed. 1997).

3. *Id.* at 466.

4. 1 LAURENCE H. TRIBE, AMERICAN CONSTITUTIONAL LAW 1344 n.4 (3d ed. 2000).

5. RICHARD J. PIERCE, JR. & ERNEST GELLHORN, REGULATED INDUSTRIES IN A NUTSHELL 80 (1994).

6. ROBERT G. MCCLOSKEY, THE AMERICAN SUPREME COURT 101 (2d rev'd ed. 1994).

7. GUNTHER & SULLIVAN, *supra* note 2, at 465 n.1; TRIBE, *supra* note 4, at 567 n.2.

8. WRIGHT, *supra* note 1, at 148.

9. *Id.* at 148 n.1.

10. *See id.* at 148–53.

11. *Id.* at 154.

12. *E.g.*, *id.* at 159, 163–64.

13. *Id.* at 155.

14. *Id.* at 172.
15. *See id.*at 154–79.
16. *Id.* at 165 n.63.
17. FRANKFURTER, *supra* note 1, at 97.
18. *See id.* at 97–137.
19. For a more detailed rendition of the following arguments, see Michael J. Phillips, *How Many Times Was* Lochner-*Era Substantive Due Process Effective?* 48 MERCER L. REV. 1049, 1057–64 (1997).
20. *See* Colgate v. Harvey, 296 U.S. 404, 419–36 (1935) (containing an equal protection discussion as well). *Colgate* is mainly remembered as a privileges and immunities case. *E.g.*, GUNTHER & SULLIVAN, *supra* note 2, at 429 n.2.
21. 273 U.S. 536, 540–41 (1927).
22. 286 U.S. 73, 89 (1932).
23. Hollins v. Oklahoma, 295 U.S. 394, 395 (1935) (jury service); Norris v. Alabama, 294 U.S. 587, 597–99 (1935) (grand and petit jury service); Rogers v. Alabama, 192 U.S. 226, 229–31 (1904) (grand jury service in a murder case); Carter v. Texas, 177 U.S. 442, 447–49 (1900) (grand jury service in a criminal prosecution against a black person).
24. Truax v. Raich, 239 U.S. 33, 39–43 (1915) (striking down an Arizona law ordering that at least eighty percent of the employees of firms employing more than five workers must be qualified electors or native-born U.S. citizens).
25. Concordia Fire Ins. Co. v. Illinois, 292 U.S. 535, 544–45 (1934) (foreign insurers taxed at higher assessed values than other firms); Iowa-Des Moines Nat'l Bank v. Bennett, 284 U.S. 239, 245–47 (1931) (tax on stock of national banks exceeds tax on stock of state banks); Hanover Fire Ins. Co. v. Harding, 272 U.S. 494, 516–17 (1926) (foreign insurance companies taxed differently than similarly situated domestic insurers); Air-Way Elec. Appliance Corp. v. Day, 266 U.S. 71, 81–85 (1924) (state corporate franchise tax; both commerce clause and equal protection violated); Bethlehem Motors Corp. v. Flynt, 256 U.S. 421, 423–26 (1921) (statute reducing license tax if at least three-quarters of manufacturer's assets invested in state's property or securities; both equal protection and commerce clause violated); F. S. Royster Guano Co. v. Virginia, 253 U.S. 412, 414–17 (1920) (statute not taxing out-of-state income of local corporations without any local business but taxing such income when earned by other local corporations); Southern Ry. v. Green, 216 U.S. 400, 411–18 (1910) (franchise tax applies to foreign corporations but not to domestic corporations doing same business).
26. Binney v. Long, 299 U.S. 280, 292–95 (1936) (state succession tax); Valentine v. Great Atl. & Pac. Tea Co., 299 U.S. 32, 33 (1936) (graduated state tax on gross receipts of chain stores); Stewart Dry Goods Co. v. Lewis, 294 U.S. 550, 555–60 (1935) (sales tax on retailers graduated according to gross sales); Cumberland Coal Co. v. Board of Revision, 284 U.S. 23, 28–30 (1931) (discriminatory assessments); Quaker City Cab Co. v. Pennsylvania, 277 U.S. 389, 400–402 (1928) (gross receipts tax that distinguishes between corporate taxi businesses and individual or partnership taxi businesses); Louisville Gas & Elec. Co. v. Coleman, 277 U.S. 32, 37–40 (1928) (tax on recording of mortgages of more than five years but not on recording of shorter mortgages); Sioux City Bridge Co. v. Dakota County, 260 U.S. 441, 445–47 (1923) (discriminatory assessment); Kansas City

Southern Ry. v. Road Improvement Dist., 256 U.S. 658, 659–61 (1921) (tax assessment that treats railroad property differently from property of individuals).

27. Hartford Steam Boiler Inspection & Ins. Co. v. Harrison, 301 U.S. 459, 460–63 (1937) (state law permitting mutual fire and casualty insurance companies, but not stock fire and casualty insurance companies, to act through their salaried employees); Mayflower Farms, Inc. v. Ten Eyck, 297 U.S. 266, 272–74 (1936) (milk control act allowing dealers without advertised trade names who were in business before April 10, 1933 to undersell similar dealers who entered the business later); Frost v. Corporation Comm'n, 278 U.S. 515, 521–25 (1929) (permit requirements for cooperative cotton gins more lenient than permit requirements for other gins); Power Mfg. Co. v. Saunders, 274 U.S. 490, 493–97 (1927) (venue statute that treats foreign corporations differently from domestic corporations); Kentucky Finance Corp. v. Paramount Auto Exchange Corp., 262 U.S. 544, 549–51 (1923) (state law imposing various requirements on nonresident corporations, but not nonresident individuals, before each can sue in-state); McFarland v. American Sugar Ref. Co., 241 U.S. 79, 85–87 (1916) (statute making it criminal offense to pay less for sugar in Louisiana than in another state); Atchison, Topeka & Santa Fe Ry. v. Vosburg, 238 U.S. 56, 59–62 (1915) (law imposes reciprocal burdens on shipper and carrier while letting shipper recover attorney's fees upon carrier's delinquency, but not vice versa); Cotting v. Kansas City Stock Yards Co., 183 U.S. 79, 102–12 (1901) (state stock yard regulations that effectively apply only to Kansas City stock yards); Gulf, C. & S. F. Ry. Co. v. Ellis, 165 U.S. 150, 154–66 (1897) (law saying that for claims of $50 or less against a railroad, plaintiff can recover costs and attorney's fees if railroad fails to pay claim within thirty days after presentation of affidavit and if plaintiff then gets a good judgment against railroad).

Frankfurter's list categorized as equal protection decisions two other cases in which the Court did not make its basis of decision clear. FRANKFURTER, *supra* note 1, at 103, 110. Neither case gives much reason to suggest that this categorization is wrong. *See* Gast Realty & Investment Co. v. Schneider Granite Co., 240 U.S. 55, 57–59 (1916) (inequitable distribution of costs for paving street); *Ex parte* Young, 209 U.S. 123, 145–48 (1908) (huge criminal penalties for violation of rate-setting law make it impracticable to challenge rates).

28. I can identify at most five such possibilities. The first two are the *Gast* and *Young* cases discussed at the end of the previous note. In the *McFarland* and *Ellis* cases from that note, furthermore, the case syllabus says that the bases of decision were due process and equal protection. Frankfurter's book says the same. FRANKFURTER, *supra* note 1, at 98, 110. But the decisions in these cases do not clearly state that they are being decided on due process grounds and do contain fairly clear equal protection reasoning. *See* McFarland, 241 U.S. at 87 (where Holmes's opinion finally descends from abstraction to make a specific reference to equal protection); Ellis, 165 U.S. at 154–66 (which I construe as containing equal protection reasoning). Finally, Frankfurter claims that the *Frost* case from the previous note was decided on due process and equal protection grounds. FRANKFURTER, *supra* note 1, at 128. Since *Frost* strikes me as entirely an equal protection decision, I fail to see the basis for this description.

29. Wayne McCormack, *Economic Substantive Due Process and the Right of Live-*

lihood, 82 KY. L.J. 397, 406–7 (1993–1994) (no member of the Court used "procedural due process" until 1934 or "substantive due process" until 1948).

30. Ohio Bell Tel. Co. v. Public Utils. Comm'n, 301 U.S. 292, 300–306 (1937) (public utilities commission order not accompanied by adequate hearing); Brown v. Mississippi, 297 U.S. 278, 285–87 (1936) (murder conviction based on confession produced by torture); Georgia Ry. & Elec. Co. v. Decatur, 295 U.S. 165, 170–71 (1935) (denial of opportunity to offer evidence on benefits of an assessment denies street railway an adequate hearing); Morrison v. California, 291 U.S. 82, 88–97 (1934) (state's imposing on defendant burden of proving either citizenship or eligibility for naturalization under California alien land law violates due process); Southern Ry. Co. v. Virginia, 290 U.S. 190, 196–99 (1933) (railroad commission order invalid because statute on which it is based did not provide for notice, hearing, or review); Brinkerhoff-Faris Trust & Sav. Co. v. Hill, 281 U.S. 673, 678–82 (1930) (procedures for challenging state tax do not afford claimant adequate hearing); Wuchter v. Pizzutti, 276 U.S. 13, 17–24 (1928) (service of process against secretary of state insufficient notice to nonresident defendant sued because of in-state auto accident); Tumey v. Ohio, 273 U.S. 510, 522–35 (1927) (state statute empowering mayor to try alleged violators of state prohibition act violates due process, where mayor had pecuniary and other interests in conviction); Browning v. Hooper, 269 U.S. 396, 405–6 (1926) (notice and opportunity to be heard required before road district can make assessments against land); Moore v. Dempsey, 261 U.S. 86, 90–91 (1923) (murder trial in which accused black man hurried to conviction under influence of mob violates due process); Turner v. Wade, 254 U.S. 64, 69–70 (1920) (tax assessment not accompanied by adequate notice or hearing); Ohio Valley Water Co. v. Ben Avon Borough, 253 U.S. 287, 290–91 (1920) (no fair opportunity to appeal water rate order to judiciary); Oklahoma Operating Co. v. Love, 252 U.S. 331, 336–37 (1920) (no effective way to challenge rate order where only vehicle is violation of order and subsequent contempt proceedings, and severe penalties for violating order tended to preclude this option); Postal Tel. Cable Co. v. City of Newport, 247 U.S. 464, 474–76 (1918) (giving conclusive effect to a prior judgment against one not a party thereto, or in privity with such a party, violates due process); Saunders v. Shaw, 244 U.S. 317, 319–20 (1917) (state supreme court violates due process where it reverses case on basis of a factual proposition ruled immaterial at trial, one on which losing party had no opportunity to offer evidence); McDonald v. Mabee, 243 U.S. 90, 90–92 (1917) (service upon out-of-state defendant by publication in in-state newspaper provides insufficient notice); Coe v. Armour Fertilizer Works, 237 U.S. 413, 422–26 (1915) (no execution against shareholder where execution against corporation returned unsatisfied and shareholder afforded no notice or opportunity to be heard); Londoner v. City & County of Denver, 210 U.S. 373, 380–86 (1908) (inadequate hearing afforded taxpayer/landowner subject to assessment); Central of Georgia Ry. v. Wright, 207 U.S. 127, 138–42 (1907) (state's system of valuing property for tax purposes does not provide adequate opportunity to be heard); Wetmore v. Karrick, 205 U.S. 141, 148–60 (1907) (judgment rendered one year after dismissal of suit against defendant is void, where no subsequent service on defendant); Old Wayne Mut. Life Ass'n v. McDonough, 204 U.S. 8, 15–23 (1907) (due process violated by giving full faith and credit to judgment, where

first state lacked jurisdiction because no notice); Roller v. Holly, 176 U.S. 398, 407–13 (1900) (five days' notice of suit insufficient for out-of-state defendant).

31. Champlin Ref'g Co. v. Corporation Comm'n, 286 U.S. 210, 240–43 (1932) (criminal provisions of Oklahoma statute forbidding waste of petroleum); Cline v. Frink Dairy Co., 274 U.S. 445, 453–65 (1927) (criminal provisions of state antitrust law); Connally v. General Constr. Co., 269 U.S. 385, 391–95 (1926) (state minimum-wage law with criminal penalties); American Seeding Mach. Co. v. Kentucky, 236 U.S. 660, 661 (1915) (state antitrust law); Collins v. Kentucky, 234 U.S. 634, 636–38 (1914) (state antitrust law); International Harvester Co. v. Kentucky, 234 U.S. 216, 221–24 (1914) (state antitrust law). On the void-for-vagueness doctrine's derivation from the fair-notice requirement, *see, e.g.*, LAURENCE H. TRIBE, AMERICAN CONSTITUTIONAL LAW 683–84 (2d ed. 1988).

32. Consolidated Textile Corp. v. Gregory, 289 U.S. 85, 87–88 (1933) (in-state sale of goods through a controlled subsidiary insufficient for jurisdiction); Flexner v. Farson, 248 U.S. 289, 292–93 (1919) (service upon defendant's local agent does not afford jurisdiction where service occurs after agency terminated); Riverside & Dan River Cotton Mills v. Menefee, 237 U.S. 189, 193–96 (1915) (assertion of jurisdiction over out-of-state corporation exceeds limits set by due process); Simon v. Southern Ry. Co., 236 U.S. 115, 129–32 (1915) (jurisdiction via service on secretary of state fails where cause of action arose outside state and foreign corporation had no in-state agent).

33. Johnson Oil Ref'g Co. v. Oklahoma, 290 U.S. 158, 161–63 (1933) (tax on railroad tank cars); First Nat'l Bank v. Maine, 284 U.S. 312, 321–31 (1932) (succession tax on shares of an in-state corporation that were owned by resident of another state); Hans Rees' Sons, Inc. v. North Carolina, 283 U.S. 123, 130–36 (1931) (state income tax based on ratio of in-state tangible property to all property); Beidler v. South Carolina Tax Comm'n, 282 U.S. 1, 7–9 (1930) (inheritance tax on transfer of indebtedness owed to out-of-state decedent by in-state corporation); Baldwin v. Missouri, 281 U.S. 586, 590–94 (1930) (inheritance tax on in-state intangibles owned by out-of-state decedent); Farmers Loan & Trust Co. v. Minnesota, 280 U.S. 204, 209–13 (1930) (inheritance tax on bonds issued by taxing state; decedent domiciled, and bonds kept, in another state); Safe Deposit & Trust Co. v. Virginia, 280 U.S. 83, 91–94 (1929) (tax on out-of-state trust); Brooke v. City of Norfolk, 277 U.S. 27, 28–29 (1928) (tax on corpus of trust created and controlled out of state); Blodgett v. Silberman, 277 U.S. 1, 18 (1928) (death tax on coins and bank notes that decedent kept in another state); Southern Ry. v. Kentucky, 274 U.S. 76, 80–84 (1927) (taxation of railroad's out-of-state intangible property); Wachovia Bank & Trust Co. v. Doughton, 272 U.S. 567, 575 (1926) (tax on in-state exercise of power of appointment in trust fund created outside state); Rhode Island Hosp. Trust Co. v. Doughton, 270 U.S. 69, 80–84 (1926) (tax on inheritance of stock of foreign corporation owned by nonresident decedent); Lee v. Osceola & Little River Road Improvement Dist., 268 U.S. 643, 645–46 (1925) (tax on improvements made to land while it was owned by the federal government); Frick v. Pennsylvania, 268 U.S. 473, 488–500 (1925) (tax on transfer of out-of-state tangible property); Provident Sav. Life Assurance Soc'y v. Kentucky, 239 U.S. 103, 113–16 (1915) (tax on insurance premiums paid by state's residents to insurer that had ceased to do business in state); Atchison, Topeka, & Santa Fe Ry. v. O'Connor, 223 U.S. 280, 285 (1912) (tax on foreign corporation's capital

stock); Buck v. Beach, 206 U.S. 392, 399–409 (1907) (tax on mortgage notes present in state but created out of state and backed by out-of-state property); Union Refrigerator Transit Co. v. Kentucky, 199 U.S. 194, 201–11 (1905) (tax on corporation's out-of-state rolling stock); Delaware, L., & W. R.R. v. Pennsylvania, 198 U.S. 341, 352–60 (1905) (tax on corporate stock cannot include portion of stock's value attributable to tangible personal property located out of state); Fargo v. Hart, 193 U.S. 490, 498–503 (1904) (tax on out-of-state corporate property); Louisville & Jeffersonsville Ferry Co. v. Kentucky, 188 U.S. 385, 394–98 (1903) (tax on out-of-state franchise); Dewey v. Des Moines, 173 U.S. 193, 196–204 (1899) (tax assessment against out-of-state party who owned property in state, for amount by which liability exceeds sum realized from sale of in-state property). *See also* Senior v. Braden, 295 U.S. 422, 429–33 (1935) (state investments tax on income from certificates entitling holder to portion of rent from real estate, where some of the real estate is within state and some not; constitutional basis of decision not clear).

34. WRIGHT, *supra* note 1, at 160.

35. *Id.*

36. Hartford Accident & Indemnity Co. v. Delta Pine Land Co., 292 U.S. 143, 149–50 (1934) (Mississippi statute invalidating fidelity bond provisions limiting time within which suit possible does not govern contract made in Tennessee, even though suit took place in Mississippi); Home Ins. Co. v. Dick, 281 U.S. 397, 407–10 (1930) (Texas statute invalidating contract provisions that limit time of suit violates due process as applied to out-of-state insurance contract with Mexican insurer); Aetna Life Ins. Co. v. Dunken, 266 U.S. 389, 399–400 (1924) (Texas statute imposing penalty and allowing recovery of attorney's fees cannot constitutionally be applied against insurance company because policy on which suit is based was made outside the state and therefore is outside the state's power).

37. *See* Railroad Retirement Bd. v. Alton R.R., 295 U.S. 330, 346–61 (1935) (striking down the compulsory retirement and pension provisions of the Railroad Retirement Act under a supposed commerce clause analysis that actually involved substantive due process); Handy v. Delaware Trust Co., 285 U.S. 352, 354–55 (1932) (federal gift tax provision violates due process because arbitrary and capricious); Heiner v. Donnan, 285 U.S. 312, 322–29 (1932) (same); Chicago, R. I. & P. Ry. v. United States, 284 U.S. 80, 96–100 (1931) (striking down as a confiscatory and arbitrary denial of Fifth Amendment due process an Interstate Commerce Commission order that exempted certain railroads from stipulated per diem charges for switching cars from railroad to railroad); Untermyer v. Anderson, 276 U.S. 440, 445–46 (1928) (federal gift tax provision violates due process as applied because arbitrary); Adkins v. Children's Hosp., 261 U.S. 525, 544–62 (1923) (striking down a District of Columbia minimum-wage law); Adair v. United States, 208 U.S. 161, 173–80 (1908) (striking down a federal law that forbade the firing of railroad employees for their union affiliation).

38. Compania General de Tabacos de Filipinas v. Collector of Internal Revenue, 275 U.S. 87, 91–98 (1927) (striking down a Philippine tax on insurance premiums that the claimant had paid to a foreign insurer outside the islands' jurisdiction); Yu Cong Eng v. Trinidad, 271 U.S. 500, 524–27 (1926) (striking down a Philippine law making it a crime to keep business acount books in any language other than English, Spanish, or a local dialect).

39. West v. Chesapeake & Potomac Tel. Co., 295 U.S. 662, 668–80 (1935) (striking down as confiscatory telephone rates set by state public service commission); West Ohio Gas Co. v. Public Utils. Comm'n, 294 U.S. 79, 80–83 (1935) (striking down as confiscatory gas rates imposed by a public utilities commission).

40. Chicago, M. & S.P. Ry. v. Kennedy, 232 U.S. 626, 627 (1914) (striking down a state statute making it easier to recover for property damaged by operation of a railroad); Duluth & Iron Range R.R. v. St. Louis County, 179 U.S. 302, 304–5 (1900) (state law amending earlier grant so as to preserve corporation's obligations to state while taking away consideration therefor denies equal protection and takes property without due process).

41. In Home Tel. & Tel. Co. v. City of Los Angeles, 227 U.S. 278 (1913), a suit attacking municipal telephone rates as confiscatory, the district court dismissed the suit on the ground that federal jurisdiction was lacking. *Id.* at 281–82. While reversing that dismissal, the Supreme Court did not rule on the constitutionality of the rates. *See id.* at 283–96. In Ludwig v. Western Union Tel. Co., 216 U.S. 146, 162–64 (1910), which used the commerce clause to strike down a state license tax on foreign corporations, the Court specifically stated that it was not applying due process or equal protection. *Id.* at 163–64. Davis v. Wallace, 257 U.S. 478, 482–85 (1922) was not decided on constitutional grounds. Finally, I do not read Willcox v. Consolidated Gas Co., 212 U.S. 19 (1909), where the Court reversed a lower court decision invalidating a state gas rate determination, as clearly striking down any state action on due process grounds.

42. Herndon v. Lowry, 301 U.S. 242, 255–61 (1937) (state anti-insurrection statute violates First Amendment freedom of speech); De Jonge v. Oregon, 299 U.S. 353, 361–66 (1937) (state criminal syndicalism law, as applied, violates First Amendment freedoms of speech and assembly); Grosjean v. American Press Co., 297 U.S. 233, 242–50 (1936) (heavy and unusual state tax on certain newspapers violates First Amendment freedom of the press); Near v. Minnesota, 283 U.S. 697, 707–22 (1931) (state statute making newspapers that regularly engage in libel public nuisances violates First Amendment freedom of the press); Stromberg v. California, 283 U.S. 359, 368–70 (1931) (state statute forbidding display of red flag violates First Amendment freedom of speech); Fiske v. Kansas, 274 U.S. 380, 386–87 (1927) (state criminal syndicalism statute violates First Amendment freedom of speech as applied).

43. Powell v. Alabama, 287 U.S. 45, 68–73 (1932) (Fourteenth Amendment due process includes Sixth Amendment right to counsel, at least in a capital case).

44. *See, e.g.*, JAMES W. ELY, JR., THE GUARDIAN OF EVERY OTHER RIGHT: A CONSTITUTIONAL HISTORY OF PROPERTY RIGHTS 115–16 (2d ed. 1998).

45. Treigle v. Acme Homestead Ass'n, 297 U.S. 189, 194–98 (1936) (state law changing building and loan association's obligation to maintain a fund to pay shareholders violates due process and contract clause); Coombes v. Getz, 285 U.S. 434, 441–48 (1932) (repeal of state constitutional provision letting creditors and shareholders of corporation recover against directors for misappropriations by firm's officers violates due process and contract clause as applied to present case); Coolidge v. Long, 282 U.S. 582, 595–606 (1931) (application of estate tax to a succession under a trust created before passage of the tax violates due process and contract clause); Missouri, K. & T. Ry. v. Oklahoma, 271 U.S. 303, 306–10

(1926) (commission order that railroad provide pass under its tracks and highway over them and to pay part of resulting cost violates due process and contract clause because it invalidated an earlier ordinance under which city had agreed to pay full cost of such improvements); Bradley v. Lightcap, 195 U.S. 1, 19–24 (1904) (state statute limiting mortgagee's ability to retain title to repossessed property both impairs a contract obligation and deprives claimant of property without due process). *Cf.* Forbes Pioneer Boat Line v. Board of Comm'rs, 258 U.S. 338, 338–42 (1922) (statute validating illegal collection of canal toll after claimant had recovered for that toll apparently violates both due process and contract clause); Duluth & Iron Range R.R. v. St. Louis County, 179 U.S. 302, 304–5 (1900) (state law amending earlier grant so as to preserve corporation's obligations to state while taking away consideration therefor denies equal protection and takes property without due process).

46. Cudahy Packing Co. v. Hinkle, 278 U.S. 460, 464–67 (1929) (filing fee and license tax for out-of-state corporations); Alpha Portland Cement Co. v. Massachusetts, 268 U.S. 203, 216–20 (1925) (state excise tax on out-of-state corporations); Wallace v. Hines, 253 U.S. 66, 66–70 (1920) (tax on out-of-state businesses); Union Tank Line Co. v. Wright, 249 U.S. 275, 282–86 (1919) (tax on railroad's rolling stock used in state); International Paper Co. v. Massachusetts, 246 U.S. 135, 142–45 (1918) (excise tax on out-of-state corporations); Looney v. Crane Co., 245 U.S. 178, 187–91 (1917) (permit charges and franchise tax on foreign corporations); West v. Kansas Natural Gas Co., 221 U.S. 229, 249–62 (1911) (state law preventing foreign corporations from building pipelines across highways to transport natural gas outside the state); Western Union Tel. Co. v. Kansas, 216 U.S. 1, 18–48 (1910) (law conditioning out-of-state corporation's doing business on its paying a charter fee based on some percentage of its authorized capital).

47. Chicago, Burlington, & Quincy R.R. v. Chicago, 166 U.S. 226, 241 (1897); *see id.* at 233–42.

48. Panhandle Eastern Pipe Line Co. v. State Highway Comm'n, 294 U.S. 613, 618–23 (1935) (state highway commission order compelling pipeline company to make changes in its transmission lines without compensation); Delaware L. & W. R.R. v. Town of Norristown, 276 U.S. 182, 193–95 (1928) (ordinance establishing a hack stand at railroad station violates due process because it is a taking of railroad's property without just compensation); Pennsylvania Coal Co. v. Mahon, 260 U.S. 393, 412–16 (1922) (state statute forbidding the mining of coal in such a way as to cause subsidence of the land). *Cf.* Sterling v. Constantin, 287 U.S. 378, 396–404 (1932) (affirming injunction against governor's order limiting oil production in parts of Texas, perhaps on basis that order is an unconstitutional deprivation of property without due process); Ettor v. City of Tacoma, 228 U.S. 148, 156–57 (1913) (which struck down a state's repeal of a statute allowing recovery of consequential damages for effects of street grading, on apparent theory that by doing so, the state took a statutory compensation right that had already accrued). *Sterling* and *Ettor* do not employ takings rhetoric, but the government action they struck down resembles a taking more than anything else.

49. 260 U.S. at 415.

50. *E.g.*, GUNTHER & SULLIVAN, *supra* note 2, at 487–90 (putting *Mahon* within a section on the takings clause).

51. *E.g.*, TRIBE, *supra* note 31, at 772.

52. JAMES W. ELY, JR., THE CHIEF JUSTICESHIP OF MELVILLE W. FULLER 1888–1910, at 104 (1995).

53. However, one might argue that takings clause and contract clause values can be found within due process. How much difference is there between a provision checking government's ability to "deprive" people of property and one limiting the taking of it? And if freedom of contract is part of due process liberty, one might derive contract clause standards from due process. Still, these takings and contract clause values obviously have a firmer basis outside due process than within it.

54. 94 U.S. 113 (1877).

55. *Id.* at 125–36. For descriptions of *Munn*, of the historical roots of the doctrine, and of its subsequent evolution, *see, e.g.*, Breck P. McAllister, *Lord Hale and Business Affected with a Public Interest*, 43 HARV. L. REV. 759 (1930); Walton H. Hamilton, *Affectation with Public Interest*, 39 YALE L. J. 1089 (1930). On the doctrine and the uses to which it was put in the 1920s, see Robert C. Post, *Defending the Lifeworld: Substantive Due Process in the Taft Court Era*, 78 B.U. L. REV. 1489, 1505–29 (1998).

56. WRIGHT, *supra* note 1, at 100–101, 156.

57. *See generally* Stephen A. Siegel, *Understanding the* Lochner *Era: Lessons from the Controversy over Railroad and Utility Rate Regulation*, 70 VA. L. REV. 187, 199–223 (1984).

58. Railroad Comm'n Cases, 116 U.S. 307, 331 (1886). This language was quoted with approval in: Covington & L. Turnpike Rd. Co. v. Sandford, 164 U.S. 578, 593 (1896); Reagan v. Farmers' Loan & Trust Co., 154 U.S. 362, 398 (1894); and Chicago, Milwaukee, & St. Paul Ry. v. Minnesota, 134 U.S. 418, 456 (1890).

59. 169 U.S. 466, 522–50 (1898). *See* Siegel, *supra* note 57, at 224–32.

60. 169 U.S. at 526.

61. *E.g.*, West v. Chesapeake & Potomac Tel. Co., 295 U.S. 662, 671 (1935).

62. Siegel, *supra* note 57, at 224. Federal Power Comm'n v. Hope Natural Gas Co., 320 U.S. 591 (1944) is generally regarded as the case that ended the *Smyth v. Ames* approach to rate regulation.

63. On these subjects, *see generally* Siegel, *supra* note 57, at 224–59.

64. Smyth v. Ames, 169 U.S. 466, 522–50 (1898) (railroad rates); The Minnesota Rate Cases, 230 U.S. 352, 433–73 (1913) (railroad rates); The Missouri Rate Cases, 230 U.S. 474, 497–509 (1913) (railroad rates); San Joaquin & Kings River Canal & Irrigation Co. v. County of Stanislaus, 233 U.S. 454, 458–61 (1914) (water rates); Northern Pac. Ry. v. North Dakota, 236 U.S. 585, 595–605 (1915) (railroad rates); Norfolk & W. Ry. v. Conley, 236 U.S. 605, 608–14 (1915) (railroad rates); Rowland v. Boyle, 244 U.S. 106, 107–11 (1917) (railroad rates); City & County of Denver v. Denver Union Water Co., 246 U.S. 178, 185–94 (1918) (water rates); Detroit United Ry. v. City of Detroit, 248 U.S. 429, 434–37 (1919) (street railway fares); Groesbeck v. Duluth South Shore & Atl. Ry., 250 U.S. 607, 611–15 (1919) (railroad rates); Vandalia R.R. v. Schnull, 255 U.S. 113, 118–22 (1921) (railroad rates); Newton v. Consolidated Gas Co., 258 U.S. 165, 174–78 (1922) (gas rates); City of Houston v. Southwestern Bell Tel. Co., 259 U.S. 318, 322–25 (1922) (telephone rates); City of Paducah v. Paducah Ry., 261 U.S. 267, 272–75 (1923) (electric street car fares); Prendergast v. New York Tel. Co., 262 U.S. 43, 50–51 (1923) (telephone rates); Missouri *ex rel.* Southwestern Bell Tel. Co. v. Public Serv.

Comm'n, 262 U.S. 276, 287–89 (1923) (telephone rates); Bluefield Waterworks & Improvement Co. v. Public Serv. Comm'n, 262 U.S. 679, 684–95 (1923) (water rates); Pacific Gas & Elec. Co. v. City & County of San Francisco, 265 U.S. 403, 405–16 (1924) (gas rates); Ohio Utils. Co. v. Public Utils. Comm'n, 267 U.S. 359, 362–64 (1925) (gas and electric rates); Northern Pac. Ry. v. Department of Pub. Works, 268 U.S. 39, 42–45 (1925) (railroad rates); Banton v. Belt Line Ry., 268 U.S. 413, 419–25 (1925) (street railway fares); Smith v. Illinois Bell Tel. Co., 270 U.S. 587, 590–92 (1926) (commission delay in eliminating confiscatory telephone rates); Board of Pub. Util. Comm'rs v. New York Tel. Co., 271 U.S. 23, 31–32 (1926) (telephone rates); Patterson v. Mobile Gas Co., 271 U.S. 131, 135 (1926) (gas rates); McCardle v. Indianapolis Water Co., 272 U.S. 400, 410–21 (1926) (water rates); Ottinger v. Brooklyn Union Gas Co., 272 U.S. 579, 580–81 (1926) (gas rates); Chicago, M. & St. P. Ry. v. Public Utils. Comm'n, 274 U.S. 344, 350–52 (1927) (railroad rates); Denney v. Pacific Tel. & Tel. Co., 276 U.S. 97, 101–4 (1928) (telephone rates); United Rys. & Elec. Co. v. West, 280 U.S. 234, 249–54 (1930) (street railway rates); Railroad Comm'n v. Maxcy, 282 U.S. 249, 250–51 (1931) (water rates); Central Kentucky Natural Gas Co. v. Railroad Comm'n, 290 U.S. 264, 275 (1933) (gas rates); Columbus Gas & Fuel Co. v. Public Utils. Comm'n, 292 U.S. 398, 404–14 (1934) (price for natural gas); West Ohio Gas Co. v. Public Utils. Comm'n, 294 U.S. 63, 67–77 (1935) (gas rates); West Ohio Gas Co. v. Public Utils. Comm'n, 294 U.S. 79, 80–83 (1935) (gas rates); West v. Chesapeake & Potomac Tel. Co., 295 U.S. 662, 668–80 (1935) (telephone rates). *See also* Chicago, Rock Island, & Pac. Ry. v. United States, 284 U.S. 80, 96–100 (1931) (ICC order regarding charges for switching cars between railroads); City of San Antonio v. San Antonio Pub. Serv. Co., 255 U.S. 547, 555–58 (1921) (confiscatory nature of rates assumed in decision holding that government and utility had not made contract on this subject); Southern Iowa Elec. Co. v. City of Chariton, 255 U.S. 539, 542–46 (1921) (same); Lake Shore & M.S. Ry. v. Smith, 173 U.S. 684, 691–99 (1899) (statute compelling railroad to sell 1,000-mile tickets for a set fee).

65. Townsend v. Yeomans, 301 U.S. 441, 449–52 (1937) (maximum charges for handling and selling leaf tobacco; tobacco business held to be affected with a public interest); Dayton Power & Light Co. v. Public Utils. Comm'n, 292 U.S. 290, 295–312 (1934) (gas rates); Lindheimer v. Illinois Bell Tel. Co., 292 U.S. 151, 154–76 (1934) (telephone rates); Clark's Ferry Bridge Co. v. Public Serv. Comm'n, 291 U.S. 227, 234–42 (1934) (tolls charged by bridge company); Los Angeles Gas & Elec. Corp. v. Railroad Comm'n, 289 U.S. 287, 304–20 (1933) (gas rates); Public Service Comm'n v. Great N.Utils., 289 U.S. 130, 134–36 (1933) (gas rates); Wabash Valley Elec. Co. v. Young, 287 U.S. 488, 495–502 (1933) (electric rates); Aetna Ins. Co. v. Hyde, 275 U.S. 440, 446–48 (1928) (insurance rates); Lincoln Gas & Elec. Light Co. v. City of Lincoln, 250 U.S. 256, 266–69 (1919) (gas rates); Pennsylvania R.R. v. Towers, 245 U.S. 6, 8–17 (1917) (railroad rates); Darnell v. Edwards, 244 U.S. 564, 568–70 (1917) (railroad rates); Newark Natural Gas & Fuel Co. v. City of Newark, 242 U.S. 405, 407–9 (1917) (gas rates); Des Moines Gas Co. v. City of Des Moines, 238 U.S. 153, 157, 162–73 (1915) (gas rates); Wood v. Vandalia R.R., 231 U.S. 1, 3–8 (1913) (railroad rates); City of Knoxville v. Knoxville Water Co., 212 U.S. 1, 6–7, 15–19 (1909) (water rates); Seaboard Air Line Ry. v. Florida *ex rel.* Ellis, 203 U.S. 261, 268–70 (1906) (railroad rates); Atlantic Coast Line R.R. v. Florida *ex rel.* Ellis, 203 U.S. 256, 259–60 (1906) (railroad rates); Stanislaus County

v. San Joaquin & King's River Canal & Irrigation Co., 192 U.S. 201, 213–17 (1904) (water rates); San Diego Land & Town Co. v. Jasper, 189 U.S. 439, 441–47 (1903) (water rates); Minneapolis & St. Louis R.R. v. Minnesota, 186 U.S. 257, 264–69 (1902) (railroad rates). *See also* Oklahoma Natural Gas Co. v. Oklahoma, 258 U.S. 234, 237–39 (1922) (commission order reducing gas bills due to gas company's poor service does not violate due process); Producers Transp. Co. v. Railroad Comm'n, 251 U.S. 228, 229–32 (1920) (oil pipeline is devoted to public use and hence state can regulate its rates); Union Dry Goods Co. v. Georgia Pub. Serv. Comm'n, 248 U.S. 372, 374–77 (1919) (rejecting a consumer's challenge to a commission order raising electric rates). *Cf.* St. Joseph Stock Yards Co. v. United States, 298 U.S. 38, 51–72 (1936) (setting of rates under federal Packers and Stockyards Act); Washington *ex rel.* Stimson Lumber Co. v. Kuykendall, 275 U.S. 207, 212 (1927) (rates for towage of logs by common carrier do not take property in violation of Fourteenth Amendment); Dayton-Goose Creek Ry. v. United States, 263 U.S. 456, 486 (1924) (ICC regulation of railroad rates); The New England Divisions Case, 261 U.S. 184, 195–96 (1923) (ICC regulation of railroad rates); O'Keefe v. United States, 240 U.S. 294, 304 (1916) (ICC regulation of railroad rates).

66. On railroad regulation during that period, *see, e.g.*, LAWRENCE M. FRIEDMAN, A HISTORY OF AMERICAN LAW 446–54 (2d paperback ed. 1985).

67. *E.g.*, Richard J. Pierce, Jr., *Public Utility Regulatory Takings: Should the Judiciary Attempt to Police the Political Institutions?* 77 GEO. L.J. 2031, 2031, 2033 (1989).

68. 217 U.S. 196, 205–8 (1910).

69. Dobbins v. City of Los Angeles, 195 U.S. 223, 235–41 (1904) (arbitrary ordinance forbidding construction of gas works that city previously granted company right to build); Cleveland Elec. Ry. v. Cleveland, 204 U.S. 116, 142 (1907) (compelled transfer of street railway's rails, poles, and appliances to another street railway after termination of first railway's franchise); Louisville & Nashville R.R. v. Central Stock Yards Co., 212 U.S. 132, 143–45 (1909) (constitutional provision compelling railroad to deliver cars to, and accept cars from, other railroads); Missouri Pac. Ry. v. Nebraska, 217 U.S. 196, 205–8 (1910) (statute requiring railroad to build or maintain side track to grain elevators); Washington *ex rel.* Oregon R.R. & Navigation Co. v. Fairchild, 224 U.S. 510, 527–33 (1912) (order that tracks of competing railroads be connected at various points); South Covington & Cincinnati Street Ry. v. City of Covington, 235 U.S. 537, 548–49 (1915) (regulation that temperature of railroad cars never should fall below fifty degrees); Great N. Ry. v. Minnesota, 238 U.S. 340, 345–47 (1915) (order for railroad to install scale at its stock yards); Southwestern Tel. & Tel. Co. v. Danaher, 238 U.S. 482, 489–91 (1915) (penalty against phone company for terminating customer); Chicago M. & St. P. R.R. v. Wisconsin, 238 U.S. 491, 497–502 (1915) (statute requiring that railroad not let down upper berth in sleeping cars before berth actually sold); Mississippi R.R. Comm'n v. Mobile & Ohio R.R., 244 U.S. 388, 393–96 (1917) (order that financially distressed railroad restore six passenger trains to service); City of Los Angeles v. Los Angeles Gas & Elec. Corp., 251 U.S. 32, 37–40 (1919) (order that electric company remove its poles and property, so that city could build its own system); Brooks-Scanlon Co. v. Railroad Comm'n, 251 U.S. 396, 398–400 (1920) (order to operate narrow-gauge railroad at a loss);

Great N. Ry. v. Cahill, 253 U.S. 71, 73–77 (1920) (order for railroad to install scales at its stock yard); Chicago, St. P., M. & O. Ry. v. Holmberg, 282 U.S. 162, 166–67 (1930) (order that railroad install underground pass to connect two portions of farmer's farm); Thompson v. Consolidated Gas Utils. Corp., 300 U.S. 55, 68–81 (1937) (gas proration order limiting wells' production).

70. Nashville, Chattanooga, & St. Louis Ry. v. Walters, 294 U.S. 405, 413–33 (1935) (commission order requiring, at commission's discretion, that railroad build underpass at grade crossings and pay half the cost); Atchison, Topeka, & Santa Fe Ry. v. Railroad Comm'n, 283 U.S. 380, 394–97 (1931) (state commission order requiring interstate railroads to build passenger station in Los Angeles); New York *ex rel.* Woodhaven Gas Light Co. v. Public Serv. Comm'n, 269 U.S. 244, 245–46, 248–49 (1925) (commission order requiring gas company to extend its service to new territories); Western & Atl. R.R. v. Public Serv. Comm'n, 267 U.S. 493, 496–97 (1925) (commission order requiring railroad to continue to furnish switching service to a shipper on an established industrial siding); Fort Smith Light & Traction Co. v. Bourland, 267 U.S. 330, 332–33 (1925) (city commission's refusal to allow street railway to abandon part of one of its lines); United States v. New River Co., 265 U.S. 533, 542 (1924) (ICC order regarding distribution of coal from mines by carriers); Norfolk & W. Ry. v. Public Serv. Comm'n, 265 U.S. 70, 74–75 (1924) (commission order requiring railroad to furnish facilities for shippers, including a crossing, at a siding); Lake Erie & W. R. R v. Public Utils. Comm'n, 249 U.S. 422, 424–25 (1919) (commission order requiring railroad to restore a siding); Chicago & N.W. Ry. v. Ochs, 249 U.S. 416, 418–22 (1919) (commission order requiring railroad to alter and extend a side track to a manufacturing plant); Chicago, M., & St. P. Ry. v. Minneapolis Civic & Commerce Ass'n, 247 U.S. 490, 501–2 (1918) (commission order that two railroads owning a third railroad charge shippers the same rates over the third railroad's tracks that they charge over their own tracks); New York *ex rel.* New York & Queens Gas Co. v. McCall, 245 U.S. 345, 348–51 (1917) (commission order requiring gas company to extend its service area); Chesapeake & Ohio Ry. v. Public Serv. Comm'n, 242 U.S. 603, 606–8 (1917) (order that railroad begin passenger service on a branch line); Phoenix Ry. Co. v. Geary, 239 U.S. 277, 280–83 (1915) (commission order to railroad to double-track a portion of its line); Michigan Cent. R.R. v. Michigan R.R. Comm'n, 236 U.S. 615, 630–34 (1915) (commission order that two railroads physically connect their tracks); Wadley S. Ry. v. Georgia, 235 U.S. 651, 658–59 (1915) (commission order requiring railroad to cease demanding prepayment from one carrier, but not from another); Chicago, M., & St. P. Ry. v. Iowa, 233 U.S. 334, 344–45 (1914) (commission order requiring railroad to accept coal cars from other railroads and transport them as directed); Grand Trunk Ry. v. Michigan R.R. Comm'n, 231 U.S. 457, 463–73 (1913) (commission order that interstate railroads use their intracity tracks for the interchange of intrastate traffic); Missouri Pac. Ry. v. Kansas, 216 U.S. 262, 273–83 (1910) (commission order that railroad institute passenger service between two points); Atlantic Coast Line R.R. v. Corporation Comm'n, 206 U.S. 1, 19–27 (1907) (railroad commission order that railroad arrange through service between two points); Chicago, B., & Q. Ry. v. Illinois *ex rel.* Drainage Comm'rs., 200 U.S. 561, 581–95 (1906) (drainage commission order that railroad remove bridge over stream); New Orleans Gas Light Co. v. Drainage Comm'n, 197 U.S. 453, 453, 460–

62 (1905) (drainage commission order that gas company change location of gas pipes to accommodate a new drainage system); Wisconsin, Minnesota, & Pac. R.R. v. Jacobson, 179 U.S. 287, 296–302 (1900) (court order to two railroads to make track connections).

71. New Orleans Pub. Serv., Inc. v. City of New Orleans, 281 U.S. 682, 686–87 (1930) (ordinance requiring street railway to remove viaduct and construct double tracks across railroad tracks); Nashville, Chattanooga, & St. Louis Ry. v. White, 278 U.S. 456, 456, 458–60 (1929) (ordinance requiring railway to keep a flagman on duty on every street crossed by its tracks); Sullivan v. City of Shreveport, 251 U.S. 169, 171–73 (1919) (ordinance requiring that street cars be operated by a motor-man and a conductor); Pacific Gas & Elec. Co. v. City of Sacramento, 251 U.S. 22, 25–26 (1919) (ordinance requiring street railway to sprinkle streets near its tracks); Denver & Rio Grande R.R. v. City & County of Denver, 250 U.S. 241, 244–45 (1919) (ordinance requiring railroad to remove track crossing crowded city thoroughfare); Columbus Ry., Power, & Light Co. v. City of Columbus, 249 U.S. 399, 407–14 (1919) (ordinance requiring street railway to continue to operate at unremunerative rates for which it had previously contracted with city); Missouri Pac. Ry. v. City of Omaha, 235 U.S. 121, 127–31 (1914) (ordinance requiring that railroad construct viaduct over streets); Atlantic Coast Line R.R. v. City of Goldsboro, 232 U.S. 548, 555–62 (1914) (ordinance regulating trains and their tracks within a municipality); Chicago, M., & St. P. Ry. v. City of Minneapolis, 232 U.S. 430, 437–42 (1914) (city may condemn portion of railroad right-of-way and compel railroad to build a bridge over that portion at its own expense, without compensating railroad); Detroit United Ry. v. City of Detroit, 229 U.S. 39, 46 (1913) (ordinance compelling street railway to remove its tracks and property from the streets upon city's failure to renew franchise); West Chicago Street R.R. v. Illinois, 201 U.S. 506, 522–27 (1906) (ordinance requiring street railway to lower tunnel beneath a river).

72. Missouri Pac. R.R. v. Norwood, 283 U.S. 249, 254–56 (1931) (state statutes regulating the size of freight train and switching crews); Fort Smith Light & Traction Co. v. Board of Improvement, 274 U.S. 387, 390 (1927) (state statute requiring that street railway pave street between its tracks); Board of Trade v. Olsen, 262 U.S. 1, 40–41 (1923) (statute regulating, *inter alia*, membership in board of trade does not take property without due process because trade association is a business affected with a public interest); Great N. Ry. v. Minnesota *ex rel.* Village of Clara City, 246 U.S. 434, 436–39 (1918) (state statute applied to require railroad to construct sidewalk across right-of-way); St. Louis, Iron Mountain, & S. Ry. v. Arkansas, 240 U.S. 518, 520–21 (1916) (state statute requiring full switching crews on railroads exceeding 100 miles in length); Chicago & Alton R.R. v. Tranbarger, 238 U.S. 67, 76–78 (1915) (state statute requiring outlets for water across rights-of-way); Minneapolis & St. Louis R.R. v. Minnesota, 193 U.S. 53, 64–65 (1904) (state statute requiring railroads to establish stations at all villages and boroughs on their roads); Gladson v. Minnesota, 166 U.S. 427, 429–32 (1897) (state statute requiring railroads to stop all passenger trains at a station within each county seat); New York, New Haven, & Hartford R.R. v. New York, 165 U.S. 628, 634 (1897) (state statute prohibiting heating of railroad passenger cars by stoves or furnaces inside the car).

73. *See generally* Michael J. Phillips, *The Slow Return of Economic Substantive Due Process*, 49 SYRACUSE L. REV. 917 (1999).

74. 517 U.S. 559, 574–85 (1996).

75. *Id.* at 574.

76. *Id.* at 599 (Scalia, J., dissenting); *id.* at 612 (Ginsburg, J., dissenting).

77. *See* the sources in Phillips, *supra* note 73, at 952 n.241.

78. Deters v. Equifax Credit Info. Servs., 981 F. Supp. 1381, 1389 (D. Kan. 1997); Langmead v. Admiral Cruises, Inc., 696 So. 2d 1189, 1191–94 (Ala. Ct. App. 1997); Owens-Corning Fiberglass Corp. v. Malone, 972 S.W.2d 35, 45 (Tex. 1998).

79. *See supra* note 29 and accompanying text.

80. Schware v. Board of Bar Examiners, 353 U.S. 232 (1957). *See* Michael J. Phillips, *Entry Restrictions in the* Lochner *Court*, 4 GEO. MASON L. REV. 405, 420–21 (1996).

81. *See* DAVID P. CURRIE, THE CONSTITUTION IN THE SUPREME COURT: THE SECOND CENTURY, 1888–1986 41–44 (1990); WRIGHT, *supra* note 1, at 102–3; James W. Ely, Jr., *The Railroad Question Revisited*: Chicago, Milwaukee & St. Paul Railway. v. Minnesota *and Constitutional Limits on State Regulations*, 12 GREAT PLAINS Q. 121, 122 (1992).

82. 134 U.S. 418, 456–58 (1890).

83. *Gore*, 517 U.S. at 587 (Breyer, J., concurring), *quoting* Pacific Mut. Life Ins. Co. v. Haslip, 499 U.S. 1, 20–21 (1991).

84. *Id.* at 596.

85. *Id.* at 597.

86. Honda Motor Co. v. Oberg, 512 U.S. 415, 420 (1994).

87. TXO Prod. Corp. v. Alliance Resources Corp., 509 U.S. 443, 453–54 (1993). I say "assertedly" primarily because one decision cited by the Court appears to be an equal protection decision rather than a substantive due process case. *See* Seaboard Air Line Ry. v. Seegers, 207 U.S. 73, 76–78 (1907).

88. 509 U.S. at 455 (quoting from the respondents' brief).

89. *Id.*

90. St. Louis, Iron Mountain, & S. Ry. v. Wynne, 224 U.S. 354, 358–61 (1912) (statute giving double liability plus attorney's fees to owner of livestock allegedly killed by railroad, if railroad refused demand for compensation); Missouri Pac. Ry. v. Tucker, 230 U.S. 340, 346–51 (1913) (civil liquidated damages provision for violating rate schedule for shipping petroleum products); Chicago, M. & St. P. Ry. v. Polt, 232 U.S. 165, 167–68 (1914) (same general kind of statute at issue in *Wynne*); Chicago, M. & St. P. Ry. v. Kennedy, 232 U.S. 626, 627 (1914) (following *Polt*); Chicago & N.W. Ry. v. Nye-Schneider-Fowler Co., 260 U.S. 35, 46–48 (1922) (statute allowing recovery of attorney's fees against carrier upon appeal, under certain circumstances).

91. 224 U.S. 354, 360 (1912).

92. Kansas City S. Ry. v. Anderson, 233 U.S. 325 (1914).

93. Atlantic Coast Line R.R. v. Ford, 287 U.S. 502, 505–9 (1933) (presumption of railroad's negligence in crossing accidents); Southern Ry. v. Clift, 260 U.S. 316, 320–22 (1922) (state law requiring railroads to pay or reject claims for loss or damage to freight within ninety days or else suffer liability for such claims); St. Louis, Iron Mountain, & S. Ry. v. Williams, 251 U.S. 63, 66–67 (1919) (state statute imposing civil penalties on railroads whose passenger fees exceed those set by

state law is not arbitrary and unreasonable); Atlantic Coast Line R.R. v. Glenn, 239 U.S. 388, 392–94 (1915) (state statute making carrier liable for certain damage to shipped property even if the loss occurred while the goods were under another carrier's control, where the defendant had tried to contract out of this liability); Yazoo & Miss. Valley R.R. v. Jackson Vinegar Co., 226 U.S. 217, 219–20 (1912) (state law penalizing common carriers for failing to settle claims for lost or damaged freight within a reasonable time period, the penalty being in addition to actual damages); St. Louis & San Francisco Ry. v. Mathews, 165 U.S. 1, 27 (1897) (state statute making railroads liable for all property damaged by fire from its locomotives).

94. Life & Cas. Ins. Co. v. McCray, 291 U.S. 566, 569–72 (1934) (state statute making insurance company liable for certain damages and for attorney's fees upon its failure to pay upon demand under a life insurance policy); Hartford Accident & Indemnity Co. v. N. O. Nelson Mfg. Co., 291 U.S. 352, 358–60 (1934) (state statute making building contractor's bond inure to benefit of laborers and materialmen even though bond itself said the contrary); Louis Pizitz Dry Goods Co. v. Yeldell, 274 U.S. 112, 114–17 (1927) (state law allowing imposition of punitive damages against employers for deaths caused by the negligence of their employees); Eiger v. Garrity, 246 U.S. 97, 102–4 (1918) (state statute allowing wife whose means of support is damaged by sale of liquor to her husband to recover against tavern and creating a lien against the owner of the premises to enforce the judgment); Western Union Tel. Co. v. Commercial Milling Co., 218 U.S. 406, 421 (1910) (state statute imposing liability for misdelivery of telegram); Shevlin-Carpenter Co. v. Minnesota, 218 U.S. 57, 67–70 (1910) (state statute criminalizing the cutting of timber on state lands and imposing multiple damages therefor, even if the cutting was involuntary); Waters-Pierce Oil Co. v. Texas, 212 U.S. 86, 111–12 (1909) (penalties for violation of state antitrust statute not so severe as to violate due process).

95. Young v. Masci, 289 U.S. 253, 258–60 (1933) (state statute making car owner liable for personal injury resulting from negligent operation of car by person to whom it was entrusted, as applied to nonresident owner); Jones v. Brim, 165 U.S. 180, 181–84 (1897) (state statute imposing liability for damage to highways constructed on a hillside upon anyone who drives a herd over such a highway).

96. Western & Atl. R.R. v. Henderson, 279 U.S. 639, 642–44 (1929) (railroad liability).

97. Manley v. Georgia, 279 U.S. 1, 5 (1929) (bank director liability).

98. Great N. Ry. v. Weeks, 297 U.S. 135, 145–53 (1936) (use of pre-Great Depression numbers to value claimant's property); Louis K. Liggett Co. v. Lee, 288 U.S. 517, 533–36 (1933) (tax on chain store violates Fourteenth Amendment); Handy v. Delaware Trust Co., 285 U.S. 352, 354–55 (1932) (presumption); Heiner v. Donnan, 285 U.S. 312, 322–29 (1932) (presumption); Hoeper v. Tax Comm'n, 284 U.S. 206, 214–18 (1931) (tax against husband based on his income plus wife's income); Untermyer v. Anderson, 276 U.S. 440, 445–46 (1928) (gift tax); Schlesinger v. Wisconsin, 270 U.S. 230, 239–40 (1926) (presumption).

99. Helvering v. City Bank Farmers Trust Co., 296 U.S. 85, 89–92 (1935) (estate tax provision); Bromley v. McCaughn, 280 U.S. 124, 138–39 (1929) (graduation and exemption schemes in federal gift tax); Barclay & Co. v. Edwards, 267 U.S.

442, 444–45 (1924) (taxation of certain foreign corporations differently from their U.S. counterparts in federal income tax); LaBelle Iron Works v. United States, 256 U.S. 377, 392–94 (1921) (federal excess profits tax). None of these cases formally incorporated equal protection standards within Fifth Amendment due process.

100. Barwise v. Sheppard, 299 U.S. 33, 36–39 (1936) (tax on oil production); Fox v. Standard Oil Co., 294 U.S. 87, 103 (1935) (tax on chain gasoline stations); A. Magano Co. v. Hamilton, 292 U.S. 40, 44–47 (1934) (excise tax on butter substitutes sold within state); Puget Sound Power & Light Co. v. Seattle, 291 U.S. 619, 622–27 (1934) (tax by city on gross receipts of private competitor of city); Salomon v. State Tax Comm'n, 278 U.S. 484, 489–90 (1929) (methods of valuing contingent remainder in estate tax); Pierce Oil Corp. v. Hopkins, 264 U.S. 137, 138–39 (1924) (law requiring gas stations to collect gas tax); Baker v. Druesedow, 263 U.S. 137, 140 (1923) (tax on railroad property); Southern Ry. Co. v. Watts & Watts, 260 U.S. 519, 527–28 (1923) (valuations made in administration of state property tax); Knights v. Jackson, 260 U.S. 12, 14–15 (1922) (state income tax's distribution to cities for increases in teacher salaries); Bowman v. Continental Oil Co., 256 U.S. 642, 649 (1921) (excise tax on sale of gasoline); Jones v. City of Portland, 245 U.S. 217, 220–25 (1917) (tax to create municipal coal and fuel yard for sale of same to city's inhabitants); Ohio Tax Cases, 232 U.S. 576, 587–90 (1914) (levy on intrastate earnings of railroads); Paddell v. City of New York, 211 U.S. 446, 448–51 (1908) (land subject to mortgage can be taxed at full value).

101. Kansas City S. Ry. v. Road Improvement Dist., 266 U.S. 379, 386 (1924).

102. *See* Standard Pipe Line Co. v. Miller County Hwy. & Bridge Dist., 277 U.S. 160, 161–63 (1928) (assessment arbitrary because claimant received relatively little benefit from the road financed by the assessment); Road Improvement Dist. v. Missouri Pac. R.R., 274 U.S. 188, 189–95 (1927) (amount assessed against railroad for road paralleling its tracks exceeds benefit railroad received from the road); Myles Salt Co. v. Board of Comm'rs., 239 U.S. 478, 479–85 (1916) (drainage district's taxation of claimant's land unconstitutional because that land did not benefit from the district's undertakings). *Cf.* Norwood v. Baker, 172 U.S. 269, 275–97 (1898) (municipality's assessment of costs of condemning property for road on landowner whose land the road crossed violates principle that land must be specially benefitted by the activity funded by the assessment; case seems to partly proceed under a takings rationale).

103. *See* Roberts v. Richland Irrigation Dist., 289 U.S. 71, 73–75 (1933); Memphis & Charleston Ry. v. Pace, 282 U.S. 241, 246–49 (1931); Missouri Pac. R.R. v. Western Crawford Road Improvement Dist., 266 U.S. 187, 189–90 (1924); Kansas City S. Ry. v. Road Improvement Dist., 266 U.S. 379, 386–89 (1924); House v. Road Improvement Dist., 266 U.S. 175, 177–78 (1924); Houck v. Little River Drainage Dist., 239 U.S. 254, 260–67 (1915); Philip Wagner, Inc. v. Leser, 239 U.S. 207, 215–17, 218–20 (1915); Briscoe v. Rudolph, 221 U.S. 547, 547, 549–51 (1911); Carson v. Brockton Sewerage Comm'n, 182 U.S. 398, 400–405 (1901); Webster v. Fargo, 181 U.S. 394, 395 (1901); Tonawanda v. Lyon, 181 U.S. 389, 391–92 (1901); French v. Barber Asphalt Paving Co., 181 U.S. 324, 329–46 (1901).

104. 272 U.S. 365, 384–95 (1926).

105. *E.g.*, Village of Belle Terre v. Boraas, 416 U.S. 1, 3–5 (1974).

106. *Euclid*, 272 U.S. at 395 (emphasis added).

107. Nectow v. City of Cambridge, 277 U.S. 183, 188–89 (1928).

108. *See* Phillips, *supra* note 73, at 929–34.

109. 5 F.3d 685, 692–702 (3d Cir. 1993), *petition for rehearing en banc denied*, 1993 U.S. App. LEXIS 33087 (3d Cir. 1993). However, the plaintiff later was ordered to remit over $4.9 million of this amount to the city, or else to submit to a new trial on the damages issue. Parkway Garage, Inc. v. City of Philadelphia, 1994 U.S. Dist. LEXIS 10900 (E.D. Pa. 1994).

110. *See* Phillips, *supra* note 73, at 935–36.

111. 46 F.3d 162 (2d Cir. 1995).

112. Gorieb v. Fox, 274 U.S. 603, 608–10 (1927) (setback provision); Zahn v. Board of Pub. Works, 274 U.S. 325, 326–28 (1927) (zoning ordinance).

113. Marcus Brown Holding Co. v. Feldman, 256 U.S. 170, 197–99 (1921); Block v. Hirsch, 256 U.S. 135, 154–58 (1921).

114. Thomas Cusak Co. v. City of Chicago, 242 U.S. 526, 527, 529–31 (1917) (law regulating the placement of billboards); Hadacheck v. Sebastian, 239 U.S. 394, 407–12 (1915) (law prohibiting the manufacture of bricks within certain areas); Reinman v. City of Little Rock, 237 U.S. 171, 177–80 (1915) (ordinance forbidding livery stables within certain parts of a city); Bown v. Walling, 204 U.S. 320, 320–21 (1907) (law regulating herding and grazing of sheep); Bacon v. Walker, 204 U.S. 311, 314–17 (1907) (same); Fischer v. St. Louis, 194 U.S. 361, 372 (1904) (ordinance forbidding erection of cow stables and dairies); L'Hote v. New Orleans, 177 U.S. 587, 595–600 (1900) (ordinance prescribing limits within which woman of lewd character could dwell).

115. 226 U.S. 137, 143–44 (1912).

116. 278 U.S. 116, 120–23 (1928).

117. 245 U.S. 60, 74–82 (1917). The relevant portion of the ordinance made it unlawful for any black person to move into and occupy any house located in any block in which the majority of homes are owned by white people. On the significance of *Buchanan v. Warley*, see James W. Ely, Jr., *Reflections on* Buchanan v. Warley, *Property Rights, and Race*, 51 VAND. L. REV. 953 (1998); Roger L. Rice, *Residential Segregation by Law, 1910–1917*, 34 J. SOUTH. HIST. 179 (1968).

118. Miller v. Schoene, 276 U.S. 272, 277–81 (1928) (law requiring that diseased trees be cut down); Northwestern Laundry v. City of Des Moines, 239 U.S. 486, 490–92 (1916) (smoke regulation); Hutchinson v. City of Valdosta, 227 U.S. 303, 307–8 (1913) (ordinance requiring people near sewer lines to install water closets and to connect with the sewer); Gardner v. Michigan, 199 U.S. 325, 330–33 (1905) (ordinance requiring all occupants of buildings to place waste in a suitable watertight vessel and to place it where it could be picked up and letting the city give some party the exclusive right to collect the waste); California Reduction Co. v. Sanitary Reduction Works, 199 U.S. 306, 317–25 (1905) (ordinance requiring the cremation of garbage and refuse at a designated place).

119. Bayside Fish Flour Co. v. Gentry, 297 U.S. 422, 427–28 (1936) (statute restricting processing of fish in order to conserve their numbers); Walls v. Midland Carbon Co., 254 U.S. 300, 318–24 (1920) (statute forbidding, *inter alia*, various uses of natural gas without its heat being fully utilized); Lindsley v. Natural Carbonic Gas Co., 220 U.S. 61, 76–78 (1911) (statute regulating the pumping of mineral waters containing an excess of carbonic gas with the aim of selling such gas as a separate commodity; aim of law is to preserve the common pool); New

York *ex rel.* Silz v. Hesterberg, 211 U.S. 31, 39–40 (1908) (statute prohibiting the possession of game during the closed season for such game, as applied to game killed in England); Ohio Oil Co. v. Indiana, 177 U.S. 190, 200–11 (1900) (law restricting flow of gas or oil from well into air to prevent waste).

120. Standard Oil Co. v. City of Marysville, 279 U.S. 582, 583–87 (1929); Pierce Oil Corp. v. City of Hope, 248 U.S. 498, 499–501 (1919).

121. Henderson Co. v. Thompson, 300 U.S. 258, 264–65 (1937) (regulation of means of production and use of natural gas); Gant v. Oklahoma City, 289 U.S. 98, 100–03 (1933) (law requiring filing of bond to drill for gas or oil within city limits); Atlantic Coast Line R.R. v. Georgia, 234 U.S. 280, 287–89 (1914) (train headlights); Norfolk & Suburban Turnpike Co. v. Virginia, 225 U.S. 264, 270–71 (1912) (toll roads); City of Chicago v. Sturges, 222 U.S. 313, 321–22 (1911) (indemnification of property owners); Jacobsen v. Massachusetts, 197 U.S. 11, 24–39 (1905) (vaccination).

122. 216 U.S. 358, 364–66 (1910).

123. *Id.* at 366.

124. *See* Crane v. Campbell, 245 U.S. 304, 306–07 (1917) (upholding a state statute forbidding, *inter alia,* the personal possession of liquor); Clark Distilling Co. v. Western Md. Ry., 242 U.S. 311, 319–20 (1917) (upholding a state prohibition law that, *inter alia,* forbade the importation of liquor by carriers); Eberle v. Michigan, 232 U.S. 700, 706–7 (1914) (upholding a local option law regarding the sale of liquor within a county against various claims that it deprived brewers and merchants of various property rights); Purity Extract & Tonic Co. v. Lynch, 226 U.S. 192, 199–205 (1912) (upholding state statute forbidding the sale of malt liquor).

125. Butler v. Perry, 240 U.S. 328, 333 (1916) (work on public roads); Waugh v. Board of Trustees, 237 U.S. 589, 593, 595–97 (1915) (fraternities); Murphy v. California, 225 U.S. 623, 628–30 (1913) (billiard halls); Marvin v. Trout, 199 U.S. 212, 224–25 (1905) (gambling).

126. 274 U.S. 200 (1927). The law was challenged on both due process and equal protection grounds, *id.* at 205, and the substantive due process discussion occurs in *id.* at 207.

127. *See, e.g.,* GUNTHER & SULLIVAN, *supra* note 2, at 516–18 (discussing the role *Meyer* and *Pierce* played in the development of modern substantive due process).

128. 262 U.S. 390, 399–403 (1923) (striking down a state statute that forbade the teaching of any subject in any language besides English in both public and private schools and that also forbade the teaching of any such language as a language to any student who had not completed the eighth grade).

129. Bartels v. Iowa, 262 U.S. 404, 409–11 (1923) (striking down, on the authority of *Meyer,* laws resembling those at issue in *Meyer*).

130. 268 U.S. 510, 534–35 (1925) (striking down a state law requiring that all students between the ages of eight and sixteen attend a public school).

131. In *Pierce,* the Court said that "[u]nder the doctrine of Meyer v. Nebraska, . . . we think it entirely plain that the [law at issue] unreasonably interferes with the liberty of parents and guardians to direct the upbringing and education of children under their control." *Id.* at 534–35 [citation omitted]. Actually, though, Justice McReynolds's *Meyer* opinion emphasized a panoply of rights, including a language teacher's right to teach a particular language to children, a parent's

right to retain him to do so, a pupil's right to acquire knowledge, and a parent's right to control her child's education. 262 U.S. at 400–401.

132. The statements about McReynolds in this paragraph come from JAMES EDWARD BOND, I DISSENT: THE LEGACY OF JUSTICE JAMES CLARK MCREYNOLDS (1992).

133. *Id.* at viii, 51.

134. *Id.* at 135.

135. 262 U.S. at 399.

136. Terrace v. Thompson, 263 U.S. 197, 216–18 (1923) (statute preventing aliens who have not declared intention to become a U.S. citizen from taking or holding interests in land); Nicchia v. New York, 254 U.S. 228, 230–31 (1920) (license fee for dog owners); Western Turf Ass'n v. Greenberg, 204 U.S. 359, 363–64 (1907) (statute preventing places of public entertainment from forbidding entry to those over twenty-one, subject to certain exceptions).

137. Sproles v. Binford, 286 U.S. 374, 388–89 (1932) (upholding weight limits for trucks against a due process attack).

138. Pacific States Box & Basket Co. v. White, 296 U.S. 176, 180–82 (1935) (state regulation of containers for raspberries and strawberries); Corn Prods. Ref. Co. v. Eddy, 249 U.S. 427, 431 (1919) (law mandating the labeling of syrups and disclosure of their ingredients on the label); Pure Oil Co. v. Minnesota, 248 U.S. 158, 161–63 (1918) (law requiring inspection of gasoline and illuminating oil before sale); Price v. Illinois, 238 U.S. 446, 451–53 (1915) (law forbidding sale of food preservatives containing boric acid); Adams v. City of Milwaukee, 228 U.S. 572, 582–84 (1913) (portion of ordinance regulating the sale of milk that requires nonconforming milk to be confiscated, forfeited, and destroyed).

139. 270 U.S. 402, 412–15 (1926). Shoddy is material spun into yarn, knit, or woven into fabric, then cut up, torn up, broken up, or ground up.

140. National Fertilizer Ass'n v. Bradley, 301 U.S. 178, 182 (1937) (state statute requiring that fertilizer manufacturers attach tags showing their products' ingredients and their proportions); Hutchinson Ice Cream Co. v. Iowa, 242 U.S. 153, 157–59 (1916) (state law forbidding sale of "ice cream" that does not contain a certain percentage of butter fat); Capital City Dairy Co. v. Ohio, 183 U.S. 238, 245–47 (1902) (law allowing manufacture and sale of oleo so long as it was free of any coloring or ingredients that would make it appear to be butter). *See also* Halter v. Nebraska, 205 U.S. 34, 38–43 (1907) (state statute forbidding, *inter alia*, sale of merchandise bearing representation of American flag).

141. Armour & Co. v. North Dakota, 240 U.S. 510, 512–16 (1916) (state law requiring that lard be sold in containers holding a specified number of pounds or even multiples thereof); Schmidinger v. City of Chicago, 226 U.S. 578, 585–90 (1913) (state law regulating sizes of bread loaves for sale); House v. Mayes, 219 U.S. 270, 278, 282–84 (1911) (state law requiring grain traders to sell at actual weight).

142. Jay Burns Baking Co. v. Bryan, 264 U.S. 504, 513–17 (1924).

143. P. F. Petersen Baking Co. v. Bryan, 290 U.S. 570, 572–75 (1934).

144. 273 U.S. 418, 429–45 (1927) (resale price of theater tickets).

145. 277 U.S. 350, 355–59 (1928) (employment agency fees).

146. 278 U.S. 235, 239–45 (1929) (retail gasoline prices).

147. *See* Nebbia v. New York, 291 U.S. 502, 521–39 (1934).

148. *See, e.g.*, Hegeman Farms Corp. v. Baldwin, 293 U.S. 163, 167–73 (1934) (upholding New York regulations establishing minimum prices for purchase and resale of milk by dealers).

149. Tagg Bros. & Moorhead v. United States, 280 U.S. 420, 437–39 (1930) (regulation of fees and prices under the Packers and Stockyards Act); Highland v. Russell Car & Snow Plow Co., 279 U.S. 253, 258–62 (1929) (federal price fixing during World War I).

150. Advance-Rumely Thresher Co. v. Jackson, 287 U.S. 283, 288–91 (1932) (striking down a state law giving purchasers of harvesting and threshing machinery a reasonable time for inspection and a warranty of fitness for the machinery's purposes and forbidding disclaimers of this implied warranty).

151. The leading case is German Alliance Ins. Co. v. Lewis, 233 U.S. 389, 404–18 (1914).

152. Hardware Dealers Mut. Fire Ins. Co. v. Glidden, 284 U.S. 151, 157–59 (1931) (statute compelling arbitration where the parties cannot agree on the loss payable under a fire insurance policy and imposing an arbitration clause in the standard fire policy); Merchants Mut. Automobile Liab. Ins. Co. v. Smart, 267 U.S. 126, 128–30 (1925) (statute saying that, in auto insurance contracts, the insurer remains liable despite the insured's insolvency or bankruptcy); National Union Fire Ins. Co. v. Wanberg, 260 U.S. 71, 73–77 (1922) (the hail-loss measure); German Alliance Ins. Co. v. Hale, 219 U.S. 307, 315–18 (1911) (statute allowing insured to recover 125 percent of covered loss from insurer connected with a tariff association that fixed rates); Northwestern Nat. Life Ins. Co. v. Riggs, 203 U.S. 243, 252–55 (1906) (statute saying that no misrepresentation in a life insurance application is material, or can void the contract, unless the matter misrepresented contributed to the contingency insured against).

153. Hodge Drive-It-Yourself Co. v. Cincinnati, 284 U.S. 335, 336–38 (1932) (law requiring that auto rental companies pay license fees on vehicles and insure against their negligent operation); Packard v. Banton, 264 U.S. 140, 145 (1924) (law requiring that taxi companies insure).

154. 165 U.S. 578, 589–93 (1897).

155. *E.g.*, GUNTHER & SULLIVAN, *supra* note 2, at 460.

156. Compania General de Tabacos de Filipinas v. Collector of Internal Revenue, 275 U.S. 87, 91–98 (1927) (striking down a Philippine tax on insurance premiums paid to a foreign insurer); Fidelity & Deposit Co. v. Tafoya, 270 U.S. 426, 433–36 (1926) (striking down state law forbidding any insurance company authorized to do business in the state from paying anyone not so authorized to place insurance on in-state risks); St. Louis Cotton Compress Co. v. Arkansas, 260 U.S. 346, 348–49 (1922) (striking down state statute imposing five percent tax on amounts paid to insure in-state property with insurer that is not registered to do business within the state).

157. New York Life Ins. Co. v. Dodge, 246 U.S. 357, 367–77 (1918) (Missouri statute forbidding the forfeiture of a life insurance policy for nonpayment of premiums, valuing the policy, and using this value to set a single premium for temporary insurance cannot govern a loan contract made in New York and stating that it would be governed by New York law).

158. Chief Justice Taft evidently thought that banking was a business affected

with a public interest. Chas. Wolff Packing Co. v. Court of Indus. Relations, 262 U.S. 522, 535 (1923).

159. Noble State Bank v. Haskell, 219 U.S. 104, 110–13 (1911) (law imposing one percent fee on bank deposits to establish fund to pay for protection of customers of failing banks); Assaria State Bank v. Dolley, 219 U.S. 121, 125–27 (1911); Shallenberger v. First State Bank, 219 U.S. 114, 120 (1911). *See also* Gibbes v. Zimmerman, 290 U.S. 326, 331–33 (1933) (state law regulating liquidation of insolvent banks).

160. Brodnax v. Missouri, 219 U.S. 285, 292–93 (1911) (state statute forbidding maintenance of any place where futures contracts traded); Otis v. Parker, 187 U.S. 606, 608–10 (1903) (state constitutional provision voiding all margin sales of, and futures contracts for, corporate stock, as applied to margin sales); Booth v. Illinois, 184 U.S. 425, 428–32 (1902) (state statute criminalizing and voiding certain options and futures contracts).

161. *See, e.g.*, 44 Liquormart, Inc. v. Rhode Island, 517 U.S. 484, 501–14 (1996).

162. Semler v. Oregon State Bd. of Dental Examiners, 294 U.S. 608, 610–13 (1935) (state law forbidding certain kinds of advertising by dentists); Packer Corp. v. Utah, 285 U.S. 105, 111 (1932) (summarily dismissing a substantive due process challenge to a state law forbidding tobacco advertising on billboards, street car signs, and placards); Fifth Avenue Coach Co. v. City of New York, 221 U.S. 467, 481–83 (1911) (prohibition of advertising on buses is within the police power).

163. *See supra* note 42 and accompanying text.

164. Yu Cong Eng v. Trinidad, 271 U.S. 500, 524–27 (1926).

165. Endicott Johnson Corp. v. Encyclopedia Press, Inc., 266 U.S. 285, 290 (1924) (statute creating lien against future wages of judgment debtor); Great Southern Fire Proof Hotel Co. v. Jones, 193 U.S. 532, 548–50 (1904) (state mechanics' lien law).

166. Lemieux v. Young, 211 U.S. 489, 494–96 (1909) (state law requiring notice of sale before merchant can sell stock-in-trade); Kidd, Dater, & Price Co. v. Musselman Grocer Co., 217 U.S. 461, 471–74 (1910) (following *Lemieux* in a case involving a similar statute).

167. Kuehner v. Irving Trust Co., 299 U.S. 445, 450–56 (1937) (federal bankruptcy provision); James-Dickinson Farm Mortgage Co. v. Harry, 273 U.S. 119, 123–24 (1927) (statute expanding fraud liability to include not only misrepresentations regarding past or existing facts but also false promises); Delaware, L., & W. R.R. v. United States, 231 U.S. 363, 369–70 (1913) (federal law forbidding railroads from transporting their own property in interstate commerce, unless the property was necessary for their business as common carriers); Rosenthal v. New York, 226 U.S. 260, 266–69 (1912) (state statute forbidding junk dealers from buying wire or copper used by a railroad or a telephone or telegraph company without first determining that the seller had a right to sell); Mutual Loan Co. v. Martell, 222 U.S. 225, 232–35 (1911) (state law restricting certain assignments of wages by employees); Ling Su Fan v. United States, 218 U.S. 302, 308, 309–12 (1910) (Philippine law forbidding the exportation of silver coins from the islands); Wilson v. Eureka City, 173 U.S. 32, 35–37 (1899) (ordinance requiring written permission from certain city officials to move a building on city streets); Sentell v. New Orleans & Carrollton R.R., 166 U.S. 698, 705–6

(1897) (state statute providing that owner not entitled to legal protection against destruction of dog unless dog placed on assessment rolls).

168. Central Lumber Co. v. South Dakota, 226 U.S. 157, 162 (1912) (state statute forbidding price discrimination in sale of commodities); Grenada Lumber Co. v. Mississippi, 217 U.S. 433, 441–43 (1910) (state antitrust law); National Cotton Oil Co. v. Texas, 197 U.S. 115, 127–30 (1905) (state antitrust law); Smiley v. Kansas, 196 U.S. 447, 453–57 (1905) (state antitrust law); Aikens v. Wisconsin, 195 U.S. 194, 203–5 (1904) (statute forbidding combinations for the purpose of willfully or maliciously injuring another in his occupation or business). At least two of the laws the old Court upheld probably suppressed competition. *See* Old Dearborn Distributing Co. v. Seagram Distillers Corp., 299 U.S. 183, 191–99 (1936) (upholding a state "fair trade" act that allowed vertical price fixing); Liberty Warehouse Co. v. Burley Tobacco Growers' Co-Operative Marketing Ass'n, 276 U.S. 71, 89–97 (1928) (upholding a state cooperative marketing act with what perhaps are some anticompetitive features).

169. 274 U.S. 1, 8–11 (1927).

170. *See id*. at 8–9.

171. *E.g.*, Kavanu v. Santa Monica Rent Control Bd., 941 P.2d 851, 857, 864–65 (Cal. 1997) (striking down Santa Monica rent control ordinance on substantive due process grounds); Guimont v. Clarke, 854 P.2d 1, 13–16 (Wash. 1993) (state statute requiring mobile home park owners to pay relocation assistance to park's tenants upon owner's closing park violates substantive due process because it is unduly oppressive to the landowner). *See* Phillips, *supra* note 73, at 944–49.

172. *E.g.*, Independent Coin Payphone Ass'n v. City of Chicago, 863 F. Supp. 744, 752 (N.D. Ill. 1994) (substantive due process challenge to ordinances severely restricting the installation of public payphones survives motion to dismiss); *In re* Forfeiture of 1969 Piper Navajo, 592 So. 2d 233, 235–36 (Fla. 1992) (state law permitting seizure of private aircraft whose fuel tanks do not conform to Federal Aviation Administration [FAA] regulations violates substantive due process because confiscation too restrictive a means of accomplishing state's concededly legitimate ends); Rivers v. State, 490 S.E.2d 261, 263–65 (S.C. 1997) (state tax law retroactively reducing refunds receivable by taxpayers under previous law violates substantive due process because the retroactivity period is too long).

173. *E.g.*, Santos v. City of Houston, 852 F. Supp. 601, 607–8 (S.D. Tex. 1994) (striking down on substantive due process grounds a Houston ordinance forbidding the operation of jitneys). *See generally* Phillips, *supra* note 73, at 936–44.

174. 244 U.S. 590, 593–97 (1917). The law struck down in *Adams v. Tanner* was a state initiative making it unlawful for employment agencies to receive fees from people seeking employment, in return for furnishing those people with employment or with information leading thereto.

175. Baccus v. Louisiana, 232 U.S. 334, 337 (1914) (state law forbidding sale of drugs by itinerant vendors).

176. *See* Phillips, *supra* note 80, at 431–34.

177. Graves v. Minnesota, 272 U.S. 425, 426–29 (1926) (dentistry); La Tourette v. McMaster, 248 U.S. 465, 467–68 (1919) (insurance brokerage); Payne v. Kansas, 248 U.S. 112, 112–13 (1918) (license to sell farm produce on commission); McNaughton v. Johnson, 242 U.S. 344, 348–49 (1917) (optometry); Gundling v. Chicago, 177 U.S. 183, 185–99 (1900) (ordinance giving mayor power to grant licenses

to sell cigarettes). *See also* Hayman v. City of Galveston, 273 U.S. 414, 416 (1927) (city hospital's exclusion of osteopathic physician from practice with hospital).

178. *See* Michael J. Phillips, *The Progressiveness of the* Lochner *Court*, 75 DENVER U. L. REV. 453, 484 n.228 (1998).

179. Rast v. Van Deman & Lewis Co., 240 U.S. 342, 363–67 (1916); Tanner v. Little, 240 U.S. 369, 381–86 (1916) (following *Rast*); Pitney v. Washington, 240 U.S. 387, 390 (1916) (same).

180. 285 U.S. 262, 273–80 (1932).

181. 278 U.S. 105, 111–14 (1928).

182. Michigan Pub. Utils. Comm'n v. Duke, 266 U.S. 570, 577–78 (1925); Frost & Frost Trucking Co. v. Railroad Comm'n, 271 U.S. 583, 592–99 (1926); Smith v. Cahoon, 283 U.S. 553, 563 (1931). Common carriers undertake to carry all persons or their goods, while private carriers undertake to carry particular people or particular goods on particular occasions.

183. Stephenson v. Binford, 287 U.S. 251, 265–69 (1932). *See also* Stanley v. Public Utils. Comm'n, 295 U.S. 76, 76–78 (1935) (state statute requiring that common carriers obtain a certificate of convenience and necessity and making this a matter of right where the applicant previously had provided good service).

184. 233 U.S. 630, 638–39 (1914). This case found the law unconstitutional on Fourteenth Amendment grounds, without specifying the specific provision on which it relied. But it evidently thought that life, liberty, property, and equal protection are closely related. *Id.* at 636.

185. WRIGHT, *supra* note 1, at 172.

186. Adkins v. Children's Hosp., 261 U.S. 525, 545–62 (1923); Coppage v. Kansas, 236 U.S. 1, 8–20 (1915); Adair v. United States, 208 U.S. 161, 172–76 (1908); Lochner v. New York, 198 U.S. 45, 57–64 (1905).

187. Morehead v. New York *ex rel.* Tipaldo, 298 U.S. 587, 603–18 (1936); Donham v. West-Nelson Mfg. Co., 273 U.S. 657 (1927); Murphy v. Sardell, 269 U.S. 530 (1925).

188. Chas. Wolff Packing Co. v. Court of Indus. Relations, 262 U.S. 522, 534–44 (1923). *Chas. Wolff* receives an extensive discussion in Post, *supra* note 55, at 1508–22.

189. Dorchy v. Kansas, 264 U.S. 286, 289–91 (1924) (accepting *Chas. Wolff* while declining to decide whether a provision of the act at issue there was separable from it and returning the case to the state for a decision on this issue); Chas. Wolff Packing Co. v. Court of Indus. Relations, 267 U.S. 552, 566–69 (1925) (striking down a maximum-hours provision contained in a writ of mandamus issued by a state supreme court following the first *Chas. Wolff* case's return to that court).

190. 257 U.S. 312, 327–30 (1921).

191. 295 U.S. 330, 347–61 (1935).

192. Bunting v. Oregon, 243 U.S. 426, 434–39 (1917) (upholding a state maximum-hours law for factory workers); Muller v. Oregon, 208 U.S. 412, 417–23 (1908) (upholding a state maximum-hours law for women); Holden v. Hardy, 169 U.S. 366, 389–98 (1898) (upholding a state maximum-hours law for mining employees).

193. Bosley v. McLaughlin, 236 U.S. 385, 392–94 (1915) (eight-hour daily maximum for women, as applied to graduate nurses in hospitals); Miller v. Wilson, 236 U.S. 373, 379–82 (1915) (eight-hour day for women in a wide range of oc-

cupations); Hawley v. Walker, 232 U.S. 718 (1914) (per curiam decision upholding a maximum-hours law for women on the authority of *Muller v. Oregon*); Riley v. Massachusetts, 232 U.S. 671, 679–81 (1914) (ten-hour daily limit for women working in manufacturing or mechanical establishments).

194. *E.g.*, Adkins v. Children's Hosp., 261 U.S. 525, 553–54 (1923) (amount of wages to be paid and received is at "the heart" of a labor contract).

195. Rail & River Coal Co. v. Yaple, 236 U.S. 338, 349–55 (1915) (state law requiring that coal miners' pay be based, generally speaking, on carloads of coal they produced); Erie R.R. v. Williams, 233 U.S. 685, 699–704 (1914) (state law requiring that railroads pay their employees semimonthly in cash); McLean v. Arkansas, 211 U.S. 539, 545–51 (1909) (state law requiring that, for payment purposes, coal produced by miners be weighed as it comes from the mine and before it is passed over a screen); Knoxville Iron Co. v. Harbison, 183 U.S. 13, 19–22 (1901) (state law requiring employer to redeem scrip in cash).

196. *Adkins*, 261 U.S. at 547. *See* Atkin v. Kansas, 191 U.S. 207, 219–24 (1903) (state law regulating wages and hours of workers employed by municipal paving contractors); Heim v. McCall, 239 U.S. 175, 191–93 (1915) (state law giving citizens a preference over aliens in employment on public works); Crane v. New York, 239 U.S. 195, 198 (1915) (a companion case to *Heim*). *Cf.* Ellis v. United States, 206 U.S. 246, 255–56 (1907) (upholding a federal statute limiting the hours worked by federal workers or employees of federal contractors to eight per day; decided on authority of *Atkin* without mentioning due process).

197. Wilson v. New, 243 U.S. 332 (1917). Among other things, the Court held that the act did not unconstitutionally interfere with the private rights of the railroads and their employees, because the industry was one charged with a public interest. *Id.* at 352–53. The affected-with-a-public-interest doctrine is usually regarded as an application of substantive due process. The Court also rejected a due process claim that seems both procedural and substantive. This is the assertion that the law was both improvidently enacted and unworkable. *Id.* at 355–59.

198. Hadley Arkes, *Who's the Laissez-Fairest of Them All? The Tradition of Natural Rights in American Law*, 60 POLICY REV. 78, 78 (1992).

199. *See, e.g.*, Miller v. Wilson, 236 U.S. 373, 380–82 (1915).

200. Radice v. New York, 264 U.S. 292, 293–95 (1924) (nighttime employment of women); Booth v. Indiana, 237 U.S. 391, 395–97 (1915) (wash houses); Sturges & Burn Mfg. Co. v. Beauchamp, 231 U.S. 320, 325–26 (1913) (child labor in hazardous occupations); Barrett v. Indiana, 229 U.S. 26, 28–29 (1913) (width of entries to coal mines). *Cf.* Wilmington Star Mining Co. v. Fulton, 205 U.S. 60, 70–74 (1907) (state law requiring licensure of mine managers and examiners and making mine liable for their willful failure to furnish a reasonably safe place for workers upheld as consistent with the Fourteenth Amendment).

201. Prudential Ins. Co. v. Cheek, 259 U.S. 530, 534–36 (1922); Chicago, Rock Island, & Pac. Ry. v. Perry, 259 U.S. 548, 555–56 (1922).

202. Carmichael v. Southern Coal & Coke Co., 301 U.S. 495, 509–27 (1937) (unemployment compensation); Virginian Ry. Co. v. American Federation of Labor, 300 U.S. 515, 557–59 (1937) (Railway Labor Act).

203. Paul Kens, *The Source of a Myth: Police Powers of the States and Laissez-Faire*

Constitutionalism 1900–1937, 35 AM. J. LEGAL HIST. 70, 83–91 (1991) is an exception to this generalization.

204. Second Employers' Liability Cases, 223 U.S. 1, 52–53 (1912) (upholding provision of federal law covering railroads' liability for their employees' on-the-job injuries that voids any contract by which employer tries to eliminate its liability under the act); Chicago, B., & Q. R.R. v. McGuire, 219 U.S. 549, 560, 563–73 (1911) (upholding provision of state law governing railroads' liability for their employees' on-the-job injuries that prevents any contract of insurance relief, benefit, or indemnity between employer and employee from operating as a defense to the statutory liability). *See also* Bowerstock v. Smith, 243 U.S. 29, 34–35 (1917) (state statute making employer liable for failure to properly guard manufacturing equipment does not violate due process as applied to employee who had contracted with the employer to provide the safeguards whose absence caused his death).

205. 243 U.S. 188, 196–208 (1917).

206. 243 U.S. 219, 235–46 (1917).

207. Crowell v. Benson, 285 U.S. 22, 41–42 (1932); Arizona Employers' Liability Cases, 250 U.S. 400, 420–31 (1919).

208. Bountiful Brick Co. v. Giles, 276 U.S. 154, 156, 158–59 (1928) (upholding workers' compensation recovery by employees killed while en route to work); Yeiser v. Dysart, 267 U.S. 540, 541 (1925) (state law restricting the fees attorneys could charge clients in workers' compensation cases); New York State Rys. v. Shuler, 265 U.S. 379, 383–84 (1924) (upholding law requiring that when employee dies without beneficiaries employer must make contribution to state workers' compensation fund); R. E. Sheehan Co. v. Shuler, 265 U.S. 371, 376–78 (1924) (same); Cudahy Packing Co. v. Parramore, 263 U.S. 418, 422–26 (1923) (same as *Bountiful Brick*); Madera Sugar Pine Co. v. Industrial Accident Comm'n, 262 U.S. 499, 500–504 (1923) (no violation of due process for otherwise-valid workers' compensation law to require that compensation for accidental death be paid to employee's nonresident alien dependents); Ward & Gow v. Krinsky, 259 U.S. 503, 510–16 (1922) (upholding the extension of the law at issue in *White* to most occupations in which four or more workers are employed); New York Central R.R. v. Bianc, 250 U.S. 596, 600–603 (1919) (rejecting employer's claim that employee recovery for disfigurement deprives employer of property without due process); New York Central R.R. v. Bianc, 250 U.S. 596, 600–603 (1919) (rejecting employer's claim that employee recovery for disfigurement deprives employer of property without due process); Middleton v. Texas Power & Light Co., 249 U.S. 152, 162–63 (1919) (employee not deprived of liberty and property without due process by requiring him to accept workers' compensation through his employer's election thereof in an elective system). *See also* Staten Island Rapid Transit Ry. v. Phoenix Indemnity Co., 281 U.S. 98, 106–8 (1930) (upholding a portion of the law at issue in the two *Shuler* cases that required that the employer or its insurer be indemnified by a third party against whom the employee had recovered outside workers' compensation).

209. *See* Phillips, *supra* note 178, at 488–90.

210. The ten cases in which the Court used express freedom-of-contract reasoning to strike down government action are: Morehead v. New York *ex rel.* Tipaldo, 298 U.S. 587, 604–18 (1936); Compania General de Tabacos de Filipinas

v. Collector of Internal Revenue, 275 U.S. 87, 91–98 (1927) (applying the due process provision contained in the Philippine Organic Act); Fairmont Creamery Co. v. Minnesota, 274 U.S. 1, 8–9 (1927); Chas. Wolff Packing Co. v. Court of Indus. Relations, 262 U.S. 522, 534–44 (1923); Adkins v. Children's Hosp., 261 U.S. 525, 545–62 (1923); New York Life Ins. Co. v. Dodge, 246 U.S. 357, 373–77 (1918); Coppage v. Kansas, 236 U.S. 1, 14–26 (1915); Adair v. United States, 208 U.S. 161, 172–76 (1908); Lochner v. New York, 198 U.S. 45, 53–64 (1905); Allgeyer v. Louisiana, 165 U.S. 578, 588–93 (1897).

The five decisions relying on earlier freedom-of-contract cases are: Donham v. West-Nelson Mfg. Co., 273 U.S. 657 (1927) (following *Adkins*); Murphy v. Sardell, 269 U.S. 530 (1925) (same); Chas. Wolff Packing Co. v. Court of Indus. Relations, 267 U.S. 552, 560–69 (1925) (applying the first *Chas. Wolff* decision to subsequent litigation under the statute at issue in that case); Dorchy v. Kansas, 264 U.S. 286, 289 (1924) (same); St. Louis Cotton Compress Co. v. Arkansas, 260 U.S. 346, 348–49 (1922) (following *Allgeyer*).

211. *See* Michael J. Phillips, *The Substantive Due Process Decisions of Mr. Justice Holmes*, 36 AM. BUS. L.J. 437, 451–52 n.81 (1999) and cases cited there.

212. Brandeis's Court tenure spanned the years 1916 to 1939. During that time, he joined at least the following eighteen "core" decisions striking down government action on substantive due process grounds: Buchanan v. Warley, 245 U.S. 60 (1917); St. Louis Cotton Compress Co. v. Arkansas, 260 U.S. 346 (1922); Meyer v. Nebraska, 262 U.S. 390 (1923); Bartels v. Iowa, 262 U.S. 404 (1923); Chas. Wolff Packing Co. v. Court of Indus. Relations, 262 U.S. 522 (1923); Dorchy v. Kansas, 264 U.S. 286 (1924); Michigan Pub. Utils. Comm'n v. Duke, 266 U.S. 570 (1925); Chas. Wolff Packing Co. v. Court of Indus. Relations, 267 U.S. 552 (1925); Pierce v. Society of Sisters, 268 U.S. 510 (1925); Yu Cong Eng v. Trinidad, 271 U.S. 500 (1926); Road Improvement Dist. v. Missouri Pac. R.R., 274 U.S. 188 (1927); Standard Pipe Line Co. v. Miller County Highway & Bridge Dist., 277 U.S. 160 (1928); Nectow v. City of Cambridge, 277 U.S. 183 (1928); Washington v. Roberge, 278 U.S. 116 (1928); Williams v. Standard Oil Co., 278 U.S. 235, 245 (1928) (concurring in the result); Manley v. Georgia, 279 U.S. 1 (1929); Western & Atl. R.R. v. Henderson, 279 U.S. 639 (1929); Smith v. Cahoon, 283 U.S. 553 (1931).

Although I will spare myself and my readers another string citation to nail down the point, Brandeis dissented in at least twenty-one such cases over the 1916 to 1937 period. Most of these cases involved more politically charged statutes than the decisions in which Brandeis joined the Court. For readers with any inclination to trust my recollections, I believe that Brandeis joined most of the decisions in which the Court used due process to strike down utility rate orders and other orders to regulated industries during the 1916–1937 period.

213. G. Edward White, *The Canonization of Holmes and Brandeis: Epistemology and Judicial Reputations*, 70 N.Y.U. L. REV. 576, 578 (1995) (citing no authority).

214. *See, e.g.*, Adkins v. Children's Hosp., 261 U.S. 525, 568–69 (1923) (Holmes, J., dissenting); Adair v. United States, 208 U.S. 161, 191 (1908) (Holmes, J., dissenting); Lochner v. New York, 198 U.S. 45, 75 (1905) (Holmes, J., dissenting).

215. Otis v. Parker, 187 U.S. 606, 608 (1903).

216. *Id.* at 609. The second quotation comes from Booth v. Illinois, 184 U.S. 425, 429 (1902).

217. Lochner v. New York, 198 U.S. 45, 76 (1905) (Holmes, J., dissenting).

218. Coppage v. Kansas, 236 U.S. 1, 27 (1915) (Holmes, J., dissenting); Adkins v. Children's Hosp., 261 U.S. 525, 570 (1923) (Holmes, J., dissenting); Bartels v. Iowa, 262 U.S. 404, 412 (1923) (Holmes, J., dissenting) (test of reasonableness); Schlesinger v. Wisconsin, 270 U.S. 230, 241 (1926) (Holmes, J., dissenting). For a different test, see Louis K. Liggett Co. v. Baldridge, 278 U.S. 105, 115 (1928) (Holmes, J., dissenting) ("It is enough if the questioned act has a manifest tendency to cure or at least to make the evil less").

219. *See* Adair v. United States, 208 U.S. 161, 191–92 (1908) (Holmes, J., dissenting); *Coppage*, 236 U.S. at 26–27 (Holmes, J., dissenting); Truax v. Corrigan, 257 U.S. 312, 343 (1921) (Holmes, J., dissenting); *Adkins*, 261 U.S. at 570–71 (Holmes, J., dissenting); *Bartels*, 262 U.S. at 412 (Holmes, J., dissenting); *Schlesinger*, 270 U.S. at 241–42 (Holmes, J., dissenting); Weaver v. Palmer Bros., 270 U.S. 402, 415 (1926) (Holmes, J., dissenting); Frost & Frost Trucking Co. v. Railroad Comm'n, 271 U.S. 583, 600–602 (1926) (Holmes, J., dissenting); *Liggett*, 278 U.S. at 114–15 (Holmes, J., dissenting). *But see* Tyson & Bro. v. Banton, 273 U.S. 418, 445–47 (1927) (Holmes, J., dissenting) (which seems not to state any real or hypothetical justification for the challenged law).

220. *Liggett*, 278 U.S. at 114–15 (Holmes, J., dissenting).

221. 260 U.S. 346, 348–49 (1922).

222. 165 U.S. 578, 589–93 (1897).

223. Fidelity & Deposit Co. v. Tafoya, 270 U.S. 426, 433–36 (1926).

224. *See* New York Life Ins. Co. v. Dodge, 246 U.S. 357, 373–77 (1918). However, in another case decided under *Allgeyer*'s authority, Compania General de Tabacos de Filipinas v. Collector of Internal Revenue, 275 U.S. 87, 92–98 (1927), Holmes dissented. *See id.* at 99–101 (Holmes, J., dissenting).

225. 261 U.S. 525 (1923). Holmes later joined two minimum-wage decisions applying *Adkins*. *See* Donham v. West-Nelson Mfg. Co., 273 U.S. 657 (1927); Murphy v. Sardell, 269 U.S. 530 (1925). *Sardell* contained a statement in which Holmes said that he concurred only because he felt himself bound by *Adkins*.

226. 262 U.S. 522 (1923).

227. Dorchy v. Kansas, 264 U.S. 286, 289 (1924).

228. Chas. Wolff Packing Co. v. Court of Indus. Relations, 267 U.S. 552, 569 (1925).

229. 260 U.S. 393, 413–16 (1922).

230. *Id.* at 415.

231. Chicago, R.I. & Pac. Ry. v. United States, 284 U.S. 80, 100–24 (1931) (Stone, J., dissenting, joined by Holmes); United Rys. & Elec. Co. v. West, 280 U.S. 234, 255–88 (1930) (Brandeis, J., dissenting, joined by Holmes); Pacific Gas & Elec. Co. v. City & County of San Francisco, 265 U.S. 403, 416 (1924) (Holmes, J., dissenting); Detroit United Ry. v. City of Detroit, 248 U.S. 429, 437–46 (1919) (Clarke, J., dissenting, joined by Holmes); City & County of Denver v. Denver Union Water Co., 246 U.S. 178, 195–98 (1918) (Holmes, J., dissenting). For the full list of cases striking down utility rate orders, see *supra* note 64.

232. Chicago, M. & St. P. R.R. v. Wisconsin, 238 U.S. 491, 502 (1915) (Holmes, J., dissenting). For the cases striking down utility regulatory orders, see *supra* note 69.

233. Brooks-Scanlon Co. v. Railroad Comm'n, 251 U.S. 396 (1920); Missouri Pac. Ry. v. Nebraska, 217 U.S. 196 (1910); Louisville & N. R.R. v. Central Stock

Yards Co., 212 U.S. 132 (1909). Holmes also wrote one of the rate cases: San Joaquin & Kings River Canal & Irrigation Co. v. County of Stanislaus, 233 U.S. 454 (1914).

234. Chicago, Milwaukee, & St. Paul Railway v. Polt, 232 U.S. 165, 167–68 (1914). On the liability and remedies and land-use cases, see *supra* notes 90–97, 112–17 and accompanying text.

235. Hoeper v. Tax Comm'n, 284 U.S. 206, 218–21 (1931) (Holmes, J., dissenting); Untermyer v. Anderson, 276 U.S. 440, 446 (1928) (Holmes, J., dissenting); Schlesinger v. Wisconsin, 270 U.S. 230, 241–42 (1926) (Holmes, J., dissenting).

236. Standard Pipe Line Co. v. Miller County Highway & Bridge Dist., 277 U.S. 160, 161–63 (1928); Road Improvement Dist. No. 1 v. Missouri Pac. R.R., 274 U.S. 188, 189–95 (1927); Myles Salt Co. v. Board of Comm'rs, 239 U.S. 478, 479–85 (1916). On the various kinds of tax cases, see *supra* notes 98–103 and accompanying text.

237. Pierce v. Soc'y of Sisters, 268 U.S. 510 (1925). Holmes dissented from two precursors to *Pierce*: Meyer v. Nebraska, 262 U.S. 390, 403 (1923) (Holmes, J., dissenting); Bartels v. Iowa, 262 U.S. 404, 412–13 (1923) (Holmes, J., dissenting).

238. Smith v. Cahoon, 283 U.S. 553, 563 (1931) (striking down a state trucking regulation that converted private carriers into public carriers). The cited portion of *Smith v. Cahoon* did not mention due process, but it explicitly relied on Michigan Pub. Util. Comm'n v. Duke, 266 U.S. 570, 577–78 (1925) and Frost & Frost Trucking Co. v. Railroad Comm'n, 271 U.S. 583, 591–99 (1926), both of which struck down trucking regulations on due process grounds. Holmes joined the majority in *Duke* but dissented in *Frost*, 271 U.S. at 600–602 (Holmes, J., dissenting). Holmes left the Court before its decision in New State Ice Co. v. Liebmann, 285 U.S. 262 (1932).

239. Yu Cong Eng v. Trinidad, 271 U.S. 500, 524–28 (1926).

240. *See supra* notes 222–24 and accompanying text.

241. *See supra* notes 226–28 and accompanying text.

242. *See supra* note 225.

243. In a previous article, I estimated that Holmes joined Court decisions using substantive due process to strike down government action on sixty-two of eighty-nine occasions during his time on the Court. The figure dropped to twenty-three of forty-four if the rate and utility order cases from the "borderline" group are excluded. Phillips, *supra* note 211, at 460–62. This book, however, includes three cases not found in that article—the *Tafoya* decision in *supra* note 223 and the two evidentiary presumption cases in *supra* notes 91–97.

244. For three less-than-successful attempts at such an explanation, see Phillips, *supra* note 211, at 462–75. On Holmes's personal political views, *see, e.g., id.* at 445.

Chapter 3

What Motivated the Old Court?

Chapter 1's rendition of the consensus view about *Lochner*-era substantive due process had a rough factual-normative organization. The chapter first presented a standard descriptive picture of those decisions. In this picture, twenty or so exemplary cases typically appear. Several of them involve employment regulations that were struck down because they restricted freedom of contract. Often the standard account implicitly suggests that the old Court's other substantive due process decisions resemble the twenty-odd cases presented. It also asserts that freedom of contract was central to *Lochner*-era substantive due process. The standard picture further suggests that the doctrine was a potent check on government regulation of the economy. This belief is reflected in the common statement that the old Court sustained substantive due process challenges on some 200 occasions. It may also be reflected in the standard picture's suggested ratio of successful to unsuccessful substantive due process challenges. Although it usually is conceded that this ratio is less than one, one sometimes gets the impression that the ratio is not *much* less than one. A final element in the standard picture appears late in the chapter, when it develops the familiar belief that Justice Oliver Wendell Holmes, Jr. was a regular dissenter from the old Court's substantive due process decisions.

These descriptive matters, however, were not the main concern of Chapter 1. Instead, much of that chapter developed three standard normative critiques of *Lochner*-era substantive due process. One of these attacks claims that the doctrine lets courts usurp powers that properly reside in legislatures, a usurpation sanctioned by neither the text nor the history of the due process clauses. The other two critiques share a common perception about the old Court's decisions but disagree in how they interpret it. The perception is that those decisions assisted business by enabling courts to strike down social legislation that limited freedom of contract. According to one critique, this occurred because the Court's conservative justices consciously set out to make it occur. According to the other critique, these justices acted as they did because they failed to see that social legislation was necessary to counteract the inequalities in bargaining power generated by the emergence of large corporations. This failure of perception, in turn, was due largely to the justices' limited intellectual powers and their simple-minded nostalgia for a laissez-faire era whose time had passed.

As Chapter 2 made clear, the standard picture of *Lochner*-era substantive due process bears some resemblance to the real thing, but not a great deal. That being the case, what happens to our three normative attacks on the doctrine? Despite the beating Chapter 2 administered to the standard picture, it did not destroy that picture's every claim. For example, while the old Court did not strike down 200 distinct laws on substantive due process grounds and while several times as many measures survived a substantive due process attack as fell, still some 110 (or fifty-six) laws did fall. Some of the 110 "core" and "borderline" substantive due process cases involved employment regulations, and others concerned laws that qualify as social legislation by almost any measure. In addition, some of these 110-odd laws were struck down because they violated freedom of contract. And Holmes indeed did dissent in many of these cases.

Thus, while Chapter 2 weakened our three critiques of the old Court's substantive due process decisions, it hardly destroyed them. In order to assess the degree of the damage, and to see what else might be said about these three attacks on the old Court, Chapters 3, 4, and 5 consider them in more detail. This chapter examines the claim that the old Court acted as a conscious and willing agent of business when it struck down social legislation on substantive due process grounds. Chapter 4 examines the assertion that this unfortunate result came about not from the justices' malevolence but rather from their failure to grasp certain elementary features of the twentieth-century social and economic landscape. Chapter 5 considers the traditional argument that *Lochner*-era substantive due process was an illegitimate exercise of judicial power.

As will become apparent soon enough, the conscious-agent-of-business critique of *Lochner*-era substantive due process faces significant objections. If it fails, what *did* motivate the old Court's conservative justices? The traditional answer, one I largely endorse, is that the justices' substantive due process decisions reflected their commitment to freedom in general and economic freedom in particular and to the protection of property. Recently, however, another interpretation of those decisions has gained currency with some academics. This is the assertion that

Lochner-era substantive due process is best understood as one manifestation of the old Court's hostility toward "class" or "partial" legislation—law making that seeks primarily to benefit particular interests rather than the general good. Before considering the traditional interpretation, therefore, the chapter examines this "class legislation" hypothesis. But first it considers the agent-of-business explanation.

WAS THE OLD COURT A CONSCIOUS AND WILLING AGENT OF BUSINESS?

The notion we are investigating is that the old Court's substantive due process decisions largely resulted from the justices' desire to suppress social legislation that reduced business's prerogatives and profits. Of all the attacks on the old Court, this one has by far the least to support it. In detailing that claim, this section makes four major arguments. Invoking Chapter 2's data on unsuccessful substantive due process claims, the section first argues that if the doctrine was intended to benefit business, it performed its mission rather poorly. As for the laws the old Court did strike down, secondly, many of those at issue in the rate cases and some of our other categories are questionable on public policy grounds. This suggests that if the justices were deciding on extraconstitutional criteria, these did not necessarily include the desire to aid business. The section's third argument is that some of the laws the old Court struck down cannot be characterized as social legislation that disadvantaged business. In fact, fourthly, some of those laws were *pro-business*, in the sense that they favored entrenched interests over new competitors. While detailing this last charge, I consider at length Justice Brandeis's vastly overrated 1932 dissent in *New State Ice Co. v. Liebmann.*

The Unsuccessful Substantive Due Process Claims

This argument that the old Court was business's agent seems to derive considerable support from the cases contained in the standard picture of *Lochner*-era substantive due process. Consider, for example, the employment decisions, which include cases striking down minimum-wage and maximum-hours laws, as well as several cases that easily can be construed as anti-union. Or consider the decisions striking down such consumer protection measures as maximum-price laws, statutes fixing the weights at which bread loaves could be sold, and measures regulating the materials used in furniture and bedding.

The old Court's apparent pro-business tilt, furthermore, hardly is limited to the cases comprising the standard picture. Some of the old Court's tax decisions probably benefitted business, or at least may have been used as precedent for that purpose. The liability and remedies cases obviously benefitted the railroads. Also assisting railroads and other regulated industries were the old Court's many decisions striking down regulatory orders telling those firms to undertake some burdensome or costly action at their own expense. This brings us to Exhibit A in the claim that the *Lochner* Court was business's agent: its many rate cases. These decisions struck down rate orders for regulated industries such as railroads; trolley companies; electric, gas, and water companies; telephone companies; and so forth. They seem to directly benefit those firms, their shareholders, and their bondholders and to disadvantage all those who had to pay the charges imposed by these regulated monopolies.

Brief as it was, the preceding recitation probably would convince many people that the old Court's substantive due process decisions were primarily intended to benefit business. Indeed, many people have had precisely that belief for quite some time. But even the most die-hard exponent of the agent-of-business view would have to admit that the old Court could have gone further than it did. The reason is the considerable number of cases in which the Court rejected substantive due process claims attacking government regulation. As Chapter 2 made clear, such cases considerably outnumber those in which the Court granted a substantive due process claim.

Figure 2.1 in Chapter 2 shows the degree to which rejected substantive due process claims exceeded successful claims during the *Lochner* era. Overall, rejected "core" and "borderline" claims exceeded successful claims by about 2.4 to 1 (269 to 110). Within the "borderline" group, the ratio was approximately 1.3 to 1 (70 to 54), whereas in the "core" group, the figure was over 3.5 to 1 (199 to 56). Within the latter group, the ratios of rejected to successful claims were fairly high for two of the categories often used as evidence for the agent-of-business argument: the employment cases and the cases involving general business regulations. For the employment cases, the ratio was about 3.6 to 1 (43 to 12); for the general business regulation cases, it was approximately 4.9 to 1 (59 to 12), and for the two combined, it was about 4.25 to 1 (102 to 24).

Justifying the Rate Cases

Even if the *Lochner* Court was business's servant, therefore, it pursued its master's interests with something less than complete dedication, ruthlessness, and efficiency. But in one context this seems not to be true. For the rate cases, the ratio of unsuccessful to successful claims was 0.72 to 1 (28 to 39). As noted earlier, these decisions seem to strongly argue for the agent-of-business position, because they so clearly pit the economic interests of regulated monopolies against other interests. But there are other reasons why the old Court might have decided the rate cases the way it did. Although these alternative explanations do not disprove the agent-of-business explanation, they at least put it in some doubt.

The rate cases rarely appear in contemporary accounts of *Lochner*-era substantive due process. As Chapter 2 maintained, they are easy to characterize as decisions incorporating the Fifth Amendment's takings clause within Fourteenth Amendment due process. Their official termination date, furthermore, is not 1937 but 1944.[1] But some of the principles and tests employed in those cases continue to be employed by modern agencies and courts.[2] More important, the problems those cases addressed remain with us as well. Central to those problems, Richard J. Pierce claimed in a 1989 article on electric utility regulation, is "the political malfunction Madison feared most—majoritarian bias based on unequal distributions of property."[3] Due to this bias, Pierce maintained, state governments "took" billions of dollars of property from utilities through the regulatory process during the 1970s and 1980s. (During the 1950s and 1960s, on the other hand, the utilities prospered due to the "minoritarian bias" resulting from their influence on then-compliant regulators.) Evidently the fear of politically biased rate decisions was one reason for the Court's original decision to review those decisions late in the nineteenth century.[4] Another factor behind the Court's decision to review rates was the fear that majoritarian bias and excessive state regulation would inhibit private investment in railroads, thus frustrating their efforts to expand and improve their services.[5] For all these reasons, perhaps it is unsurprising that even Holmes joined most of the rate cases decided during his tenure on the Court.[6]

The upshot of the preceding remarks is that while the old Court's rate decisions no doubt favored the affected businesses, those decisions may nonetheless have been justified as a matter of public policy. This casts some doubt on the familiar claim that they were expressions of probusiness sentiment and nothing else. Maybe the same arguments could support the Court's decisions striking down regulatory orders directed at these public utilities. As for the cases striking down laws allowing enhanced recoveries against railroads and other businesses, perhaps it is sufficient to note that, as we saw in Chapter 2, the modern Court acted similarly in *BMW v. Gore*. Some of the other measures the old Court struck down arguably have their infirmities as well. For instance, laws regulating the price of consumer goods, three of which fell during the 1920s, are routinely criticized for creating artificial shortages of the controlled product or service.[7] And the minimum wage comes under continual fire for reducing employment, especially among marginal workers such as minorities, young people, and middle-aged women.[8]

Some Cases the Agent-of-Business Theory Cannot Explain

As I understand it, the agent-of-business argument criticizes *Lochner*-era substantive due process *as a doctrine*. It does so in the belief that this doctrine enabled the old Court to willfully and knowingly strike down social legislation that disadvantaged business. But what happens if some applications of *Lochner*-era substantive due process simply cannot be explained in that way? In that event, one must wonder whether the desire to assist business was the doctrine's real inspiration. If that motive really was substantive due process's mainspring, why did it not manifest itself in all of that doctrine's applications?

In fact, some of our "core" substantive due process cases cannot plausibly be attributed to the justices' desire to assist business. The most obvious examples are the three decisions tucked away under the "general police" heading in Chapter 2's Figure 2.1. These are the three "personal rights" cases that provided some inspiration for modern substantive due process. It is almost impossible to explain *Meyer v. Nebraska* and *Pierce v. Society of Sisters*—both of which affirmed parents' right to control the upbringing and education of children—as manifestations of a drive to protect business against social legislation.[9] The old Court's land-use cases also are difficult to label in this way. One of them is easily characterized as a civil rights case.[10] Two more involved ordinances that effectively ceded sovereign power to the arbitrary wills of certain private property owners.[11] Finally, at least some of the tax cases seem difficult to tar with the agent-of-business brush. These are the decisions striking down state action allocating the costs of certain public improvements among the landowners ostensibly benefitted by the improvement in question. In those cases, the Court typically concluded that the aggrieved taxpayer either did not benefit from the improvement or did not benefit in proportion to his share of the tax burden.

Cases That Conflict with the Agent-of-Business Theory

In the immediately preceding section, I tried to undermine the agent-of-business theory by demonstrating that it cannot explain some applications of *Lochner*-era substantive due process. But the theory is in deeper trouble than that. Not only does it fail to explain one significant group of *Lochner*-era substantive due process decisions, but in those decisions the old Court sometimes was attacking established business interests. The cases in question are the old Court's entry restriction decisions. Here I concentrate primarily on two prominent examples from the 1920s and early 1930s.

The Liggett *and* Liebmann *Cases.* In 1973, the Supreme Court rejected a due process attack on a North Dakota statute requiring that in order to operate a pharmacy within the state any applicant must be either a registered pharmacist, or a business entity the majority of whose stock was owned by registered pharmacists actively engaged in running the business. Toward the end of his opinion for a unanimous Court, Justice William O. Douglas overruled a 1928 case that struck down an almost identical Pennsylvania statute, terming it "a derelict in the stream of the law."[12] That case, *Louis K. Liggett Co. v. Baldridge*, usually plays a minor role in standard accounts of *Lochner*-era substantive due process. There, Justice Sutherland's opinion for a 7–2 majority maintained that a drug store's stock ownership lacked a real or substantial relation to the public health. Immediately after that, Sutherland got down to brass tacks.

> It is a matter of public notoriety that chain drug stores in great numbers, owned and operated by corporations, are to be found throughout the United States. They have been in operation for many years. We take judicial notice of the fact that the stock in these corporations is bought and sold upon the various stock exchanges of the country and, in the nature of things, must be held and owned to a large extent by persons who are not registered pharmacists.[13]

In other words, Pennsylvania's ostensible effort to protect the public health looked suspiciously like an effort by in-state pharmacists to block competition from chain stores. Against all this, Holmes's dissent, joined by Brandeis, asserted that the Pennsylvania law need only have a "manifest tendency" to cure a recognized evil and that a drug store's ownership has *some* effect on the safety with which it operates.[14]

Sutherland sounded the same notes four years later in *New State Ice Co. v. Liebmann*. In that case, the Court considered a due process attack on an Oklahoma statute blocking an applicant's entry into the ice business if existing facilities within the relevant territory were sufficient to meet the public's need for ice. The challenge arose after an existing ice business sued to block entry by a new competitor named Liebmann. Sutherland's opinion for a 6–2 Court majority striking down the statute spun its wheels for several pages before finally concluding that the ice business was not affected with a public interest and instead was a lawful private business.[15] Immediately thereafter, he said that a law denying or unreasonably curtailing the right to engage in such a private business is inconsistent with the Fourteenth Amendment. Then Sutherland concluded that the challenged regulation indeed was such a law, and said why.

> Stated succinctly, a private corporation here seeks to prevent a competitor from entering the business of making and selling ice. It claims to be endowed with state authority to achieve this exclusion. There is no question now before us of any regulation by the state to protect the consuming public either with respect to conditions of manufacture and distribution or to insure purity of product or to prevent extortion. The control here asserted does not protect against monopoly, but tends to foster it. The aim is not to encourage competition, but to prevent it; not to regulate the business, but to preclude persons from engaging in it. There is no difference in principle between this case and the attempt of the dairyman under state authority to prevent another from keeping cows and selling milk on

the ground that there are enough dairymen in the business; or to prevent a shoemaker from making or selling shoes because shoemakers already in that occupation can make and sell all the shoes that are needed.[16]

As we will see below, Justice Brandeis's renowned dissent in *Liebmann* tried to defend the Oklahoma statute as a justified legislative experiment, but Sutherland was having none of that. Instead, he maintained, "[t]here are certain essentials of liberty with which the state is not entitled to dispense in the interest of experiments."[17] He concluded by observing that no "theory of experimentation in censorship" could interfere with the freedom of the press and that "[t]he opportunity to apply one's labor and skill in an ordinary occupation with proper regard for all reasonable regulations is no less entitled to protection."[18]

The Case against Entry Restrictions. Sutherland's remarks echo the standard economic criticisms of occupational licensing schemes and other restrictions on entry into a trade, business, profession, or occupation.[19] (These criticisms do not apply, or apply with less force, to the entry restrictions accompanying the regulation of natural monopolies such as electrical power generation, natural gas service, water service, and telephone service; and of "regulated industries" such as transportation and communications.) As one foe of occupational licensing summarized the matter: "Occupational regulation has served to limit consumer choice, raise consumer costs, increase practitioner income, limit practitioner mobility, deprive the poor of adequate services, and restrict job opportunities for minorities."[20] Occupational licensing has these effects because it exists less to protect the public than to advance private economic interests by restricting entry to the business and thus limiting competition. All things being equal, this tends to raise prices and practitioner incomes, while giving consumers less return per dollar spent. These higher prices also tend to reduce the licensed service's availability to poor people. Occupational licensing disadvantages poor people, minorities especially, in other ways as well. Because they sometimes are less able to pass the tests or meet the other criteria used to limit entry, occupational licensing tends to limit minority employment. This is one example of a larger criticism of occupational licensing: that it tends to block people from doing the jobs they perform most capably. For this reason, and because it restrains competition, occupational licensing also tends to lessen innovation.

According to the standard wisdom, the old Court's substantive due process cases suppressed social legislation designed to protect weaker parties, and the general public, from business's depredations. This presupposes a certain degree of legislative concern for such parties. Yet if the preceding criticisms are accurate, that concern is nowhere to be found when legislatures pass restrictions on entry. Why is this so? The standard explanation is that the political impetus for occupational licensing normally comes from within the regulated business or profession and not from the people licensing is supposed to protect. But how can these isolated minority interests foist disadvantageous laws on the majority? They normally get their way because they benefit significantly from those laws and thus have an intense interest in getting them passed. In addition, existing practitioners of the trade typically are knowledgeable about the advantages of licensing and organized to promote its passage. The general public, on the other hand, is far more scattered and far less aware. In comparison to the potential benefit for individual practitioners, furthermore, each member of the public individually suffers relatively little from an occupational licensing law. Under these circumstances, rational, self-interested legislators normally give the occupational group what it wants. Because the general public is indifferent, the costs of acceding are minimal. And why anger an intensely motivated minority for relatively little gain? By acceding, moreover, legislators may get that group's votes and, more important, its financial support.

Brandeis's Dissent in Liebmann. The assertion that the old Court acted as business's agent assumes that the rise of corporate power required corrective social legislation. Because the need for such legislation was so obvious, the argument continues, the old Court's justices must have known what they were doing when they used substantive due process to strike it down. But this argument has no application to entry restrictions. Here, instead of counteracting private economic power, government regulation protects and furthers it. And rather than ratifying superior economic power when it struck down a regulation, the Supreme Court instead undermined such power. As Herbert Hovenkamp summarizes the matter: "These [entry restriction] decisions simply cannot be characterized as a judicial choice to side with business against labor, immigrants, and the poor. On the contrary, they permitted such groups increased entry into established markets in the face of protectionist legislation designed either to exclude newcomers directly or to give established firms a cost advantage over prospective entrants."[21] This observation raises the question I asked earlier: If *Lochner*-era substantive due process was concocted mainly to aid business, why did the doctrine not do so in all of its applications?

Of course, occupational licensing sometimes does serve the public interest—most importantly, perhaps, by protecting consumers against incompetent or unethical practitioners. Restrictions on entry to the health-care professions are probably the best example. Although these benefits may be accompanied by the costs just enumerated, in many cases they arguably outweigh those costs. Perhaps for these reasons, even the *Lochner* Court usually rejected constitutional attacks on occupational licensing laws for the standard professions.[22] But I find it difficult to identify any significant public interests that were served by the laws at issue in *Liggett* and *Liebmann*. Here, though, some readers will enter an obvious objection. Surely, I will be told, Justice Brandeis's celebrated dissent in *Liebmann* provided the necessary justifications.[23]

Brandeis's *Liebmann* dissent made page one of the *New York Times* when it was written[24] and continues to inspire liberals to this day. That inspiration, I think, comes primarily from the hymn to experimentalism with which Brandeis concluded his dissent. Brandeis began that dissent's finale by maintaining that, despite the weakness of social science knowledge and the problems this poses for regulators, the triumphs of the physical sciences still leave room for hope. "[T]he advances in the exact sciences and the achievements in invention remind us that the seemingly impossible sometimes happens." These advances and achievements, Brandeis continued, have in large measure "been due to experimentation." Thus, "[t]here must be power in the states and the nation to remould, through experimentation, our economic practices and institutions to meet changing social and economic needs." Due to their numbers, their diversity, and their separateness, the states apparently had a special role in this process. "It is one of the happy incidents of the federal system that a single courageous state may, if its citizens choose, serve as a laboratory; and try novel social and economic experiments without risk to the rest of the country." For all these reasons, "[t]o stay experimentation in things social and economic is a grave responsibility."

But what was experimental about the statute at issue in *Liebmann*, which looks like special-interest legislation of the most obvious kind? The main body of Brandeis's dissent identified several ills that the Oklahoma statute might be thought to have addressed. In discussing them, Brandeis made abundant use of social science data and other factual information. Indeed, his dissent was the archetypal "Brandeis Brief," exceeding Sutherland's page count by a ratio of about three to one, and outfootnoting him fifty-seven to zero. It even was divided into numbered sections. The standard view about Brandeis's approach is that it destroyed the conservatives' sterile conceptualism and their primitive economics by highlighting the social realities that their abstractions obscured and that justified government regulation. However, Hadley Arkes takes a different view in a recent book about Sutherland. According to Arkes, Brandeis

> amassed facts, as though the assembly of facts was an accomplishment in itself, or as though the facts generated their own conclusion. . . . The mass of statistics formed a thickly embellished screen, comparable to the screens cast up by magicians or masters of illusion, to dazzle and distract the onlookers. The screen could preserve the illusion of mastery, abetted over the years by adoring writers and publicists. And what was concealed behind the screen was a prosaic shallowness, amplified at times to a stunning mediocrity.[25]

Arkes delivered this attack during a discussion of *New State Ice Co. v. Liebmann*. As applied to that case, at least, his indictment is correct. In *Liebmann*, that is, this supposed master policy scientist failed either to justify Oklahoma's entry restriction or to undermine Sutherland's arguments against it. At one point, in fact, he lent crucial support to Sutherland's position. In detailing these contentions, I rely to a considerable degree on arguments already made by Arkes, Bernard Siegan, and Judge Richard Posner.[26]

Its numbered sections to the contrary notwithstanding, Brandeis's *Liebmann* dissent is not well organized. Most of its critical arguments are contained within two relatively small portions of the opinion's thirty-plus pages.[27] To a greater or lesser extent, the rest looks like surplusage—especially a five-page section toward the middle of the opinion recounting Oklahoma's past regulation of the ice industry.[28] In trying to come to terms with Brandeis's tome, I begin with the one place where he seems to confront Sutherland's main argument.

> It is no objection to the validity of the statute here assailed that it fosters monopoly. That, indeed, is its design. The certificate of public convenience and invention [*sic*] is a device—a recent social-economic invention—through which the monopoly is kept under effective control by vesting in a commission the power to terminate it whenever that course is required in the public interest. To grant any monopoly to any person as a favor is forbidden, even if terminable. But where, as here, there is reasonable ground for the legislative conclusion that, in order to secure a necessary service at reasonable rates, it may be necessary to curtail the right to enter the calling. It is, in my opinion, consistent with the due process clause to do so, whatever the nature of the business.[29]

But why was there a reasonable ground for the Oklahoma legislature to believe that its entry restriction was needed to secure a necessary service at reasonable rates? So far as I can tell from Brandeis's disjointed presentation, he made four major arguments that the entry restriction was reasonable.

1. *The Absence of Ice Service in Some Areas*. On two different occasions in his dissent, Brandeis seemed to say that before the advent of regulation some parts of Oklahoma had no ice service at all.[30] It is unclear whether this was due to low demand or to other factors. It also is not clear from Brandeis's opinion how regulation had solved, or would solve, this problem. One possibility is that the state could compel existing ice companies to serve areas outside their original territory. But it is not clear that Oklahoma's regulatory scheme even permitted this. Furthermore, such a step probably would have been very expensive. Maybe Oklahoma could have addressed this problem by mandating higher ice prices. But this probably would have made ice consumers in areas al-

ready served subsidize those to whom service was being extended. This arguably is neither efficient nor just and hence not reasonable either.

2. *Local Monopoly*. According to testimony before the district court, Brandeis said, "in only six or seven localities in the state . . . was there 'a semblance of competition'; and . . . even in those localities the prices of ice were ordinarily uniform. The balance of the population was, and still is, served by companies enjoying complete monopoly."[31] As long as the product sold is uniform, however, one would expect uniform prices in a competitive market. But the argument that much of Oklahoma's population was served by local monopolies deserves more attention. At first glance, this seems the classic case where regulation is needed to curb monopoly pricing and other abuses of monopoly power. And Oklahoma's statute permitted the state's Corporation Commission to regulate ice prices.[32]

Potential competition from new entrants, however, can deter local monopolists from abusing their position. Specifically, monopolists attract competition if they raise prices too high. As the Tenth Circuit's *Liebmann* opinion noted, "[I]f an ice manufacturer in a town having only one plant should demand excessive prices, manufacturers in nearby towns, in the absence of monopolistic trade agreements, would normally compete by shipping in ice by rail or trucks."[33] Brandeis's rejoinder was that, due primarily to melting, ice manufactured at a distance could not compete with locally manufactured ice.[34] But the Tenth Circuit had already suggested that many of the towns where this was likely to be true could not have supported even one ice plant and thus would have had to be served by truck from plants in larger cities.[35]

For his part, Sutherland tried to meet the local-monopoly argument by observing that the increasing availability of refrigerators made consumers less dependent on the ice companies.[36] In response to this apparent favoritism for the well-to-do, Brandeis claimed the refrigerators still were luxury items in Oklahoma and that "[l]egislation essential to the protection of individuals of limited or no means is not invalidated by the circumstance that other individuals are financially able to protect themselves."[37] But while this may be a good argument, Brandeis was in little position to make it. As we will see very shortly, it is hard to believe that Brandeis's *Liebmann* dissent was really much concerned with consumer welfare.

3. *Ruinous Competition*. So far, the opposing arguments on the local-monopoly question strike me as a standoff. But Brandeis's local-monopoly argument faces another problem, one of his own making. This was his belief that it was easy to enter the Oklahoma ice industry.[38] In that event, obviously, local monopolists would have even more to fear if they decided to abuse their position by raising prices. Brandeis made his ease-of-entry argument—and thereby undercut his local-monopoly

rationale—while maintaining that regulation was necessary to prevent ruinous competition in Oklahoma's ice industry. That argument is worth quoting at length.

> [T]he relative ease and cheapness with which an ice plant may be constructed exposes the industry to destructive and frequently ruinous competition. Competition in the industry tends to be destructive because ice plants have a determinate capacity, and inflexible fixed charges and operating costs, and because in a market of limited area the volume of sales is not readily expanded. Thus, the erection of a new plant in a locality already adequately served often causes managers to go to extremes in cutting prices in order to secure business. Trade journals and reports of association meetings of ice manufacturers bear ample witness to the hostility of the industry to such competition, and to its unremitting efforts, through trade associations, informal agreements, combination of delivery systems, and in particular through the consolidation of plants, to protect markets and prices against competition of any character.[39]

Given all this, it hardly was surprising that "the ice industry as a whole in Oklahoma has acquiesced in and accepted the act and the status which it creates."[40]

Evidently this sort of argument enjoyed wider acceptance during the 1930s than it does now. Today, claims of ruinous competition usually are met with a snicker and the observation that ruinous competition is nothing more than competition. To contemporary eyes, furthermore, it looks very much as if Brandeis made Sutherland's case for him. That is, Brandeis's ruinous competition argument detailed Sutherland's assertion that Oklahoma's regulatory scheme was little more than anticompetitive special-interest legislation. That argument also undermines the common belief that the old Court's conservatives invariably sided with business and that their Progressive foes just as invariably sought to advance the public interest.

As I noted earlier, Brandeis's ruinous competition argument also coexists uneasily with some of the other claims he made in his *Liebmann* dissent. If the Oklahoma ice industry was easy to enter, would that not help keep local monopolists on their toes? More important, Brandeis's alarm about price cutting renders hollow his expressed concern for impecunious ice consumers who could not afford refrigerators. As Posner remarked, "The people actually wronged by the statute were the poor, who were compelled to pay more for ice; the well-to-do, as Brandeis pointed out, were more likely to have refrigerators."[41]

4. *Excess Productive Capacity*. To my mind, not only does Brandeis's ruinous-competition argument fail to provide a reasonable basis for legislative intervention, but it undermines his local-monopoly argument too. But maybe the preceding discussion does Brandeis an injustice. When *Liebmann* was decided, the Great Depression was already well

under way. In an environment where businesses are failing, taking jobs and consumer spending down with them, perhaps there really is such a thing as ruinous competition. In any event, Brandeis obviously thought so. Toward the end of his dissent, he remarked that "[t]he people of the United States are now confronted with an emergency more serious than war."[42] Then he provided a diagnosis.

> [M]any persons think that one of the major contributing causes has been unbridled competition. Increasingly, doubt is expressed whether it is economically wise, or morally right, that men should be permitted to add to the producing facilities of an industry which is already suffering from overcapacity. In justification of that doubt, men point to the excess capacity of our productive facilities resulting from their vast expansion without corresponding increase in the consumptive capacity of the people.[43]

As a result, Brandeis concluded, "some thoughtful men of wide business experience insist that all projects for stabilization and proration must prove futile unless, in some way, the equivalent of the certificate of public convenience and necessity is made a prerequisite to embarking new capital in an industry in which the capacity already exceeds the production schedules."[44] After that came the peroration extolling legislative experimentalism.

Of course, as Brandeis's dissent had made clear, these almost certainly were not the reasons Oklahoma's entry restriction was enacted. The law was passed in 1925, well before the crash and the depression that followed it. Its apparent inspiration was the industry's concern over falling prices and profits brought about by competition. No doubt existing competitors preferred that there be less capacity in the industry, but only because that would have meant less competition. This alone, I think, is enough to doom any claim that Brandeis's excessive-capacity argument could render the Oklahoma statute rational.

But maybe Brandeis's dissent should be read as setting guideposts for the future—as stating the attitude the Court ought to take toward government's efforts to save capitalism from itself. In that event, its evaluation depends in part on the soundness of Brandeis's views about excess productive capacity. I say "Brandeis's views" because evidently that is what they were. As G. Edward White suggested in a recent article, Brandeis evidently had had these ideas for some time. And as White notes, he "injected these views into his *Liebmann* dissent by attributing them to 'economists,' 'many persons,' 'all,' and 'some thoughtful men.' "[45] I do not know whether Brandeis ever criticized his conservative brethren for injecting their economic views into the Constitution, but he would have been most hypocritical if he had. Maybe that word does apply to liberals, such as Justice Hugo Black, who praise Brandeis for his restraint while condemning the old Court's conservatives for constitutionalizing their economic theories.[46]

If Brandeis's economic views were sound, however, perhaps all this should be forgiven and forgotten. But this seems unlikely. The main reason is that it is difficult to see how higher prices would increase "the consumptive capacity of the people." After observing that the overcapacity of which Brandeis complained was due to diminished demand rather than overbuilding, Posner argues that "limiting competition would not have increased purchasing power and therefore demand; it would just have impaired the efficiency of economic activity at its reduced level."[47] Interestingly, Posner also claims that the view that the depression was caused by excessive competition eventually gave way to a competing, if equally erroneous, view that was almost its polar opposite. "Soon the pendulum of opinion swung the other way and it was argued that monopoly rather than competition had been responsible for the depression, or at least for its severity."[48]

More than anything else, Brandeis's *Liebmann* dissent seems the product of a man possessed by an idea so strong that it finds corroboration everywhere he looks. The idea in question, of course, was governmental experimentation with the economy. Fueling it was Brandeis's faith in the social sciences and in the political system's ability to put them to good use. Oklahoma's regulation was justified, he apparently thought, by the absence of ice producers in some localities, by excessive ice production capacity over the state as a whole, by local monopolies in some areas, and by excessive and ruinous price competition in others. At this point it is natural to ask what would *not* have justified regulation for Brandeis. The likely answer is: nothing. Under his approach in *Liebmann*, after all, even the most irrational assertions of government power could be justified as experiments.

THE OLD COURT AND CLASS LEGISLATION

For all the reasons just adduced, the agent-of-business hypothesis has little to recommend it. Another piece of evidence against the hypothesis is the low esteem into which it has fallen among certain people whose politics are far from conservative. Other examples will appear later, but for now I limit myself to the Harvard legal historian Morton Horwitz. Horwitz opened a 1987 article with a startling admission: "As I study the constitutional history of this period," he said, "I have increasingly come to believe that to a surprising extent, the picture we have of the Court between 1880 and 1937 is largely the product of winner's history."[49] In that piece, he went on the argue that this consensus picture helped Progressives legitimize the New Deal by portraying it, not as a radical break with tradition, but as a return to a long-standing practice of democracy and judicial restraint.[50] Although Horwitz had relatively little to say about the nature of that consensus picture in 1987, five years later he elaborated a bit. "Although in every other field of American history, Progressive historiography, premised on a conflict between the 'people' and the 'interests,' has been overthrown as simplistic, in the constitutional history of the *Lochner* era it has continued to be the standard mode of explanation."[51] "The result," he continued, "has been to buttress historical interpretations that, for example, continue to treat the late-nineteenth century judiciary as having capitulated to big business." "In fact," however, "it is quite clear . . . that the *Lochner* Court was strongly representative of the old conservative view that big business was unnatural and illegitimate."

At this point, some readers may feel that revisionism has gone far enough. It is one thing, they might say, to suggest that the old Court was not, or was not merely, a tool of business. But what conceivable sense can it make to say that it saw big business as "unnatural" and "illegitimate"? Although I am uncertain what Horwitz meant when he used those terms, maybe the key word in his statement is "big" rather than "business." Because a private actor's political power roughly correlates with its size, large corporations have some ability to bend the law to their purposes. But this means that government cannot be neutral among its subjects. Yet such neutrality is a traditional American ideal. One way to preserve it is to empower the courts to strike down nonneutral government action. More than the advancement of personal freedom, Horwitz suggests, it is this goal that inspired the old Court. "An earlier generation [of twentieth-century observers] saw the post-bellum rise of laissez-faire as a Lochnerian wish to let a free market trump protective governmental regulation. Revisionists see instead a continuation of the Jacksonian wish for a neutral state that would prevent 'the interests' from using government to feather their own nests."[52] He also suggested that government neutrality was one component within "an astonishingly constant underlying vision" that the Court maintained during its first 150 years.[53] Only after 1937, he added, was there a decisive break with that tradition.

Gillman's Version of the "Class Legislation" Argument

So far as I am aware, a 1995 book by Howard Gillman is the most complete statement of the view that the old Court is best understood as an enemy of nonneutral lawmaking.[54] "The hypothesis advanced in these pages," Gillman states late in his book, is that "the justices were by and large motivated by a principled commitment to the application of a constitutional ideology of state neutrality."[55] To elaborate:

> Police powers jurisprudence during the *Lochner* era had its origins in the founders' desire to delegitimize "factional politics," attempts by competing classes to use public power to gain unfair or unnatural advantages over their market adversaries. The object of this agenda was not to promote the value of market liberty per se, nor to reduce government intervention in the market to a bare minimum; rather, the goal was to prohibit the government from passing laws designed merely to promote the interests of certain classes at the expense of their competitors, to impose special burdens and benefits on particular groups without linking these burdens and benefits to the welfare of the community as a whole.[56]

The traditional term for such measures is "class legislation." To Gillman, then, an opposition to class legislation is the central feature of the old Court's police power cases.

The position just stated has two corollaries, and it requires one important elaboration. The first corollary, which Gillman made explicit in the previous quotation, is that the old Court was at best only secondarily or derivatively devoted to the expansion of individual liberty and the minimization of state power. The second is that the *Lochner* Court did not act to further business interests when it struck down government action on Fourteenth Amendment grounds. Gillman is explicit on this point. On the same page that he states his main hypothesis, for example, Gillman also says that "the story of the *Lochner* era is not about how reactionary justices in the late nineteenth century became more daring in their willingness to exploit legal materials in order to protect or promote their personal class or policy biases."[57]

However, one should not infer from all this that Gillman is an admirer of the old Court's jurisprudence or that he urges its revival.[58] The reason is familiar: While the old Court indeed did act from principle, its beliefs were outmoded by the beginning of the twentieth century, if not earlier.[59] Specifically, the emergence of large corporations, the growing personal dependency on such institutions, and the associated increase in class conflict all required affirmative government regulation on a vast scale. If it was to adequately protect weaker parties, this regulation had to be nonneutral: that is, it had to be class legislation. A commitment to government neutrality, on the other hand, would only have ratified the profound power imbalances that existed in the private sphere. Chapter 4 considers some aspects of this argument.

According to Gillman, then, the old Court basically was asking whether the law before it was a police measure that advanced general public interests, on the one hand, or a "class" or "partial" law that benefitted relatively narrow interests, on the other. His evidence for this thesis consists primarily of relatively familiar federal substantive due process cases, some of which make regular appearances in the standard picture, plus some state cases and some cases involving other provisions of the U.S. Constitution. For the most part, the following exposition of that evidence limits itself to clear federal substantive due process decisions. From that exposition, we can begin to form some estimate of his thesis's strengths and weaknesses. Throughout, the question is whether Gillman's hypothesis explains—or at least illuminates—the case considered.

Gillman begins with a decision that was the Court's first important exposition of the Fourteenth Amendment but that did not particularly feature substantive due process. In the *Slaughterhouse Cases,*[60] a 5–4 Court majority upheld a Louisiana law that chartered a company and gave it a twenty-five-year monopoly to maintain slaughterhouses in and around the city of New Orleans. The law's proponents claimed that its aims were to make New Orleans the commercial center through which Texas cattle would move to the rest of the nation and to eliminate the sanitation and disease-control problems created by the existing slaughterhouses; its opponents saw the law as an illegitimate and exclusionary grant of special privileges that had been procured by bribery. In Gillman's view, each view was partially acccurate, which explains why the justices split 5–4. This claim seems at least plausible, and for that reason the *Slaughterhouse Cases* seem hospitable to Gillman's mode of analysis. This also seems true of the next case on Gillman's list, *Munn v. Illinois,*[61] which upheld state regulation of the rates charged by grain elevators and established that businesses "affected with a public interest" could be regulated in ways that other businesses could not. Since the grain business was affected with a public interest, the rate regulation evidently was not class legislation. Therefore, it deserved to be upheld under Gillman's criterion. In an 1894 case that Gillman examines a bit later, the Court explicitly stated that one test for a valid police power regulation is "that the interests of the public generally, as distinguished from those of a particular class, require such interference."[62]

Some of the other cases Gillman discusses, however, pose greater difficulties for his argument. For example, the state law at issue in *Powell v. Pennsylvania,*[63] which forbade the manufacture and sale of oleomargarine on public health grounds, would seem an obvious piece of class legislation. Yet the Court upheld the measure. Although it involved a much more defensible statute, the Court's 1898 decision in *Holden v. Hardy*[64] should also have gone the other way if Gillman's thesis governed it. In that case, the Court upheld a Utah statute limiting the hours of work in underground mines. Because it benefitted a discrete group of people, this law was attacked as class legislation,[65] but the Court upheld it nonetheless. Also suggesting the irrelevance of Gillman's thesis is the virtual absence of "class legislation" language in the relevant portion of the Court's opinion.[66]

This brings us to *Lochner*, where the Court struck down New York's maximum-hours law for bakery employees.[67] Gillman admits that Justice Peckham's majority opinion did not employ "class legislation" rhetoric. As he apparently recognizes, however, one portion of Peckham's opinion might be read that way. After establishing that the New York statute interfered with contractual liberty and that laws of that kind needed some justification, Peckham first inquired whether the statute "is valid as a labor law, pure and simple."[68] As suggested in Chapter 1, by a "labor law, pure and simple" Peckham apparently meant a measure that regarded shorter working hours for bakery employees as an intrinsic good and not as a law that was good because it promoted more general, public aims. To Gillman, saying that the act was "purely a labor law" suggested that it was promoting a class interest in singling out for special treatment certain market competitors.[69] Consistent with this belief and with Gillman's general thesis, the Court refused to sustain the New York law as a labor law. "Viewed in the light of a purely labor law, with no reference whatever to the question of health, we think that a law like the one before us involves neither the safety, the morals nor the welfare of the public, and that the interest of the public is not in the slightest degree affected by such an act."[70]

The remainder of Peckham's opinion, however, proceeded on the assumption that the purpose necessary to support police power regulation need not be general or public. Thus it implicitly sanctioned apparent class legislation like the maximum-hours law for miners in *Holden v. Hardy*. Immediately after the preceding quotation, Peckham said that "[t]he law must be upheld, if at all, as a law pertaining to the health of the individual engaged in the occupation of a baker. It does not affect any other portion of the public than those who are engaged in that occupation."[71] On at least three occasions thereafter, Peckham suggested that either some connection to the *public* health or to the health of *bakery employees* would justify the New York statute.[72] As things turned out, the law failed because it lacked a sufficiently close connection with employee health. In Peckham's words, that measure "has no such direct relation to and no such substantial effect upon the health of the employee, as to justify us in regarding the section as really a health law."[73] Here, of course, Peckham was applying a means-ends test. As originally formulated in *Lochner*, that test said nothing about general or public purposes. Instead, Peckham wrote that "[t]he act must have a more direct relation, as a means to an end, and the end itself must be appropriate and legitimate."[74] And as we have just seen, the health of bakery employees clearly was an appropriate and legitimate purpose in Peckam's eyes. This means that on some occasions the law might legitimately protect the interests of a particular class, even if the general public did not benefit in any obvious way.

Lochner, then, provides some assistance to Gillman's cause but detracts from it even more by recognizing that laws that directly and substantially promote the health of a discrete class (bakery employees) satisfy due process. (As we will see in Chapter 4, however, the law at issue in *Lochner* may have been class legislation of a wholly different kind than Gillman envisions.) Following *Lochner*, Gillman discusses about a dozen substantive due process decisions, most of them employment cases, some of them famous, and all at least reasonably well known.[75] By this time, he seems at least as much concerned with showing the deficiencies of the old Court's jurisprudence as with advancing his basic argument that it attacked class legislation. In fact, I detected only three instances in which Gillman directly argues for that thesis. One of these arguments seems effective, one appears to be a stretch, and one looks like a wash.

In *Coppage v. Kansas*, the Court struck down a state law that forbade yellow-dog contracts: contracts under which an employee agrees not to join or remain a labor union member. As Gillman observes, at one point in his majority opinion Justice Mahlon Pitney asked what possible relation there could be between that law and the *public* health, safety, morals, or *general* welfare and concluded that there was none.[76] Shortly thereafter, Pitney added that the strengthening of labor unions—or indeed the strengthening of any voluntary association—is not a legitimate purpose of government. To strengthen any particular association, of course, is to benefit a class.

A year later, in *Adams v. Tanner*, the Court invalidated a Washington initiative preventing employment agencies from collecting fees for their services. Evidently this measure was inspired by various abuses that were prevalent in the business. Even so, at one point in his opinion for the Court Justice James B. McReynolds launched the following extended sentence:

> A suggestion in behalf of the state, that while a pursuit of this kind "may be beneficial to some particular individuals or in specific cases, economically it is certainly nonuseful, if not vicious, because it compels the needy and unfortunate to pay for that which they are entitled to without fee or price, that is, the right to work," while possibly indicative of the purpose held by those who originated the legislation, in reason, gives it no support.[77]

Gillman evidently takes this to support his assertion that, to McReynolds, "rather than promoting legitimate health and safety, the state was interested simply in providing special benefits (free job placement) to certain classes (the unemployed) at the expense of competing classes (employment agents for hire)."[78] But while McReynolds no doubt thought such a purpose illegitimate, that belief had little to do with his decision in *Adams v. Tanner*. It is difficult to believe that he really thought that the initiative's aim was to make employment agencies provide services for free. The law did not command anyone to furnish such services. And who would voluntarily do so for nothing? Instead, McReynolds obviously thought that, practically speaking, the Washington measure was a prohibition of employment agencies.[79] As such, it unduly and arbitrarily restricted the right to engage in a useful business.[80]

Adkins v. Children's Hospital,[81] the last case in our trio, struck down a District of Columbia minimum-wage law for women and children. Gillman quotes a sentence from Justice Sutherland's majority opinion, in which Sutherland says that the minimum wage "amounts to a compulsory exaction from the employer for the support of a partially indigent person, for whose condition there rests upon him no peculiar responsibility, and therefore, in effect, arbitrarily shifts to his shoulders a burden which, if it belongs to anybody, belongs to society as a whole."[82] "Rather than burden one class with the responsibility to care for another," Gillman continues, Sutherland thought that "the society as a whole should bear the burden by passing poor-relief laws."[83] This sounds the "class legislation" theme, but note that here the benefitted classes (working women and children) probably comprised a fairly large portion of the D.C. population. At what point does legislation unconstitutionally benefitting a class become a law that instead promotes the health, safety, and welfare of the general public? Like *Lochner*, finally, *Adkins* might be class legislation of a rather different sort than Gillman envisions. Chapter 4 discusses this possibility.

The "Class Legislation" Thesis and the "Core" and "Borderline" Substantive Due Process Cases

The aim of this section is to determine whether a hostility toward class legislation actually motivated the old Court; it is not to determine whether this was a good or a bad thing. From the evidence presented thus far, this hypothesis obviously has some explanatory power, but it just as obviously fails in some cases. Among these failures, of course, is one that the theory shares with its two competitors: inconsistency with the sizable group of decisions in which the old Court *rejected* a substantive due process attack on government action. Perhaps the biggest weakness of Gillman's presentation, however, is the range of substantive due process cases he does not consider. Like most writers on the *Lochner* Court, he mainly examines the familiar cases that comprise the standard picture, plus some others that are reasonably well known. And while Gillman also considers some other federal constitutional decisions and some state cases, he does not comprehensively address either group. In particular, he does not comprehensively discuss the old Court's equal protection cases, which might have proven useful to him. (Nor, to my knowledge, has anyone else done so.) Gillman's fairly slim evidentiary base naturally raises a question: How well does the "class legislation" argument fare when considered against the full rage of *Lochner*-era substantive due process cases striking down government action? In trying to answer that question, this subsection necessarily paints with a broader brush than its predecessor. Overall, it is a mixed bag for Gillman's thesis.

Perhaps the most curious defect of Gillman's book is his failure to emphasize the old Court's decisions striking down restrictions on entry, some of which are class legislation through and through. As we have seen earlier in this chapter, in *Louis K. Liggett Co. v. Baldridge* and *New State Ice Co. v. Liebmann* the Court overturned state laws that advanced the economic interests of established firms within certain industries, to the disadvantage both of potential competitors and of the general public. Gillman briefly mentions *Liebmann* but seems not to appreciate its significance;[84] of the *Liggett* case he says nothing at all. Of course, neither case supports his general argument that industrialization, large corporations, dependency, unequal bargaining power, and class conflict necessitated class legislation for society's victims—and thus ultimately doomed economic substantive due process. Rather, in these two cases the classes benefitted were established in-state pharmacists and ice producers, respectively.

Providing even more dramatic support for Gillman's thesis are the old Court's decisions striking down land-use regulations. In two of these cases, the challenged measure went beyond favoring a partial private interest by effectively handing over sovereign power to private actors and allowing that power to be exercised at their discretion. In each, that exercise of power was to the potential disadvantage of other property owners. *Eubank v. City of Richmond*[85] struck down an ordinance requiring the city to set a particular building line on a street once two-thirds of the property owners on the street requested that line. *Washington* ex rel. *Seattle Title Trust Co. v. Roberge*[86] invalidated another ordinance that made construction of a home for elderly poor people contingent on the consent of two-thirds of the property owners living within 400 feet of the planned home.

Although it is difficult to generalize about the group without a lengthy case-by-case discussion, at least one of the regulatory orders directed at businesses affected with a public interest looks like class legislation. In *Missouri Pacific Railway Co. v. Nebraska*,[87] which was discussed in Chapter 2, the Court struck down a Nebraska statute requiring that, at their own expense, railroads construct and maintain a side track to any grain elevator requesting one. Perhaps there was a public policy justification for this compelled gift to the elevators, but the Court did not suggest one. The Court also did not discuss the legislative processes that gave rise to this measure, but one probably can make a reasonable guess. In a 1904 case,[88] moreover, the Court struck down an ordinance that effectively revoked a permit to construct gas works that the city of Los Angeles had previously granted the plaintiff. In that case, the plaintiff alleged that the ordinance had been enacted at the behest of a monopoly competitor, and the Court employed "class legislation" rhetoric. Later, it said that the ordinance "was not demanded by the public welfare" and "seems rather to have been actuated by the purpose to exclude the plaintiff . . . from further prosecution of the enterprise."[89]

Some other categories of *Lochner*-era substantive decisions also contain individual cases that arguably struck down class legislation. Hopefully enough has already been said in this chapter to make clear that this is true of the employment decisions. Turning to some additional classes of cases discussed in Chapter 2, the tax cases striking down laws that inequitably allocated the burdens of public improvements also can be read as involving "partial" laws. Maybe the decisions invalidating laws that imposed special liability on railroads and other businesses can be regarded as class legislation whose main aim was to give unjustified windfalls to undeserving plaintiffs and their counsel. As *BMW v. Gore* suggests, in an age of predatory plaintiff's attorneys and self-aggrandizing state attorney-generals, these cases have a contemporary feel. Last but not least, some of the business regulations the old Court struck down look very much like class legislation. The clearest examples are *Allgeyer v. Louisiana* and the cases following it, which can easily be read as invalidating special-interest legislation that favored in-state insurers.

Some of the business regulations the old Court struck down, however, do not look like class legislation. The three maximum-price regulations that it overturned, for example, probably gave the general public a short-term pecuniary advantage. The same is true for the many rate orders for regulated industries that the old Court struck down. Finally, one category (or subcategory) of *Lochner*-era substantive due process cases involves laws that are as remote from class legislation as one could imagine. I refer to the three "personal rights" cases sequestered within the general police regulations in Chapter 2. If statutes mandating public school attendance and regulating the teaching of languages are class legislation, what would not qualify?

The Old Court's Language

One could, of course, extend the preceding section's analysis to include all the many cases in which the old Court rejected substantive due process claims. Almost certainly, however, this tedious exercise would only confirm the conclusion already reached: Some of the *Lochner* Court's substantive due process cases support the class legislation hypothesis and some do not. For the most part, though, they support that hypothesis through what they do rather than what they say. Only infrequently, in other words, do the cases striking down government action explicitly say that the challenged law failed because it advanced the interests of a particular class rather than the public good. This will become plainly evident to anyone who actually reads all the relevant cases. Due to the large number of such decisions and the difficulty of proving a negative, readers who forgo this treat must take my claim on faith. But I can offer some evidence that makes it plausible.

The previous discussion provided some examples of "class legislation" rhetoric, but such language was the exception rather than the rule during the *Lochner* era. For the years 1902–1932 inclusive, I have been able to find only six substantive due process decisions that used the terms "class legislation," "class law," "partial legislation," or "partial law."[90] (A few equal protection cases did so as well.) In none of these cases were the quoted terms critical to the Court's decision. What do we find if we extend the inquiry further? A crude decade-by-decade LEXIS search for the Supreme Court—one including all kinds of cases and not merely substantive due process decisions, plus the parties' briefs—revealed the following:

Decade	*Number of Times One of the Four Terms Used*
1860–1870	7
1870–1880	7
1880–1890	18
1890–1900	19
1900–1910	33
1910–1920	27
1920–1930	15
1930–1940	5

Lochner-era substantive due process probably reached peak intensity during the 1920s—the decade during which the minimum wage was declared unconstitutional, the doctrine came to include personal as well as economic rights, three state price regulations were overturned, and *Liggett* was decided. Yet "class legislation" rhetoric apparently was on the wane by then.

THE PROTECTION OF LIBERTY AND PROPERTY

If the old Court's substantive due process cases did not usually justify themselves through class legislation themes, how did they justify themselves? Almost invariably, they said that the challenged measure deprived the claimant of liberty or property. By a potpourri of different means, these opinions then tried to determine whether that deprivation was substantively justified. When the challenged law failed whatever test the Court applied, it ceased to have force. So far as threats from the government are concerned, this increased the claimant's liberty or the security of his property in one fashion or another. From all this, one might conclude that the justices' motives aligned with their words: that they were trying to protect liberty and property against government action that would deprive people of either or both. Of course, this desire could not be absolutized: It had to be accommodated to society's interest in regulating to promote the public's health, safety, morals, and general welfare. Thus, we might amend the previous statement to say that the Court's aim was to protect liberty and property against arbitrary or unreasonable restraints.

The previous argument seems embarrassingly short. Why should anyone believe it? The better question, I think, is why anyone should *not* believe that the main inspiration for *Lochner*-era substantive due process was the justices' desire to protect liberty and property against government action. Whatever else it may have accomplished, the old Court at least protected the claimant's liberty or property in the cases where it granted a substantive due process claim. That, furthermore, is what the justices said they were doing in such cases. Sometimes people's stated reasons for doing something are their real ones, and sometimes the superficially plausible explanation for a social phenomenon is the real one, too.

The thesis that the old Court wanted to protect liberty and property against government, therefore, coheres with what its substantive due process cases said and what they did. It also explains the substantive due process decisions striking down government action better than its two competitors. Figure 3.1 states how well each of our three explanations of *Lochner*-era substantive due process explains the cases striking down government action within each category of "core" and "borderline" substantive due process case. Needless to say, it does so in broad, crude strokes.

Broadest and crudest of all, it first seems, are my conclusions about the thesis that the inspiration for the old Court's substantive due process cases was its desire to protect liberty and property. The figure asserts that this motive explains each category of substantive due process case. (The parenthesized liberty and property designations state the right a particular set of cases generally advanced and not necessarily the right of which the claimant technically was deprived in the Court's opinion.) But as argued previously, this almost necessarily is true. All the cases in question struck down government action that deprived the claimant of liberty or property. In each of them, the Court described itself as doing

Figure 3.1
Explaining the Old Court's Substantive Due Process Cases

Type of Substantive Due Process Case	Explained by Agent-of-Business Thesis?	Explained by "Class Legislation" Thesis?	Explained by "Liberty and Property"Thesis?
Utility rate	Yes	No	Yes (property)
Utility order	Yes	Partly	Yes (freedom to conduct business)
Liability and Remedy	Yes	Slightly	Yes (property)
Tax	Partly	Partly	Yes (property)
Land use	No	Yes	Yes (property)
General police (personal rights)	No	No	Yes (familial liberties)
General business regulations	Yes	Partly	Yes (various liberty and property rights)
Entry restriction and occupational freedom	No	Yes	Yes (occupational freedom)
Employment	Yes	Partly	Yes (mainly freedom of contract)

exactly that. If the Court's true motives matched its self-description, the liberty and property thesis obviously explains the substantive due process decisions striking down government action.

The other two theories would not deny—indeed, could not deny—that the old Court's substantive due process decisions struck down government action depriving someone of liberty and property and that they described themselves as doing just that. But they would deny that this was the real or ultimate reason the Court acted as it did. More precisely, they would say that beneath the superficial desire to strike down government action denying liberty or property lay a deeper desire and that, rather than being the Court's primary aim, the former was merely instrumental to the latter. For the agent-of-business theory, that deeper aim was the desire to benefit business by striking down Progressive social legislation that frustrated its economic interests. For the "class legislation" theory, it was the desire to eliminate laws that benefitted narrowly based groups rather than the public interest. How well are the various kinds of substantive due process decisions explained on each of these two theories? I begin with the agent-of-business hypothesis.

As noted earlier in the chapter, the rate cases are Exhibit A in the argument that the old Court knowingly and willingly acted as business's agent. In those decisions, the Court struck down government action limiting the rates charged by various regulated industries on the theory that the challenged regulations denied the business a fair rate of return. These decisions worked to the regulated firm's financial advantage—as well as the financial advantage of its shareholders and bondholders—in the most obvious way possible. On a smaller scale, the same might be said of the liability and remedy cases—and perhaps some of the tax cases as well. In addition to the rate cases, also high on the agent-of-business theory's list are the cases striking down laws that regulated business in various ways—cases that almost by definition worked to the affected firms' advantage. The same is true of the employment cases, which included decisions striking down minimum-wage and maximum-hours statutes, as well as laws forbidding yellow-dog contracts and other kinds of employer retaliation against union members. Finally, the decisions striking down regulatory orders directed at businesses affected with a public interest at least enhanced those firms' ability to run the business as they saw fit and probably assisted them financially as well.

Three classes of *Lochner*-era substantive due process cases, however, do not fit the agent-of-business theory at all. Of the old Court's four decisions striking down land-use regulations, not one clearly involves a conventional business. The three "personal rights" cases contained within the general police category (*Meyer v. Nebraska, Pierce v. Society of Sisters*, and a companion case to *Meyer*) have nothing at all to do with business. Finally, as argued at length earlier, the cases striking down restrictions on entry contradict the agent-of-business thesis. The reason is that in some of these cases the old Court struck down laws through which existing firms within an industry sought to benefit themselves by stifling competition from new entrants. Of course, these cases did tend to benefit the businesses that were seeking entry, but this obviously was done not to assist those firms but to promote competition.

In some respects, the virtues and defects of the class legislation thesis mirror those of the agent-of-business argument. While the latter theory foundered in explaining the entry restriction cases and the land-use cases, those decisions are entirely consistent with the belief that the old Court's main aim was to eliminate class legislation. For all the reasons stated earlier, the laws at issue in the entry restriction cases obviously are class legislation. And because they delegated sovereign power to private parties rather than merely letting those parties bend the law to their advantage, some of the measures struck down in the land-use cases are even more offensive from an anti–class legislation perspective. On the other hand, the "class legislation" hypothesis does poorly with the rate cases. The reason is that if the people benefitted by the rate orders struck down in those decisions (the general public) count as a "class," the theory explains almost any law and hence becomes vacuous. This is true whether (as the agent-of-business theory would have it) rate regulation was a justified exaction from powerful and predatory natural monopolies or instead was an example of "majoritarian bias" against politically vulnerable firms.

As Figure 3.1's frequent use of the words "partly" and "probably" suggests, the class legislation hypothesis is only partly consistent with most of the other classes of *Lochner*-era substantive due process decisions. (On the whole, it fares somewhat less well than the agent-of-business theory in these instances.) As we have seen, some of the regulatory orders that the old Court struck down look like partial laws. As this chapter's lengthy discussion of the subject made clear, the same is true for some of the employment laws the Court invalidated. Of the tax measures that fell on substantive due process grounds, one subgroup seems consistent with the class legislation argument. Here I refer to the laws creating inequitable assessments against landowners for public improvements that ostensibly benefitted their land. Because the laws they struck down arguably benefitted plaintiff's attorneys, the liability and remedy cases provide some support for the class legislation thesis. (Under the agent-of-business theory, on the other hand, these cases are explained by the old Court's desire to help out the railroads.) As discussed earlier, finally, of the general business regulations that fell to substantive due process, some look like class legislation, and some do not.

Of course, neither the agent-of-business thesis nor the class legislation argument can get much of a handle on the old Court's three personal rights cases. These cases, however, are entirely consistent with the idea that the old Court was trying to protect liberty and property against government action. As we have seen, the liberty and property theory explains all the major classes of cases in which substantive due process was used to strike down government action during the *Lochner* era. For that reason, and because it expresses what the justices said they were doing, that theory is superior to its two competitors. As we have seen, proponents of those two views might assert that the liberty and property theory is only trivially true, because the old Court was protecting liberty and property in order to advance more important goals. But since when has the protection of liberty and property been intrinsically unimportant? One might also argue that the old Court cannot have been too concerned about protecting liberty and property, since its substantive due process cases sustained considerably more regulations than they struck down. But this means only that the Court did not make liberty and property absolutes. And as we have seen, this argument also cuts against the other two explanations for *Lochner*-era substantive due process.

Of the two also-rans, which theory is preferable? As Figure 3.1 suggests, the agent-of-business thesis probably has a bit more explanatory power than the class legislation hypothesis. For two reasons, however, the latter seems the better of the two. As Gillman's book made clear, firstly, the old Court sometimes used class legislation rhetoric to justify its substantive due process decisions. Secondly, the class legislation hypothesis seems easier to reconcile with our preferred explanation, the liberty and property thesis, than does the agent-of-business theory. Here, perhaps it is sufficient to note that economic freedom, private property, and equal competition on a level playing field are traditional American ideals that have coexisted in many minds. To reconcile the agent-of-business thesis with the liberty and property theory, on the other hand, we might have to assume a devotion to laissez-faire so extreme as to favor business simply because it won out in the social struggle. Maybe this is why some critics of the old Court assert, with little or no apparent evidence, that its conservative justices were influenced by Social Darwinism.[91]

NOTES

1. *E.g.*, RICHARD J. PIERCE, JR. & ERNEST GELLHORN, REGULATED INDUSTRIES IN A NUTSHELL 98–99 (3d ed. 1994). The case marking the shift was Federal Power Comm'n v. Hope Natural Gas Co., 320 U.S. 591 (1944).

2. PIERCE & GELLHORN, *supra* note 1, at 101–2.

3. Richard J. Pierce, Jr., *Public Utility Regulatory Takings: Should the Judiciary Attempt to Police the Political Institutions?*, 77 GEO. L.J. 2031, 2051 (1989).

4. *Id.* at 2044–45. *See also* JAMES W. ELY, JR., THE CHIEF JUSTICESHIP OF MELVILLE W. FULLER 1888–1910 88 (1995); Stephen A. Siegel, *Understanding the* Lochner *Era: Lessons from the Controversy over Railroad and Utility Rate Regulation*, 70 VA. L. REV. 187, 207–9 (1984).

5. *E.g.*, JAMES W. ELY, JR., THE GUARDIAN OF EVERY OTHER RIGHT: A CONSTITUTIONAL HISTORY OF PROPERTY RIGHTS 89–90 (2d ed. 1998); Siegel, *supra* note 4, at 208.

6. Michael J. Phillips, *The Substantive Due Process Decisions of Mr. Justice Holmes*, 36 AM. BUS. L.J. 437, 456 & n.111 (1999).

7. *See, e.g.*, WALTER NICHOLSON, MICROECONOMIC THEORY: BASIC PRINCIPLES AND EXTENSIONS 432–34 (4th ed. 1989).

8. *See, e.g.*, RICHARD A. POSNER, ECONOMIC ANALYSIS OF LAW 308–10 (3d ed. 1986).

9. *See* Meyer v. Nebraska, 262 U.S. 390, 399–403 (1923) (striking down a state law regulating the teaching of foreign languages in public and private schools); Pierce v. Society of Sisters, 268 U.S. 510, 534–35 (1925) (striking down a state law requiring public school attendance for all students between the ages of eight and sixteen). *See also* Bartels v. Iowa, 262 U.S. 404, 409–11 (1923) (a companion case to *Meyer*). Actually, *Meyer* emphasized other rights besides the parental control right stressed in the text). *See* 262 U.S. at 400–401.

10. Buchanan v. Warley, 245 U.S. 60, 73–82 (1917) (striking down an ordinance making it unlawful for any black person to move into any house located in a block in which a majority of the homes were owned by whites).

11. Washington *ex rel.* Seattle Title Trust Co. v. Roberge, 278 U.S. 116, 120–23 (1928) (striking down an ordinance that conditioned construction of a home for elderly poor people on the consent of two-thirds of the property owners living within 400 feet of the planned home); Eubank v. City of Richmond, 226 U.S. 137, 143–44 (1912) (striking down an ordinance requiring that the city set a certain building line on a street at the request of two-thirds of the property owners living on the street).

12. North Dakota State Bd. of Pharmacy v. Snyder's Drug Stores, Inc., 414 U.S. 156, 167 (1973).

13. Louis K. Liggett Co. v. Baldridge, 278 U.S. 105, 113–14 (1928).

14. *Id.* at 114–15 (Holmes, J., dissenting).

15. New State Ice Co. v. Liebmann, 285 U.S. 262, 273–78 (1932). Actually, Sutherland used the term "charged with a public use." But this term almost certainly was the functional equivalent of "affected with a public interest." On this point and on the details of Sutherland's discussion, see Michael J. Phillips, *Entry Restrictions in the* Lochner *Court*, 4 GEO MASON L. REV. 405, 440–41 n.198 (1996).

16. 285 U.S. at 278–79.

17. *Id.* at 280.

18. *Id.*

19. The following remarks come from Phillips, *supra* note 15, at 411–13, and the sources cited there. These include: S. DAVID YOUNG, THE RULE OF EXPERTS: OCCUPATIONAL LICENSING IN AMERICA (1987); Walter Gellhorn, *The Abuse of Occupational Licensing*, 44 U. CHI. L. REV. 6 (1976); Mark Green & Ralph Nader, *Economic Regulation vs. Competition: Uncle Sam the Monopoly Man*, 82 YALE L.J. 871 (1973); Christopher T. Wonnell, *Economic Due Process and the Preservation of Competition*, 11 HASTINGS CONST. L.Q. 91 (1983).

20. YOUNG, *supra* note 19, at 1.

21. Herbert Hovenkamp, *The Political Economy of Substantive Due Process*, 40 STAN. L. REV. 379, 390 (1988).

22. *See* Phillips, *supra* note 15, at 431–34.

23. All the quotations in the next paragraph come from New State Ice Co. v. Liebmann, 285 U.S. 262, 310–11 (1932) (Brandeis, J., dissenting).

24. G. Edward White, *The Canonization of Holmes and Brandeis: Epistemology and Judicial Reputations*, 70 N.Y.U. L. REV. 576, 600 (1995).

25. HADLEY ARKES, THE RETURN OF GEORGE SUTHERLAND: RESTORING A JURISPRUDENCE OF NATURAL RIGHTS 55 (1994).

26. *See id.* at 54–58; POSNER, *supra* note 8, at 93; BERNARD H. SIEGAN, ECONOMIC LIBERTIES AND THE CONSTITUTION 132–38 (paperback ed. 1980).

27. *See* 285 U.S. at 287–94, 306–11 (Brandeis, J., dissenting).

28. *Id.* at 294–300.

29. *Id.* at 304.

30. *Id.* at 294, 300.

31. *Id.* at 293.

32. Southwest Utility Ice Co. v. Liebmann, 52 F.2d 349, 350–51n.1 (10th Cir. 1931).

33. *Id.* at 355.

34. 285 U.S. at 292 & n.20 (Brandeis, J., dissenting).

35. *See* 52 F.2d at 355.

36. 285 U.S. at 278 (Sutherland, J., for the majority).

37. *Id.* at 290 (Brandeis, J., dissenting).

38. Brandeis's belief in easy entry also creates difficulties for another argument that he may or may not have made: that the manufacture of ice is a natural monopoly. *See, e.g.*, SIEGAN, *supra* note 26, at 135–36. A natural monopoly is a business whose high fixed costs create economies of scale so great that the operation is most efficiently conducted by a single firm. In theory, government regulation of such a monopoly enables society both to capture this efficiency and to prevent the natural monopolist from abusing its position. But if the ice industry was a natural monopoly, how could it also be easy to enter? An industry with high fixed costs and economies of scale should be difficult, rather than easy, for competitors to join. Conversely, should we regard an easy-to-enter industry as a true natural monopoly? *See, e.g.*, POSNER, *supra* note 8, at 317, 591, 592.

39. 285 U.S. at 292–93 (Brandeis, J., dissenting).

40. *Id.* at 294.

41. POSNER, *supra* note 8, at 592.

42. 285 U.S. at 306 (Brandeis, J., dissenting).

43. *Id.* at 307–8.

44. *Id.* at 309.

45. White, *supra* note 24, at 602.

46. *See* Ferguson v. Skrupa, 372 U.S. 726, 729–32 (1963).

47. POSNER, *supra* note 8, at 592.

48. *Id.*

49. Morton J. Horwitz, *Republicanism and Liberalism in American Constitutional Thought*, 29 WM. & MARY L. REV. 57, 57 (1987).

50. *Id.* at 61–63.

51. MORTON J. HORWITZ, THE TRANSFORMATION OF AMERICAN LAW 1870–1960: THE CRISIS OF LEGAL ORTHODOXY 7 (1992). The remaining quotations in this paragraph come from this page.

52. Horwitz, *supra* note 50, at 59.

53. *Id.* at 57.

54. HOWARD GILLMAN, THE CONSTITUTION BESIEGED: THE RISE AND DEMISE OF *LOCHNER* ERA POLICE POWERS JURISPRUDENCE (paperback ed. 1995). This book was originally published in 1993. For what appears to be an earlier statement of

this general view, see Michael Les Benedict, *Laissez Faire and Liberty: A Re-Evaluation of the Meaning and Origins of Laissez-Faire Constitutionalism*, 3 LAW & HIST. REV. 293, 305–31 (1985).

55. *Id.* at 199.

56. *Id.* at 61.

57. *Id.* at 199; *see id.* at 3–7.

58. *E.g.*, *id.* at 11.

59. For the points made in the remainder of this paragraph, see *id.* at 11–13, 21–22, 63–64, 76–86, 147–58, 158–60.

60. 83 U.S. 36 (1873). *See* GILLMAN, *supra* note 54, at 64–69.

61. 94 U.S. 113 (1877). *See* GILLMAN, *supra* note 54, at 68–69.

62. Lawton v. Steele, 152 U.S. 133, 137 (1894) (upholding a state law regulating methods of fishing). *See* GILLMAN, *supra* note 54, at 104–5.

63. 127 U.S. 678 (1888). *See* GILLMAN, *supra* note 54, at 73–75.

64. 169 U.S. 366 (1898). *See* GILLMAN, *supra* note 54, at 120–25.

65. GILLMAN, *supra* note 54, at 120–21.

66. *See* 169 U.S. at 389–98.

67. Lochner v. New York, 198 U.S. 45 (1905). *See* GILLMAN, *supra* note 54, at 125–31.

68. 198 U.S. at 57.

69. GILLMAN, *supra* note 54, at 127.

70. 198 U.S. at 57.

71. *Id.*

72. *Id.* at 58, 61.

73. *Id.* at 64. For all the reasons, see *id.* at 57–64.

74. *Id.* at 57.

75. GILLMAN, *supra* note 54, at 137–46, 167–75, 180–81, 185–93.

76. Coppage v. Kansas, 236 U.S. 1, 16 (1915); GILLMAN, *supra* note 54, at 139.

77. Adams v. Tanner, 244 U.S. 590, 594 (1917).

78. GILLMAN, *supra* note 54, at 143.

79. 244 U.S. at 593.

80. *See id.* at 596–97.

81. 261 U.S. 525 (1923).

82. *Id.* at 557–58 (quotation marks omitted); *see* GILLMAN, *supra* note 54, at 170.

83. GILLMAN, *supra* note 54, at 170.

84. *Id.* at 181.

85. 226 U.S. 137, 143–44 (1912).

86. 278 U.S. 116, 120–23 (1928).

87. 217 U.S. 196, 205–8 (1910).

88. Dobbins v. Los Angeles, 195 U.S. 223, 236–37 (1904).

89. *Id.* at 239.

90. Southern Ry. Co. v. Clift, 260 U.S. 316, 320 (1922); Truax v. Corrigan, 257 U.S. 312, 333 (1921); Payne v. Kansas *ex rel.* Brewster, 248 U.S. 112, 113 (1918); Mountain Timber Co. v. Washington, 243 U.S. 219, 239 (1917); Rosenthal v. New York, 226 U.S. 260, 267 (1912); Muller v. Oregon, 208 U.S. 412, 418 (1908). These cases were identified through a LEXIS search using the terms quoted in the text.

91. *E.g.*, JOEL FRANCIS PASCHAL, MR. JUSTICE SUTHERLAND: A MAN AGAINST THE STATE 6–20, 28–31, 126–27, 242 (1951) (continually attributing George Sutherland's politics and judicial decisions to his brief exposure to Herbert Spencer's ideas while attending the University of Michigan as a young man).

Chapter 4

The Question of Unequal Bargaining Power

Moral philosophers sometimes distinguish between deontological and consequentialist ethical theories. Both tell us how to evaluate the rightness or wrongness of actions. Strict or strong deontological theories say that the morality of actions is determined by those actions' intrinsic nature, or by the motives that inspired them, but never by their consequences.[1] The classic example is the ethical philosophy of Immanuel Kant. Early in his *Foundations of the Metaphysics of Morals*, Kant declared that "[n]othing in the world—indeed nothing even beyond the world—can possibly be conceived which could be called good without qualification except a GOOD WILL."[2] "The good will," he continued, "is not good because of what it effects or accomplishes or because of its competence to achieve some intended end; it is good only because of the willing (i.e., it is good in itself)." Even if it was utterly ineffectual, Kant concluded, the good will still "would sparkle like a jewel all by itself, as something that had its full worth in itself."

Pronouncements like Kant's rub some people the wrong way. Their reaction to such statements resembles the rage many feel when, after some fool's blunders have brought disaster to the community, a defender chirps the inevitable "but he *meant well.*" Rather than judging the worth of actions by their nature or the motives that inspired them, such people look only at their consequences. In moral theory, the main example is utilitarianism, most of whose many varieties evaluate actions by their tendency to promote utility. For this reason, utilitarianism is called a consequentialist moral theory.

To consequentialist eyes, Chapter 3's attack on the claim that the *Lochner* Court acted as business's agent no doubt looks like a puny "they meant well" defense. "Who cares," these people would declare, "whether the old Court's justices acted from sincere beliefs?" In context, those beliefs were rubbish. In an economy dominated by large corporations, traditional laissez-faire loses much of its former relevance. "The main reason," our consequentialists would explain, "is that isolated, powerless individuals cannot bargain on equal terms with giant corporations." To correct for this disadvantage, Progressive social legislation was essential. Yet by constitutionalizing freedom of contract, the old Court impeded such regulations. "Maybe the justices were sincere," these interlocutors would conclude, "but the consequences of their blindness and stupidity were very serious."

Readers will recognize this line of argument from Chapter 1. There, the argument bore a more or less deontological label, being described as an "innocent" explanation for the old Court's decisions. This, of course, was to contrast it with the agent-of-business thesis. A significant strand in this "innocent" explanation is that the Court's unfortunate substantive due process decisions resulted from the justices' nostalgic attachment to outmoded laissez-faire ideas. This is broadly consistent with Chapter 3's conclusion that the best explanation for *Lochner*-era substantive due process is the justices' devotion to liberty and property. The present point, however, is consequentialist: that the old Court may as well have been business's agent as freedom's friend because the results were the same in either case. And those results were most unfortunate.

This chapter examines the very familiar charge that, whatever the justices' reasons for creating and applying it, *Lochner*-era substantive due process ratified business's superior bargaining power by striking down social legislation that would have helped correct the imbalance. The chapter concludes that this charge packs less punch than is commonly believed. This is not, I should emphasize, to say that unequal bargaining power is a meaningless concept, that the *Lochner* era was without such inequalities, or that the old Court was sufficiently sensitive to them. But it is to say that the charge is overdrawn. In support of that conclusion, I begin with a point that may already have occurred to some readers. Even if the old Court really did ratify unequal bargaining power on all the occasions when it is believed to have done so, these cases were far from the whole of *Lochner*-era substantive due process.

THE INSIGNIFICANCE OF THE UNEQUAL BARGAINING POWER CASES

Most of the decisions striking down laws that might be thought to address unequal bargaining power appear in Chapter 1's standard picture of *Lochner*-era substantive due process. As one might expect, they mainly are employment cases. *Lochner* itself, which invalidated a maximum-hours law for bakery employees, is perhaps the most familiar example. Other examples include *Adkins v. Children's Hospital* and the cases following it to strike down minimum-wage laws.[3] Also worth a mention are a lesser-known minimum-wage case, *Chas. Wolff Packing Co. v. Court of Industrial Relations*, and two subsequent decisions involving the same state measure at issue in *Chas. Wolff*.[4] Because union membership is generally thought to improve an employee's bargaining position, two much-recognized cases involving organized labor deserve inclusion as well. *Adair v. United States*[5] struck down a federal law that prevented certain common carriers from firing or otherwise discriminating against an employee because of his union affiliation, and *Coppage v. Kansas*[6] overturned a state statute banning yellow-dog contracts.

Some of the laws the old Court struck down regulated business firms' contractual relations with customers rather than employees. These laws also might be regarded as legislative responses to superior corporate bargaining power. The best examples are the three late-1920s decisions striking down maximum-price laws for various consumer goods and services.[7] Another fairly good example is *Jay Burns Baking Co. v. Bryan*,[8] in which the Court invalidated a state law whose apparent aim was to protect consumers against short-weight bread loaves. *Weaver v. Palmer Brothers*,[9] which struck down a consumer protection measure that may have been either a health or an antideception provision, also may qualify for inclusion here.

At first glance, the old Court's rate cases and its decisions striking down other laws controlling regulated industries also seem to involve government action for the correction of unequal bargaining power. But while consumers almost surely could not bargain on equal terms with the firms subject to these regulations, the old Court had effectively conceded the point much earlier. The businesses in question were actual or likely natural monopolies such as railroads, electric and gas utilities, telephone companies, trolley companies, and so forth. The Court had affirmed the states' extensive powers to regulate these businesses affected with a public interest at least as early as *Munn v. Illinois*.[10] The rate cases and the utility order cases did not seriously question those powers. This is illustrated by Chapter 2's list of the large number of rate orders and other regulations that the old Court upheld. The cases striking down such regulations, on the other hand, generally did so because the challenged laws were confiscatory or otherwise worked an unjustifiable deprivation of property. The question in these cases was not whether the states could regulate to counteract superior corporate power but the permissible extent of such regulation.

The other classes of cases comprising *Lochner*-era substantive due process either do not support the charge that the old Court's substantive due process cases ratified unequal bargaining power or actively confound it. The liability and remedies cases may have pitted railroads and other businesses against smaller businesses and isolated individuals, but the laws they struck down did not attack *contractual* inequalities between these parties. Even if the tax cases implicated the distribution of wealth between rich and poor, these distributional consequences hardly had their origins in unequal *bargaining* power. The four land-use regulations the old Court struck down also were not efforts to correct for unequal bargaining power; if they had any common theme, it was the standardless delegation of government power to private parties. Finally, the three decisions involving "general police regulations" were familial rights cases.

This brings us to the old Court's decisions striking down restrictions on entry to a trade, profession, or business. As Chapter 3 argued at some length, entry restrictions are not responses to unequal private power. If anything, they are products of such power; more precisely, they often are efforts by existing practitioners to thwart potential competition. For that reason, as Chapter 3 also argued, the entry decision cases confound the standard notion that the *Lochner* Court was business's witting or unwitting servant. The same may well be true, albeit to a lesser extent, of *Allgeyer v. Louisiana* and certain other decisions involving the insurance industry.[11] *Allgeyer* struck down a state statute that imposed a fine for obtaining marine insurance on in-state property from any insurer that had not complied in all respects with Louisiana insurance law, and the other decisions invalidated similar measures. These laws are easy to construe as efforts by in-state insurers to suppress competition from outside the state, or at least as the state's own effort to boost its resources at the expense of foreign insurers and their clients. Consider, for example, Holmes's comment in a 1922 decision that overturned an Arkansas statute taxing monies paid to insure in-state property with an insurer that was not registered to do business within the state. Analogizing the case before him to *Allgeyer*, Holmes said that "[t]he Arkansas tax manifests no less plainly than the Louisiana fine a purpose to discourage insuring in companies that do not pay tribute to the State."[12]

THE PROGRESSIVISM OF THE *LOCHNER* COURT

Thus, a good many of the laws struck down on substantive due process grounds during the *Lochner* era were not efforts to correct for unequal bargaining power. For that reason, the charge that the old Court unwittingly ratified such inequalities simply has no application to those decisions. This, in turn, helps undermine the charge's accuracy as a general characterization of *Lochner*-era substantive due process. Further blunting that charge are the cases in which the old Court *upheld* laws intended to protect weaker parties against exercises of superior bargaining power. In the interests of economy and relevance, here I limit myself to cases involving employment laws.

Chapter 2 estimated that during the *Lochner* era unsuccessful substantive due process attacks on employment regulations exceeded successful challenges by forty-three to twelve. Some of these laws involved matters that normally are an explicit part of any employment contract. Minimum-wage and maximum-hours laws are the obvious examples. As we have seen, the old Court invalidated some measures of each kind. But as Chapter 2 revealed, it upheld some as well. Indeed, *Lochner* apparently involved the only maximum-hours law that the Court struck down. It sustained at least seven others.[13] Although the old Court did draw the line more firmly when wages were at issue, there were chinks in its armor here as well. It upheld one law regulating wages in public works contracts (plus three others regulating other matters in the same context).[14] On at least four occasions, moreover, the Court sustained laws prescribing the character, methods, and time for the payment of wages.[15]

As Chapter 2 revealed, the *Lochner* Court also upheld a variety of other employment regulations, many of them health and safety measures. These might be said to involve bargaining power in the sense that had employees possessed more of it, they would have been able to get the benefits the law provided on their own. For example, in *Booth v. Indiana*[16] the Court upheld a state law requiring that, at the request of twenty or more workers, coal mines provide them with wash houses. Employees with sufficient bargaining power might also want their employers to provide them with insurance against on-the-job injuries, and eventually the law did so in the form of workers' compensation. As detailed in Chapter 2, on something like eighteen occasions, the old Court rejected substantive due process attacks on various features of workers' compensation laws and similar statutes. At least three of these decisions upheld measures that any employer with superior power would abhor: laws preventing employer and employee from contracting to eliminate the former's statutory liability for on-the-job injuries.[17]

WHAT CAUSES UNEQUAL BARGAINING POWER?

If I were writing a brief for the conventional wisdom about *Lochner*-era substantive due process, I would dismiss the previous two sections as irrelevant. The point, I would maintain, is not that many of the old Court's substantive due process decisions had nothing to do with unequal bargaining power, or that it upheld many measures intended to correct such imbalances. Instead, the critical thing is that the Court struck down any such measures at all. Any decision of that kind, I would continue, most likely had repercussions in the lower federal courts and the state courts. It might also have deterred some states from enacting certain kinds of social legislation. Furthermore, I would conclude, the decisions striking down laws that corrected for unequal bargaining power say volumes about the real motives behind *Lochner*-era substantive due process. During the first third of this century, the reality of unequal bargaining power was so palpable that no one could have failed to recognize its existence. Maybe this means that the old Court's justices were conscious agents of business after all.

The effect of the Supreme Court's substantive due process cases in other courts is beyond the scope of this book, as is the highly conjectural subject of their effect on state legislatures. But the bargaining power question is not. This section and the two that follow maintain that during the *Lochner* era unequal bargaining power was somewhat less real, palpable, and pervasive than is commonly imagined. In fact, the previous two sections probably overstate its magnitude and prevalence a bit. The present section considers the factors that might reasonably be said to create—and not create—unequal bargaining power. The next section reconsiders a few of the famous cases in which the Court supposedly ratified a power imbalance in the private sphere. This chapter's last section inquires about the real origins of the maximum-hours law struck down in *Lochner*. My overall conclusion is that while the old Court's understanding of bargaining power questions left something to be desired, the same is true of those who criticize it for lacking such an understanding.

The Supposed Causes

The prevalence of unequal bargaining power naturally played a significant role in Chapter 1's statement of the conventional wisdom about *Lochner*-era substantive due process. In that discussion four sources of inequality were emphasized with some regularity. These sources, one or more of which might appear together in particular accounts, are: the imbalance in size between corporations and natural persons, the absence of bargaining in contracts concluded between these parties, the increasing dependence of employees on their employers, and the necessitousness of those employees. The people making these arguments often describe their position as simple realism. Unlike the laissez-faire abstractions that infatuated and blinded the old Court, they seem to say, these arguments appeal to plainly observable fact. As things turn out, however, the arguments fail mainly because they remain on the surface of things. The main reason for their superficiality, in turn, is their proponents' utter inability or unwillingness to think the way economists do. (One reason I can speak with such assurance here is that I have so often sinned in such ways myself.)[18] Although someone might say in reply that the real problem is with the economic way of thinking, the way to beat an argument is with a better argument—and not with name-calling.

Superior Size. Early in his well-known article on freedom of contract, Roscoe Pound remarked that "[t]o everyone acquainted at first hand with actual industrial conditions," freedom of contract obviously is an illusion.[19] In elaboration of that idea, he criticized a case "dealing with the relation between employer and employee in railway transportation, as if the parties were individuals—as if they were farmers haggling over the sale of a horse." One might wonder about Dean Pound's firsthand acquaintance with "actual industrial conditions." In any event, what was it about those conditions that made a contract for railroad employment and the sale of a horse quite different phenomena in Pound's eyes? Two distinctions readily suggest themselves. The first and most obvious is that railroads are corporate, rather than natural, persons and, as such, usually are much bigger than the employees who contract with them for employment. As Theodore Roosevelt once put it, "[A] rich and complex industrial society cannot exist [as a democracy]; for some individuals, and especially those artificial individuals called corporations, become so very big that the ordinary individual is utterly dwarfed beside them, and cannot deal with them on terms of equality."[20] The second distinction, suggested by the word "haggling," is that the terms of contracts for railroad employment typically are not bargained but instead are offered to would-be employees on a take-it-or-leave-it basis. This subsection considers the size issue; its successor examines the absence of bargaining.

Roosevelt seemed to be saying that superior size conveys superior bargaining power all by itself. The picture his statement suggests is one in which greater mass means greater physical strength, which in turn means power over others. In this view of things, a big corporation dealing with an isolated natural person is much like Arnold Schwarzenegger arm wrestling an eighty-five-year-old grandmother into submission. But of course the grandmother need not submit to this process if she has something to sell and has other choices besides Arnold. Even though they are much smaller than the firms that eventually employ them, for example, no one would say that Harvard J.D.s and M.B.A.s lack bargaining power. With respect to price, at least, no one would say this of contemporary computer shoppers either—even when they finally buy from Dell or Compaq. The point of these trite little examples is that superior size does not automatically convey superior bargaining power. Of course, size may help provide some of the things that *do* create such power; we consider some examples later. But size *as such* is not one of these things.

The Absence of Genuine Bargaining. As we saw, Pound evidently thought that another mark of unequal bargaining power is the absence of real bargaining between the parties. Of course, such negotiations are strikingly absent from the ubiquitous modern "contract of adhesion"—typically a complex standard-form agreement drafted by one party and offered to the other on a take-it-or-leave-it basis. And genuine bargaining no doubt was conspicuous by its absence in many labor contracts during the *Lochner* era. To Melvin Urofsky, this means that with the industrialization of the United States workers lost the bargaining power previous generations had enjoyed.

> In the preindustrial age, the ideal of the labor contract and its reality merged fairly well. A would-be employer would bargain at arm's length on terms of relative equality with a would-be laborer; taking into account the customs of the local market, they would strike a bargain. . . .With the rise of factories, the legal notion that both employer and employee enjoyed parity in bargaining power diverged from the fact that the thousands of workers in any particular textile mill or copper mine did not bargain, but had to accept whatever the employer offered. Their only freedom consisted of walking away and seeking other employment—where inevitably they would face the same circumstances.[21]

Urofsky may be wrong about the preindustrial United States, when indentured servitude and black slavery were common forms of employment.[22] But he raises a point that may have occurred to some readers when I stressed how the availability of choices undermines the claim that unequal size means unequal bargaining power. How can the ability to say no and to seek work elsewhere increase workers' bargaining power when other employers offer them the same terms as the first employer and thus provide them no real choice at all? But this argument assumes that a uniform price for a commodity or service implies no competition among providers of that commodity or service. In other words, Urofsky's description is consistent with a genuinely competitive market, because in such a market competitors tend to offer the same terms at any particular point in time. As Chapter 3 observes, Brandeis made the same mistake in *New State Ice Co. v. Liebmann*. There, one of his arguments for Oklahoma's entry restriction was that even in the counties where competition existed "the prices of ice were ordinarily uniform."[23] But, Judge Richard Posner once remarked, since "the product is uniform, one would expect competitive sellers to charge the same price."[24]

Urofsky's error, then, was his failure to consider the possibility that because workers could always reject an employer's terms and all employers knew this, employers would be fearful of underbidding their competitors and most of them eventually would offer workers much the same wage for the same work. To put the matter yet another way, Urofsky fails to consider the possibility that the similar terms offered by different employers *already* reflected employees' power to choose among them. If things were otherwise, we would have to say that a member of the *Harvard Law Review* lacks bargaining power in a city where the big law firms have established a going rate for first-year associates or that internet computer shoppers are without such power just because most computer manufacturers charge roughly the same price for the same equipment. Of course, a uniform price for a commodity or service may also be due to monopoly, collusion among competitors, or some other market failure. Such possibilities are considered later in the chapter.

Dependency. By itself, therefore, neither superior size nor the absence of bargaining implies unequal bargaining power. Like its two predecessors, the third major argument for unequal bargaining power's prevalence during the *Lochner* era looks much more at the employer-employee relation than at other employers who compete with the first employer for labor. This argument basically says that because with the industrialization of the United States workers became increasingly dependent on business for their livelihood, they had to accept whatever terms their employers offered. Archibald Cox once stated it fairly succinctly: "Industrialization," he asserted, "created an ever-growing class of urban wage earners dependent for survival on factory employment and rates of pay."[25] "Not only was the factory or railroad worker dependent upon his job, but he had no power alone to affect his wages, hours, or other conditions of employment." In a far more lengthy and diffuse fashion, Gillman has made what appears to be the same argument.[26]

Gillman's account suffers from some internal tensions. At one point, for example, he complains that industrialization "imposed brutalizing burdens on masses of people at the same time it showered unprecedented splendors on a select few."[27] His immediately preceding sentence, however, observes that with increasing industrialization and increased output came "the steady movement of foreign immigrants, southern blacks, and farmers into the cities and manufacturing centers." But why did these people voluntarily accept such "brutalizing burdens"? Was it because things were even worse down on the farm? If so, why argue that industrialization harmed the working class?

In addition to its internal problems, the "dependency" argument may prove too much. There is a sense, after all, in which Michael Jordan was dependent on the Chicago Bulls. And just as industrial workers are dependent on their corporate employers, so too are those employers dependent on their employees. The real problem with the dependence argument, however, resembles those faced by its two predecessors. At most, the argument only shows that workers were dependent on *industrial employment in general*. Normally, however, the dependence that allows employers to exploit employees is dependence on *a particular employer*. As I have been arguing all along, under competitive conditions employees who have genuine options and the capacity to make use of them are difficult to describe as victims of their employers' superior power.

Necessitousness. The same basic objections apply to another contention that might be thought to complement the "dependency" argument. This is the assertion that because workers were necessitous, employers could extract from them almost any terms they desired. According to Arthur Selwyn Miller, for instance, Alexander Hamilton once asserted that "the power over a man's subsistence amounts to a power over his will."[28] This has been taken to mean that employers could obtain the labor of necessitous workers at virtually any price. For example, Urofsky quotes a British lord who maintained that "necessitous men are not, truly speaking, free men, but, to answer a present exigency, will submit to any terms that the crafty may impose on them."[29] And those terms could be onerous indeed. As Justice Stone remarked in 1936, "There is grim irony in speaking of the freedom of contract of those who, because of their economic necessities, give their service for less than is needful to keep body and soul together."[30]

Like too many other claims about the *Lochner* era's inequities and iniquities, Stone's remark suffers from excessive hyperbole. Was he saying that, as a general matter, workers literally starved to death due to their lack of bargaining power? If not, what was he saying? In any event, the claim that necessitousness *as such* puts workers at a disadvantage has little to recommend it. In other words, necessitousness gives an employer superior power and disadvantages workers only where those workers lack genuine options. Some recently graduated Harvard J.D.s and M.B.A.s may be fairly impecunious, but few would describe them as victims of corporate power.

What Some Economists Say

Readers who are offended by my constantly comparing turn-of-the-century industrial workers with contemporary Harvard J.D.s, Harvard M.B.A.s, and computer shoppers should keep in mind that the aim of the comparison is to expose four bad arguments for the claim that the former lacked bargaining power. The point, of course, was that if the arguments were valid, both the Harvard graduates and the shoppers likewise are exploited by business. But maybe we have reason to think that the two sets of cases are distinguishable. Perhaps we can find some bases for distinction by examining what labor economists have to say about unequal bargaining power.[31]

As the labor economists see things, employers get an edge over employees not from superior size, the absence of bargaining, or employee dependency as such but from market power. An employer who possesses such power is called a *monopsonist*: a monopoly or oligopoly purchaser of labor. The economists seem to be in substantial agreement about the things that produce monopsony. The first and most obvious is the situation where one firm or a small group of firms are the sole employers within a particular locality. The classic example is the company town, but almost any firm that dominates a local economy should qualify as well. But a technical monopsony within a narrowly defined territory means little if workers can easily get work outside the territory. Thus, the proximity of competing employers and the availability and cost of transportation are critical in defining what counts as an appropriate territory or locality. Today, it appears that relatively few such territories are dominated by one or a few employers.

Monopsony also can arise from a collusive agreement among employers. In such cases, Urofsky's complaint that workers who refused one employer's terms encountered the same terms elsewhere would have validity. However, such agreements are difficult to create and, once created, are even more difficult to enforce. A third factor sometimes thought to create monopsony is job specialization. For example, suppose that the XYZ Corporation is the only firm within 200 miles that employs people with specialty A. Presumably XYZ has some ability to dictate terms to people with specialty A and no other abilities of note. Because specialized skills often are difficult to acquire, however, this factor cuts both ways. In the words of one labor economics text, while "workers have nowhere else to go without leaving the area . . . the employer has no local labor supply beyond present employees."[32] In such circumstances, an exploited employee who threatens to pack up and leave unless she gets better terms may have some leverage. The result, in Judge Richard Posner's words, is "a game of chicken, likely to end in a stand-off."[33]

As the preceding discussion should suggest, labor economists appear to agree that, as compared with conditions 75 or 100 years ago, monopsony situations are fairly infrequent occurrences today. This suggests that monopsony may have been more common during much of the *Lochner* era. Maybe there were fewer employers per locality than is the case now. The main difference, though, is that the relevant locality or territory for determining monopsony almost certainly was smaller then than today. The most important reason for the change is improved transportation, especially superior roads and near-universal automobile ownership. Perhaps information about alternative job opportunities is more available today as well. In this connection, the language barriers confronting immigrants during the late nineteenth and early twentieth centuries may have prevented them from fully exploiting such information as did exist.

All these reasons for thinking monopsony more common during the *Lochner* era almost had to vary considerably with time and place. This means that inquiries about the extent to which the old Court ratified unequal bargaining power normally must be context specific. The same is true for another alleged source of unequal bargaining power—a high unemployment rate, whether brought about by mass immigration or by other factors. (Despite wave upon wave of immigration, labor shortages apparently were common and wages steadily increased during the late nineteenth and early twentieth centuries, although unemployment rose sharply immediately after World War I.)[34] Where no evidence about bargaining power is available, however, maybe considerations raised in the previous paragraph suggest a presumption that unequal bargaining power did exist. With all this in mind, the next section examines a few of the old Court's best-known substantive due process cases in some detail.

To conclude with a digression, it is at least worth noting that, under the previous criteria, large firms are more likely to be monopsonists than small ones. Such companies are more likely to dominate particular employment markets and may employ more specialized workers, too. Thus the common perception that size and bargaining power correlate may have some basis—but not the basis some people apparently imagine. Even though it has limited relevance to *Lochner*-era substantive due process, another consideration that probably correlates with firm size deserves mention in any discussion of unequal bargaining power. This is the ubiquitous standard-form contract. Larger firms are more likely to need standard forms because these forms enable top managers to impose optimum policies throughout the firm, facilitate communication across departments, and prevent lower-level managers from making suboptimum deals with employees or other third parties.[35] Larger firms are also more likely to have—or to purchase—the skills necessary to produce standard forms. Standard forms give their users an edge not so much because they are rammed down the throats of unwilling parties, as because those parties do not read them, could not penetrate their legalese if they tried, miss critical but well-hidden fine-print clauses, or fail to appreciate the significance of particular contract language. Because genuine bargaining would prevent some of these things from occurring, it is not completely wrong to say that no bargaining means unequal bargaining power. But the issue is largely beside the point here. Few, if any, of the cases striking down government action on substantive due process grounds involved laws regulating standard-form contracts and their more arcane terms.

The Paternalistic Alternative

Some readers probably feel that this section's focus on bargaining power badly misses the point. The real concern, they would say, is not whether workers' terms and conditions of employment were products of a free, fair, and equal bargaining process between employer and employee; whether those workers had other employment options and the capacity to make use of them; or whether the employer was a monopsonist. Instead, the real concern is those terms and conditions themselves. In an expanding economy with growing disparities in wealth, they would continue, it was unconscionable that workers toiled long hours for meager pay under unsafe and degrading conditions. To say that such terms and conditions are acceptable just because they were freely and equally bargained, these readers would conclude, is to worship procedure at the expense of substance. And to call their position paternalistic begs the question whether paternalism sometimes is justified.

I have only three brief comments to make about this argument. The first is that I preoccupy myself with the bargaining power question mainly because it may be the single most important basis for attacking the old Court's substantive due process cases. In other words, it is the *Lochner* Court's enemies who originally made unequal bargaining power such an issue. My second remark is that this paternalistic or substantive argument is a more difficult target than the unequal bargaining power charge and that foes of the old Court might be advised to make it more often. My third point is that the old Court did not seriously disagree with this argument. Because the bargaining power issue is not discussed in most of the Court's substantive due process decisions, it seems reasonable to assume that the justices thought most contracts were the product of a relatively free, fair, and equal bargaining process. Yet as Chapter 2 makes clear, they upheld innumerable laws regulating such contracts. In the employment area, the most notable examples were workers' compensation and (*Lochner* excepted) maximum-hours laws. The most plausible explanation for such decisions is the justices' belief that some concerns trump economic liberty.

REVISITING SOME EXEMPLARY CASES

This chapter examines the familiar claim that even if the *Lochner* Court did not deliberately seek to aid business when it struck down social legislation on substantive due process grounds, nonetheless that was what those decisions did. By striking down laws designed to correct for unequal bargaining power, this view asserts, the old Court ratified exercises of this private power. So far, the chapter has responded to this charge (1) by noting that it applies to only a small portion of the cases striking down government action on substantive due process grounds and that it ignores the much greater number of *Lochner*-era cases rejecting substantive due process challenges to social legislation and (2) by arguing that familiar ideas about the sources of unequal bargaining power will not stand much scrutiny. Also, the preceding section has developed some rough-and-ready criteria for determining when unequal bargaining power may or may not exist. Under those criteria, how should we evaluate the portion of the old Court's substantive due process work product that apparently did strike down laws intended to correct for unequal bargaining power? Did those cases really exhibit disparities in bargaining power? Overall, the results are a mixed bag.

The Cases

We begin with a decision in which the Court rejected a substantive due process claim but that deserves attention because it sets a context for a case where the Court granted one. Earlier I remarked that the bargaining power issue is not explicitly discussed in most of the old Court's substantive due process decisions, but *Holden v. Hardy*[36] is an exception. This 1898 decision involved the constitutionality of a Utah statute mandating an eight-hour day in underground mines, smelters, and ore reduction works. Justice Brown's opinion for a 7–2 majority upholding the statute explicitly justified itself on both bargaining power grounds and paternalistic grounds. "[T]he fact that both parties are of full age and competent to contract does not necessarily deprive the State of the power to interfere where the parties do not stand upon an equality, or where the public health demands that one party to the contract shall be protected against himself."[37]

The second, paternalistic, justification for Utah's law involved the special nature of mining, smelting, and ore reduction. After noting that this measure did not limit the hours of all workers, Brown stated:

> While the general experience of mankind may justify us in believing that men may engage in ordinary employments more than eight hours per day without injury to their health, it does not follow that labor for the same length of time is innocuous when carried on beneath the surface of the earth, where the operative is deprived of fresh air and sunlight, and is frequently subjected to foul atmospheres and a very high temperature, or to the influence of noxious gases, generated by the processes of refining or smelting.[38]

After that, Brown got to the first justification for the Utah statute: the unequal bargaining power rationale.

> The legislature has also recognized the fact, which the experience of legislators in many States has corroborated, that the proprietors of these establishments and their operatives do not stand upon an equality, and that their interests are, to a certain extent, conflicting. The former naturally desire to obtain as much labor as possible from their employes [*sic*], while the latter are often induced by the fear of discharge to conform to regulations which their judgment, fairly exercised, would pronounce to be detrimental to their health or strength. In other words, the proprietors lay down the rules and the laborers are practically constrained

to obey them. In such cases self-interest is often an unsafe guide, and the legislature may properly interpose its authority.[39]

Brown did not say exactly why mining, smelting, and ore refining companies had superior power and why workers necessarily had to fear discharge, but it is easy to speculate about why it was plausible for him to do so. Utah is a large state, and even today its thinly populated areas contain small towns that are considerable distances apart. This obviously was all the more true 100 years ago. Needless to say, methods of transportation were less advanced then as well. Under such circumstances, it is easy to imagine situations in which some mining, smelting, or ore refining business could provide much of the employment within a particular area. And even when it was feasible for a worker to move, he might well encounter the same situation elsewhere. Because this similarity in uniform employment terms probably resulted from monopsony rather than competition, Urofsky's objection has some force here.

Things apparently were quite different in the turn-of-the-century New York baking industry. In a 1990 book devoted to the *Lochner* case, Paul Kens states that "between 1895 and 1905, the period during which the battles over the [New York] Bakeshop Act were fought, the supply of retail bread came from innumerable small businesses."[40] "They were," Kens immediately adds, "very small indeed. In 1899, 78 percent employed four or fewer people." In a 1980 book, Bernard Siegan concurred in part but also noted the existence of some larger bakeries.

In New York, as elsewhere, the baking industry was split between sizable bakeries whose plants had been specifically built or fully converted for such purposes, and small bakeries, operating out of limited, often subterranean quarters not originally intended for such use. The Bureau of the Census reports that in 1905, there were 3,164 bakeries in New York State, of which 2,870 were owned by individuals, 228 by firms, and 64 by corporations. In that year, the individuals employed 10,804 workers, the firms 1,672, and the corporations 5,232—averaging 3.76, 7.33, and 81.75 workers per enterprise, respectively. Percentage of total bakery output maintained by each group was 62.5, 9.7, and 27.8.[41]

As we will see in the next section, the larger bakeries are critical to Siegan's explanation for passage of the maximum-hours law at issue in *Lochner*.

Either way, it does not appear that the state's baking industry was marked by widespread monopsony power when New York enacted its maximum-hours law late in the nineteenth century. Kens suggests as much when he says that in that industry "[t]here was not a struggle pitting workers against a corporate giant."[42] As Kens also observes, moreover, baking was a growth industry at that time, with aggregate employment increasing from about 7,000 in 1850 to some 60,000 in 1900.[43] This might have augmented workers' bargaining position a bit. There is nothing to indicate that bakery employment was particularly specialized work. Unlike (say) pension terms in modern employment markets, moreover, in *Lochner* the regulated contract term (hours) was one that employees are more than capable of evaluating and understanding on their own. Contrary to an almost universal belief, therefore, *Lochner* does not present obvious evidence of unequal bargaining power. At the very least, its facts provide much less compelling arguments for legislative intervention to correct such inequalities than did *Holden v. Hardy*.

This brings us to *Adair v. United States*[44] and *Coppage v. Kansas*,[45] each of which struck down a state law blocking employers' efforts to disadvantage union members. In *Adair*, the measure in question was a federal statute prohibiting interstate carriers from discriminating against union members in various ways; in *Coppage*, the relevant law was a Kansas statute forbidding yellow-dog contracts under which employees agreed not to join a union or remain a union member while in the employer's employ. The various opinions in *Adair* had little or nothing to say about the bargaining power question. But the case primarily involved the railroads, and it is not difficult to cast railroads as monopsonists. (And if this characterization fails, we are left without much evidence on the bargaining power question, which means that our general presumption of unequal bargaining power applies.) If bargaining power is the only relevant criterion, therefore, *Adair* most likely was wrongly decided.

Coppage did explicitly address the bargaining power question, but not in a perspicuous fashion. Justice Day's dissent probably can be taken as asserting that unequal bargaining power prevailed in Kansas, that unionism would help alleviate it, and that for this reason the state's ban on yellow-dog contracts was justified.[46] But he provided little evidence for these assertions. The bargaining power discussion in Justice Pitney's majority opinion had far more serious deficiencies. Basically, Pitney conceded too much to his opponents, and then tried to correct the error by running roughshod over them. After observing that the Kansas Supreme Court thought unequal bargaining power's existence a matter of common knowledge, Pitney delivered his own wisdom on that subject:

> No doubt, wherever the right of private property exists, there must and will be inequalities of fortune; and thus it naturally happens that parties negotiating about a contract are not equally unhampered by circumstances. . . . Indeed, a little reflection will show that wherever the right of private property and the right of free contract coexist, each party when contracting is inevitably more or less influenced by the question whether he has much property, or little, or none.[47]

Some people might think that by this admission Pitney had delegitimized either freedom of contract or private property. But he took the opposite tack, arguing that freedom of contract was supreme and that inequalities of fortune (and, by inference, unequal bargaining power) simply had to be accepted.[48] This is not an appealing position. Worse yet, it is one Pitney need not have taken, because his initial assumption is dubious. For the reasons developed earlier, what primarily counts in determining whether someone has bargaining power are the choices available to him and his capacity to make use of them, not his wealth or necessitousness. But to Pitney, as to Roscoe Pound, the paradigm case of equal bargaining power was two farmers haggling over the sale of a horse. And by tacitly accepting that assumption, Pitney harmed his own cause.

Even so, one might argue that the *Coppage* majority was correct because free and equal bargaining was the norm in Kansas during the early part of the century. Lacking any particularized evidence on that subject, however, we are again left with the general presumption that inequality was the norm instead. From a bargaining power perspective alone, therefore, the case seems incorrectly decided for much the same reasons that *Adair* was incorrectly decided. Because unionism was necessary to make freedom of contract meaningful, that is, a pro-union measure should not have fallen on freedom-of-contract grounds.

In any list of *Lochner*-era substantive due process decisions that ignored unequal bargaining power, the Court's 1923 decision in *Adkins v. Children's Hospital*[49] would have to rank high. *Adkins* struck down a District of Columbia minimum-wage law for women (and children). Chief Justice Taft's dissent from that decision strongly emphasized the presence of unequal bargaining power, and Justice Holmes's dissent thought it an opinion one might reasonably hold.[50] Justice Sutherland's opinion for the majority, however, scarcely mentioned the subject. And on one occasion where it did arise, Sutherland seemed to accept the Progressive equation of size and bargaining power.[51] For the reasons just stated, that concession is insufficient to condemn *Adkins* on bargaining power grounds, but other considerations most likely do. Many of the people to whom the D.C. measure applied were young, single women living at home with their parents.[52] Those who were married presumably were tied to a male breadwinner. For these reasons, most women subject to the D.C. law probably had little geographic mobility and thus relatively little ability to shop among competing employers. It also seems likely that, as a group, they lacked any special skills that would give them a bargaining edge. Viewed solely through the bargaining power prism, therefore, *Adkins* also seems a suspect decision.

Although the event is rather less well remembered than *Adkins*, the Court struck down another wage regulation in 1923. In *Chas. Wolff Packing Co. v. Court of Industrial Relations*,[53] it invalidated a Kansas measure that declared food preparation a business affected with a public interest and empowered a three-judge industrial court to fix wages within that industry. *Chas. Wolff* was a unanimous decision in which Holmes and Brandeis joined. Looking at things solely from a bargaining power angle, this unanimity is easy to understand, because the redress of contractual inequality evidently was not the challenged measure's concern. The rationale for the Kansas law was not that workers needed protection against their employers but that the public peace, health, and comfort demanded the compulsory resolution of wage disputes.[54] To that end, the law prohibited strikes by workers dissatisfied with their pay. In Chief Justice Taft's words, "[W]hile the worker is not required to work, at the wages fixed, he is forbidden, on penalty of fine or imprisonment, to strike against them and thus is compelled to give up that means of putting himself on an equality with his employer, which action in concert with his fellows gives him."[55] What has any of this to do with unequal bargaining power?

Now we move to several cases that involve relations between businesses and their customers. In *Jay Burns Baking Co. v. Bryan*,[56] the Court struck down a Nebraska antideception measure limiting the sizes of loaves of bread that could be sold. Just as firms that use standard forms might possess superior power when the individuals with whom they deal fail to understand the importance of some preset term, firms that market short-weight loaves might have it when consumers have difficulty detecting the difference in weight. The same might be thought true of *Weaver v. Palmer Brothers*,[57] where the Court struck down a state statute forbidding the use of "shoddy" in mattresses, pillows, cushions, bolsters, and the like. (Shoddy is any fabric or yarn that has been cut up, torn up, broken up, or ground up.) But the law seems to lack a bargaining power rationale and, indeed, may be an example of misguided paternalism. As for the first point, the bulk of the Court's short opinion discussed whether the law could be justified as a health measure, rather than as an antideception provision. Regarding the second, state law also required tags that disclosed, among other relevant information, the composition of these products, as well as inspections of their place of manufacture to ensure that they satisfied state law. Also, products made with shoddy were cheaper than those made with other materials.

We conclude with three late-1920s decisions in which the Court struck down laws fixing maximum prices for services or commodities sold to the public.[58] In each, Sutherland wrote for the majority. Chapter 2 observed that the states had broad powers to regulate businesses affected with a public interest and that these powers generally include the ability to regulate the prices these businesses charged. The present cases applied what might be regarded as a corollary of this rule: that the states were without power to regulate the prices charged by businesses *not* affected with a public interest.[59] In these cases, Sutherland concluded that the performance of plays and other entertainments, the procuring of employment for others, and the retail sale of gasoline were not businesses affected with a public interest and that the states therefore could not regulate the resale price of theater tickets, the fees charged by employment agencies, and the retail price of gasoline. He did so with little or no reference to the market power and bargaining power the parties challenging these laws may or may not have possessed.

Sutherland's conceptualism stands in marked contrast to the approach taken by Justice Stone's dissents in two of the price regulation cases. According to Stone, the key factor in determining the constitutionality of price regulations is

> a situation or a combination of circumstances materially restricting the regulative flow of competition, so that buyers or sellers are placed at such a disadvantage in the bargaining struggle that serious economic consequences result to a very large number of members of the community. Whether this situation arises from the monopoly conferred upon public service companies or from the circumstances that the strategical position of a group is such as to enable it to impose its will in matters of price upon those who sell, buy or consume . . . or from the predetermination of prices in the councils of those who sell, promulgated in schedules of practically controlling constancy . . . or from a housing shortage growing out of a public emergency . . . the result is the same. Self interest is not permitted to involve constitutional protection at the expense of the public interest and reasonable regulation of price is upheld.[60]

While all these possibilities are real enough, two contrary considerations also deserve mention. The first is the perennial economists' objection that price regulations tend to create artificial shortages of the regulated product or service.[61] The second is the common conservative suspicion that, in some cases, price caps represent nothing more than the majority's effort to vote itself a free lunch.

With all this in mind, what can be said about the three cases in question? In *Tyson & Brother v. Banton*, which involved the resale price of theater tickets, Stone had a ready justification for the challenged price regulation: "[a] virtual monopoly of the best seats" by certain brokers.[62] However, Stone was more equivocal in *Ribnik v. McBride*, which involved restrictions on the fees charged by employment agencies. There, he mainly trotted out the supposed sources of unequal bargaining power that were discussed earlier in the chapter. "[E]mployment agencies, admittedly subject to regulation in other respects . . . and in fact very generally regulated, deal with a necessitous class, the members of which are often dependent on them for opportunity to earn a livelihood, are not free to move from place to place, and are often under exceptional economic compulsion to accept such terms as the agencies offer."[63] But as we have seen, this begs the relevant questions. Was there sufficient competition for workers to have reasonable choices? If so, did they have the information and the capacity to make good use of those choices? On the latter point, Stone quoted the New Jersey Supreme Court to the effect that employment agencies dealt primarily "with a great body of our population, native and foreign born, which is susceptible to imposition, deception, and immoral influences."[64] Most of this dissent, however, was devoted to describing the evils practiced by employment agencies rather than their power over their customers.[65] (Much the same, by the way, is true of Brandeis's dissent in *Adams v. Tanner*, which struck down a state initiative provision that had the practical effect of virtually outlawing employment agencies.[66]) Maybe these evils should have been sufficient to carry the day for New Jersey's regulation, but that is far from a sure thing.

The last case in our trio, *Williams v. Standard Oil Co.*, involved Tennessee's scheme for fixing the retail price of gasoline. From the bargaining power–centered perspective that dominates this section, the regulation at issue in *Williams* seems the least justified and the opinion striking it down the most so. Contemporary experience, at least, suggests that gasoline retailing is a fairly competitive business. Apparently it was not a monopoly in the Tennessee of the late 1920s,[67] although oligopolistic conditions and/or collusion among sellers cannot be ruled out. More important, Stone and Brandeis concurred in the result in *Williams.*[68] They did so without commenting on Sutherland's opinion. But since Stone had dissented in *Tyson* and *Ribnik* and Brandeis had joined those dissents, it appears unlikely that they merely were following precedent.

In Summary

This section has proceeded as if the presence or absence of unequal bargaining power is the key to determining whether certain *Lochner*-era substantive due process cases were correctly decided. Obviously this does not preclude other reasons for judging those cases good or bad. For example, one might declare bargaining power irrelevant while condemning the previous decisions on the paternalistic basis mentioned earlier. Or one might sympathize with the economic laissez-faire so evident in these cases, yet reject them on the originalist or interpretivist grounds discussed in Chapter 5.

Assuming that bargaining power is the sole criterion, how do the preceding cases stack up? (I leave *Holden v. Hardy* out of the equation because there the Court upheld the challenged law.) Of these ten decisions, most of them much maligned over the years, a clear majority indeed do appear to have been wrongly decided. The reason, of course, is that they present more or less persuasive evidence of unequal bargaining power and of a statute that might have rectified it. The cases in question are

Adair, *Coppage*, *Adkins*, *Jay Burns*, *Tyson*, and perhaps *Ribnik*. (Presently, however, we will get another perspective on *Adkins*.) However, disparities in bargaining power do not typify the other cases on our list. *Chas. Wolff* involved a law whose ostensible aim was not so much to protect workers as to subordinate their interests and those of business to a supposed public good. There is little to suggest that the statutes struck down in *Weaver* and *Williams* were responses to conditions of unequal bargaining power. The same, surprisingly, also seems true of the maximum-hours law at issue in *Lochner*. Shortly, we will be examining that measure's history in more detail.

ULTERIOR MOTIVES

At various points in Howard Gillman's recent book on the old Court, he seems to say that while social legislation aimed at conditions of dependency might be characterized as class legislation, this is no basis for condemning it.[69] Although such laws might benefit partial interests rather than the general good, the argument would run, those interests need and deserve the law's protection. But there is another, less benign way in which social legislation might amount to class legislation. In these cases, social legislation is the means through which one group benefits itself at the expense of another, less powerful group. In such situations, it is more difficult to argue that the old Court inadvertently helped business dominate the downtrodden when it struck down laws ostensibly intended to assist the powerless.

Worker Protection Legislation in General

How might alleged protective regulations be something different than they seem? Consider, for example, the standard charge that minimum-wage laws tend to reduce the jobs available to marginal workers such as middle-aged women, young people, and minorities.[70] To the extent that this is true, minimum-wage laws look less like measures to protect society's victims than as means by which one set of workers disadvantages another. Note, however, that here the marginal workers' jobs might not have been the law's target; instead those lost jobs may have been the incidental by-product of other workers' enriching themselves. In other cases, though, social legislation may have been aimed directly at certain kinds of workers. During the *Lochner* era, the main examples probably were measures with the ostensible aim of protecting women. It has often been argued that these laws were intended to make it less desirable for firms to employ women and thus to limit the competitive threat they posed to male workers and male-dominated unions.[71] In an empirical study covering the early 1920s, for instance, Elisabeth M. Landes concluded that maximum-hours laws significantly reduced female employment in manufacturing, with foreign-born and first-generation women being the hardest hit and native white women escaping almost unscathed.[72] For reasons like these, the Women's Party filed a brief urging the Court to strike down the minimum-wage law for women at issue in *Adkins*.[73] In fact, one of the *Adkins* plaintiffs was a female elevator operator who had lost her job due to that measure.[74]

According to David Bryden, some *Lochner*-era Progessives evidently believed that worker protection laws like the measure at issue in *Adkins* were justified even if their aim was to exclude marginal workers.[75] For example, he quotes Walter Lippman as asserting that low-productivity workers "should not be permitted to debauch the labor market, to wreck by their competition the standards of other workers." Felix Frankfurter's brief for the District of Columbia in *Adkins*, furthermore, suggested that those blocked from employment by the minimum wage may "accept the status of a defective to be segregated for special treatment as a dependent" of the government, which was to "determine how defectives shall be supported." Frankfurter added that "Congress therefore, may use means, like the present law, for sorting the normal self-supporting workers from the semi-employables or the unemployables and then deal with the latter appropriately as a special class, instead of permitting an indiscriminate, unscientific lumping of all workers, with a resulting wasteful confusion of standards."

As Bryden remarks, "[a]fter Hitler, such language went out of fashion." Another matter on which some Progressives depart from modern perspectives is their apparent indifference to consumer welfare. All things being relatively equal, manufacturers forced to pay higher wages probably will pass those costs on to those who buy their products, but this seems not to have concerned Frankfurter. Instead, he thought that employees who sell their labor too cheaply are guilty of unfair competition and that employers who hire them at such wages engage in "cutthroat competition." As we saw in Chapter 2, Brandeis said similar things in *New State Ice Co. v. Liebmann*.

The Statute at Issue in *Lochner*

Do the preceding arguments mean that, contrary to my previous suggestion, the law at issue in *Adkins* was a bad one after all? Perhaps this is so, but there the female workers probably did lack bargaining power. Furthermore, both the reasons for the D.C. wage law's enactment and its subsequent effect on female employment are unclear. But even if *Adkins* was justified in public policy terms, this cannot vindicate the other cases discussed in the preceding section. The one possible exception is *Lochner*. In considering the claim that the *Lochner* statute was unjustified special-interest legislation, I begin with Bernard Siegan's 1980 hypothesis about the origins of New York's maximum-hours law, before developing Paul Kens's utterly different 1990 account. As we will see, Siegan has a hypothesis but little direct evidence to support it, whereas Kens's abundance of evidence still leaves the reasons for the law's passage unclear.

Siegan's Explanation. As is reasonably well known by now, business opposition to government regulation is a sometime thing. In order to gain a relative advantage, for example, a firm may support new regulations that bear harder on its competitors than itself.[76] Siegan's explanation of New York's maximum-hours law follows this pattern.[77] As I related earlier in the chapter, according to Siegan, the turn-of-the-century New York bakery industry was divided between small-scale bakeries, of which there were many, and larger, more mechanized bakeries, of which there were fewer. Along with their less efficient technology, sanitary, health, and working conditions in the small bakeries fell far below conditions in their larger counterparts. Many of their employees were recent immigrants with little command of English.

More to the present point, working hours were much longer in the small bakeries than in the large ones. This meant that a maximum-hours law would burden the former more than the latter. As Siegan summarizes the dilemma confronting the small bakeries:

> The small owners frequently provided their laborers with sleeping quarters, enabling them to spend long hours on the job. The time limitation on working hours would have forced the small owners to hire additional help. Because the reduction in hours might be less than a day's work, it might be difficult to hire someone at the existing rate of pay. As for current employees, it is unlikely that weekly wages, which already were very low, could be cut proportionately to approximate the decrease in working hours, or that worker productivity would increase sufficiently to compensate for this difference. Consequently the restrictions on working hours meant higher labor costs for the small bakers, who, due to competition from the corporate bakers, were limited in the amount they could pass on in the form of higher prices. A number of the small bakers would have to terminate their businesses.[78]

The law's effect on the larger bakeries, by contrast, was less severe. For one thing, they evidently were closer to compliance with the new maximum-hours standard. In addition, they were in a better position to absorb the costs of hiring more workers. Most important, "extra production costs would be offset by the lessened competition from the small bakeries, which would lead to higher prices."[79]

Kens's Account. Siegan provides persuasive reasons why the larger bakeries should have supported New York's maximum-hours law. Unfortunately, he provides no evidence that they did support it, let alone that their support was decisive in its passage. Indeed, he admits the deficiency.[80] In an effort to remedy that deficiency, we now turn to Kens's more detailed, if less clear-cut, account.[81] As noted earlier, Siegan and Kens disagree about the structure of the New York baking industry at the time the New York act was passed. To Siegan, the industry was divided between small bakeries and larger, mechanized ones, whereas to Kens it consisted almost entirely of the former. As we will see, this difference may be important.

The bill that became the New York Bakeshop Act, Kens says, was introduced in February 1895. Although bakery workers had long complained about working hours in the industry and bakers from New York's East Side were striking for that reason and others when the bill appeared,[82] its limitation of hours worked to ten per day and sixty per week was not its most conspicuous feature. Indeed, most of its provisions—those involving sanitation, plumbing, floors, and storage—concerned the *public* health.[83] Furthermore, organized labor seemed ambivalent about the bill and, in any event, lacked the political power to get that measure enacted on its own.[84] So why did it pass? The place "where an explanation of the Bakeshop Act may be found," Kens suggests, is "[a] rush of popular support" that "induce[d] labor to adopt the issue and to pursue it successfully."[85] That popular support came from several sources. As Kens summarizes the matter: "Bakeshop reform in 1895 was unquestionably a joint venture. A newspaper reporter supplied the opportunity and much of the drive. An element of organized labor participated, and a labor leader took on some of the responsibility for organization and direction. Finally, and probably most important, prominent and influential mainstream reformers provided the political clout."[86]

This collection of influences, however, hardly explains the ease and speed with which the proposal was enacted. After the bill was introduced on February 12, New York's assembly and senate unanimously passed it on March 19 and April 1, respectively.[87] As Kens notes, these unanimous votes strongly suggest that somewhere along the line the legislature's leadership had put its weight behind the bill. The dominant figure in that leadership—and the man whose opposition would have killed the Bakeshop Act—was Republican boss Thomas Collier Platt.[88] But why would Platt and his Republican colleagues endorse this measure? Kens suggests several reasons: the unlikelihood that the bill would harm their organization's major contributors, its appeal to the working class and to German-American bakery workers, their desire to get some labor support in an upcoming election, and their uneasy alliances with independents and reformers.[89]

Who Is Right? As James W. Ely, Jr. remarked in a review of Kens's book, he "does not address squarely the argument, advanced by defenders of *Lochner*, that the Bakeshop Act was special interest legislation designed to have an anticompetitive impact on the baking trade."[90] In particular, Kens does not address Siegan's different account of the structure of the New York baking industry. If that account can be torpedoed, Siegan's argument obviously falls apart. Information from the only source cited by Kens and Siegan that I have been able to access—William G. Panschar's two-volume 1956 history of the U.S. baking industry—goes some way toward achieving that end but ultimately falls a bit short.

Panschar paints a by-now-familiar picture of the American baking industry around the year 1900.

> [T]he baking industry at the turn of the century was a study in contrasts. At one end of the spectrum, and still by all counts the largest segment of the industry, were the small-scale retail bakeries, little different from their counterparts in the colonial period. At the other end were the industrial bakers using large-scale baking techniques and distributing their products in ways that would be familiar to their successors half a century later.[91]

These new techniques arose out of various technological advances in ovens, materials, and the like, beginning after 1850.[92] The baking industry, then, obviously was in transition as the new century began. How far had these changes proceeded by 1895 in New York? As we saw earlier, Siegan cites 1905 Bureau of the Census figures for New York reporting that of the 3,164 bakeries in the state 2,870 were owned by individuals, 228 by firms, and 64 by corporations. The individual bakers employed 10,804 workers (3.76 per enterprise), the firms 1,672 (7.33 per enterprise), and the corporations 5,232 (81.75 per enterprise). But what were things like in 1895? It is difficult to say for certain, but most likely New York had appreciably fewer large, mechanized bakeries then. At one point, Panschar remarks that "the new technology had not encompassed more than a fraction of the industry by 1900."[93] To demonstrate the point, he produced *national* figures showing, among other things, that in 1899 only 167 of the nation's 14,917 bakeries employed 51 or more people. If that figure is valid and if New York had 64 large bakeries in 1895, then that state had nearly forty percent of the country's biggest bakeries during that year. This seems unlikely.

Still, New York almost certainly had some large, mechanized bakeries in 1895, and even then it no doubt was plain that these concerns represented the industry's future. It is not unlikely that these firms had the resources to make substantial campaign contributions. Perhaps, then, such contributions were the *X* factor that explains the Republican leadership's endorsement of the Bakeshop Act and the New York legislature's remarkable unanimity on that measure. Nonetheless, when all is said and done, I would have to give Kens the decision on points. For one thing, it is unclear how many of the new-style bakeries existed in New York in 1895. More important, there appears to be no direct evidence that such bakeries exerted themselves on behalf of the Bakeshop Act. One might also wonder whether such exertions were decisive even if they did occur.

One final point may deserve reemphasis. Readers should recall that if Kens is correct, one of the conventional reasons for assuming unequal bargaining power in the New York baking industry—employers' superior size—almost entirely collapses. According to Panschar's 1899 national figures, for example, some sixty-five percent of the nation's bakeries employed one to four workers, and almost thirteen percent employed none.[94] For critics of *Lochner*, in other words, the cost of eliminating any claim that the New York statute was illegitimate class legislation is the admission that New York bakery employees were not victims of unequal bargaining power.

SUMMING UP

As Chapter 3 maintained, it is most unlikely that the old Court was business's conscious agent. But its commitment to laissez-faire still might seem culpably ignorant. The reason, the argument begins, is that conditions of unequal bargaining power brought about by the emergence of large corporations made the justices' traditional verities irrelevant. Worse yet, it continues, the Court's mindless persistence in those beliefs led it to strike down social legislation that would have gone some way toward correcting the weaker parties' position. According to this view of things, then, the old Court's justices may not have been malign, but their ignorance and their nostalgic attachment to a lost world were about as bad.

The position just described has some validity, but much less than is generally believed. For one thing, it ignores the many occasions on which the old Court voted to reject a substantive due process attack on social legislation. For another, the decisions in which the Court did overturn these remedial measures comprise a relatively small subset of the cases in which it struck down government action. Furthermore, not all the laws struck down within this subset really were responses to unequal bargaining power. For some of them, it is difficult to find such an inequality. Traditional arguments to the contrary—those involving size, bargaining, dependency, and necessitousness—reflect assumptions that are at least as thoughtless as any made by the old Court. Finally, some portion of the "social legislation" the old Court struck down may have been nothing of the kind. Such laws, that is, may have represented efforts by business or labor to disadvantage competing firms or workers. Indeed, *Lochner* itself may fit within one or both of these categories.

NOTES

1. The more common kind of deontological ethics, however, says merely that the morality of actions is not *entirely*, or even mainly, determined by their consequences. *See* PETER A. ANGELES, DICTIONARY OF PHILOSOPHY 82–83 (1981).

2. All the quotations in this paragraph are from IMMANUEL KANT, FOUNDATIONS OF THE METAPHYSICS OF MORALS 9–10 (2d rev'd Macmillan paperback ed. 1990). The translation is by Lewis Beck White.

3. Adkins v. Children's Hosp., 261 U.S. 525 (1923). The progeny are Morehead v. New York *ex rel.* Tipaldo, 298 U.S. 587 (1936); Dunham v. West-Nelson Mfg. Co., 273 U.S. 657 (1927); Murphy v. Sardell, 269 U.S. 530 (1925).

4. Chas. Wolff Packing Co. v. Court of Indus. Relations, 262 U.S. 522 (1923) (striking down a Kansas law giving a state agency the power to fix wages within industries affected with a public interest); Dorchy v. Kansas, 264 U.S. 286 (1924) (refusing to decide whether another provision of the act was separable from the provision struck down in *Chas. Wolff*); Chas. Wolff Packing Co. v. Court of Indus. Relations, 267 U.S. 552 (1925) (striking down a maximum-hours provision contained in a writ of mandamus issued by the Kansas Supreme Court following *Chas Wolff*'s return to that court).

5. 208 U.S. 161 (1908).

6. 236 U.S. 1 (1915).

7. Williams v. Standard Oil Co., 278 U.S. 235 (1929) (retail sale of gasoline); Ribnik v. McBride, 277 U.S. 350 (1928) (employment agency fees); Tyson & Bro. v. Banton, 273 U.S. 418 (1927) (resale price of theater tickets).

8. 264 U.S. 504 (1924).

9. 270 U.S. 402 (1926) (state law forbidding the use of "shoddy" in mattresses, pillows, bolsters, featherbeds, and the like).

10. 94 U.S. 113 (1877).

11. The clearest examples are Allgeyer v. Louisiana, 165 U.S. 578 (1897); Fidelity & Deposit Co. v. Tafoya, 270 U.S. 426 (1926); and St. Louis Cotton Compress Co. v. Arkansas, 260 U.S. 346 (1922). *Allgeyer* and *Cotton Compress* are described in the text; *Tafoya* struck down a state law forbidding any registered insurance agency from paying anyone to place insurance on in-state risks, where that other entity was not authorized to do business within the state.

12. *Cotton Compress*, 260 U.S. at 348–49.

13. Bunting v. Oregon, 243 U.S. 426, 434–39 (1917) (factory workers); Bosley v. McLaughlin, 236 U.S. 385, 392–94 (1915) (women); Miller v. Wilson, 236 U.S. 373, 379–82 (1915) (women); Hawley v. Walker, 232 U.S. 718 (1914) (women); Riley v. Massachusetts, 232 U.S. 671, 679–81 (1914) (women); Muller v. Oregon, 208 U.S. 412, 417–23 (1908) (women); Holden v. Hardy, 169 U.S. 366, 389–98 (1898) (mining employees).

14. Atkin v. Kansas, 191 U.S. 207, 219–24 (1903) (state law regulating wages and hours of workers employed by municipal paving contractors). *See also* Heim v. McCall, 239 U.S. 175, 191–93 (1915) (state law giving citizens a preference over aliens in employment on public works); Crane v. New York, 239 U.S. 195, 198 (1915) (a companion case to *Heim*). *Cf.* Ellis v. United States, 206 U.S. 246, 255–56 (1907) (upholding a federal statute limiting the hours worked by federal work-

ers or employees of federal contractors to eight per day; decided on authority of *Atkin* without mentioning due process).

15. Rail & River Coal Co. v. Yaple, 236 U.S. 338, 349–55 (1915) (state law requiring that coal miners' pay be based, generally speaking, on carloads of coal they produced); Erie R.R. v. Williams, 233 U.S. 685, 699–704 (1914) (state law requiring that railroads pay their employees semimonthly in cash); McLean v. Arkansas, 211 U.S. 539, 545–51 (1909) (state law requiring that, for payment purposes, coal produced by miners be weighed as it comes from the mine and before it is passed over a screen); Knoxville Iron Co. v. Harbison, 183 U.S. 13, 19–22 (1901) (state law requiring employers redeem scrip, stores orders, etc. in cash).

16. 237 U.S. 391, 395–97 (1915).

17. Second Employers' Liability Cases, 223 U.S. 1, 52–53 (1912) (upholding provision of federal law covering railroads' liability for their employees' on-the-job injuries that voids any contract by which employer tries to eliminate its liability under the act); Chicago, B., & Q. R. R. v. McGuire, 219 U.S. 549, 560, 563–73 (1911) (upholding provision of state law governing railroads' liability for their employees' on-the-job injuries that prevents any contract of insurance relief, benefit, or indemnity between employer and employee from operating as a defense to the statutory liability). *See also* Bowerstock v. Smith, 243 U.S. 29, 34–35 (1917) (state statute making employer liable for failure to properly guard manufacturing equipment does not violate due process as applied to employee who had contracted with the employer to provide the safeguards whose absence caused his death).

18. *See, e.g.*, Michael J. Phillips, *Another Look at Economic Substantive Due Process*, 1987 WIS. L. REV. 265, 301–3.

19. Roscoe Pound, *Liberty of Contract*, 18 YALE L.J. 454, 454 (1909).

20. HOWARD GILLMAN, THE CONSTITUTION BESIEGED: THE RISE AND DEMISE OF *LOCHNER* ERA POLICE POWERS JURISPRUDENCE 151 (paperback ed. 1995), quoting THEODORE ROOSEVELT, AN AUTOBIOGRAPHY 276 (1926).

21. MELVIN I. UROFSKY, A MARCH OF LIBERTY: A CONSTITUTIONAL HISTORY OF THE UNITED STATES 503 (1988).

22. *See* LAWRENCE M. FRIEDMAN, A HISTORY OF AMERICAN LAW 81–85 (2d paperback ed. 1985).

23. New State Ice Co. v. Liebmann, 285 U.S. 262, 293 (1932) (Brandeis, J., dissenting).

24. RICHARD A. POSNER, ECONOMIC ANALYSIS OF LAW 591 (1986).

25. ARCHIBALD COX, THE COURT AND THE CONSTITUTION 129 (1987). The following quotation appears on the same page,

26. *See* GILLMAN, *supra* note 20, at 63–64, 76–86, 114–18, 147–59.

27. *Id.* at 76.

28. ARTHUR SELWYN MILLER, THE MODERN CORPORATE STATE: PRIVATE GOVERNMENTS AND THE AMERICAN CONSTITUTION 45–46 (1976). Miller says that Hamilton made this remark in *The Federalist* but does not provide a citation.

29. UROFSKY, *supra* note 21, at 503, citing Vernon v. Bethel, 2 Eden 110, 119 (1762).

30. Morehead v. New York *ex rel.* Tipaldo, 298 U.S. 587, 632 (1936) (Stone, J., dissenting).

31. The material in the following paragraphs comes from the sources cited in

Michael J. Phillips, *Toward a Middle Way in the Polarized Debate over Employment at Will*, 30 AM. BUS. L.J. 441, 464–66 (1992).

32. DANIEL S. HAMERMESH & ALBERT REES, THE ECONOMICS OF WORK AND PAY 122 (3d ed. 1984).

33. Richard A. Posner, *Hegel and Employment at Will: A Comment*, 10 CARDOZO L. REV. 1625, 1632 (1989).

34. *See* Barry Cushman, *Doctrinal Synergies and Liberal Dilemmas: The Case of the Yellow-Dog Contract*, 1992 SUP. CT. REV. 235, 250–54.

35. *See* Todd Rakoff, *Contracts of Adhesion: An Essay in Reconstruction*, 96 HARV. L. REV. 1174, 1222–23 (1983).

36. 169 U.S. 366 (1898).

37. *Id.* at 397.

38. *Id.* at 396.

39. *Id.* at 397.

40. PAUL KENS, JUDICIAL POWER AND REFORM POLITICS: THE ANATOMY OF *LOCHNER V. NEW YORK* 7 (1990).

41. BERNARD H. SIEGAN, ECONOMIC LIBERTIES AND THE CONSTITUTION 116 (paperback ed. 1980).

42. KENS, *supra* note 40, at 13.

43. *Id.* at 6.

44. 208 U.S. 161 (1908).

45. 236 U.S. 1 (1915).

46. *See* 236 U.S. at 41–42 (Day, J., dissenting).

47. *Id.* at 17 (Pitney, J., for the majority).

48. *See id.* at 17–18.

49. 261 U.S. 525 (1923).

50. *Id.* at 562–63 (Taft, C.J., dissenting); *id.* at 571 (Holmes, J., dissenting).

51. "The law is not confined to the great and powerful employers but embraces those whose bargaining power may be as weak as that of the employee." *Id.* at 557 (Sutherland, J., for the majority).

52. David P. Bryden, *Brandeis's Facts*, 1 CONSTITUTIONAL COMMENTARY 281, 287, 313–14 (1984).

53. 262 U.S. 522 (1923).

54. *Id.* at 533–34.

55. *Id.* at 540.

56. 264 U.S. 504, 513–17 (1924). The Court *upheld* similar measures in 1934 and 1913. P. F. Petersen Baking Co. v. Bryan, 290 U.S. 570, 572–75 (1934); Schmidinger v. City of Chicago, 226 U.S. 578, 585–90 (1913).

57. 270 U.S. 402, 411–15 (1926).

58. Williams v. Standard Oil Co., 278 U.S. 235, 239–45 (1929) (retail price of gasoline); Ribnik v. McBride, 277 U.S. 350, 355–59 (1928) (employment agency fees); Tyson & Bro. v. Banton, 273 U.S. 418, 429–45 (1927) (resale of theater tickets).

59. *E.g.*, *Tyson*, 273 U.S. at 430. On the affected with a public interest doctrine and the uses to which it was put in the 1920s, see Robert C. Post, *Defending the Lifeworld: Substantive Due Process in the Taft Court Era*, 78 B.U. L. REV. 1489, 1505–29 (1998).

60. *Tyson*, 273 U.S. at 451–52 (Stone, J., dissenting) (case citations omitted). *See also Ribnik*, 277 U.S. at 359–60 (Stone, J., dissenting).

61. *E.g.*, WALTER NICHOLSON, MICROECONOMIC THEORY: BASIC PRINCIPLES AND EXTENSIONS 432–34 (4th ed. 1989).

62. *Tyson*, 273 U.S. at 450 (Stone, J., dissenting).

63. *Ribnik*, 277 U.S. at 361 (Stone, J., dissenting).

64. *Id.* at 361–62.

65. *See id.* at 363–70.

66. *See* Adams v. Tanner, 244 U.S. 590, 597–617 (1917) (Brandeis, J., dissenting). At one point, in fact, Brandeis complained that employment agencies were too numerous, "necessarily competitive," and therefore uncooperative with each other. *Id.* at 604.

67. *Williams*, 278 U.S. at 240.

68. *Id.* at 245.

69. *See, e.g.*, GILLMAN, *supra* note 20, at 13.

70. *E.g.*, POSNER, *supra* note 24, at 309. *See also* Bryden, *supra* note 52, at 316–21.

71. *See, e.g.*, POSNER, *supra* note 24, at 310, 593; SIEGAN, *supra* note 41, at 148–49.

72. Elisabeth M. Landes, *The Effect of State Maximum-Hours Laws on the Employment of Women in 1920*, 88 J. POL. ECON. 476 (1980).

73. SIEGAN, *supra* note 41, at 148.

74. HADLEY ARKES, THE RETURN OF GEORGE SUTHERLAND: RESTORING A JURISPRUDENCE OF NATURAL RIGHTS 13–14 (1994).

75. Everything in this paragraph and its successor is from Bryden, *supra* note 52, at 318.

76. *See generally* ROBERT A. LEONE, WHO PROFITS: WINNERS, LOSERS, AND GOVERNMENT REGULATION (1986).

77. The following discussion comes from SIEGAN, *supra* note 41, at 116–19.

78. *Id.* at 117.

79. *Id.* at 118.

80. "I have been unable to learn the large bakeries' position on New York's statute, but their support for all of its provisions would certainly not be surprising." *Id.*

81. *See generally* KENS, *supra* note 40, chs. 2–5.

82. *Id.* at 12–13, 44.

83. *Id.* at 44.

84. *See id.* at 44–47.

85. *Id.* at 47.

86. *Id.* at 57. For the details, see *id.* at 47–57.

87. *Id.* at 57.

88. *Id.* at 26; *see id.* at 27–34.

89. *Id.* at 57–58.

90. James W. Ely, Jr., *Economic Due Process Revisited*, 44 VAND. L. REV. 213, 220 (1991).

91. 1 WILLIAM G. PANSCHAR, BAKING IN AMERICA 45 (1956).

92. *See id.* at 55–66.

93. *Id.* at 68.

94. *Id.*

Chapter 5

The Originalist Challenge

In "about the strangest turnabout in jurisprudence," Hadley Arkes wrote in 1994, "[t]he most conservative of our judges have absorbed the jurisprudence of the New Deal and the jural reflexes of Hugo Black."[1] That jurisprudence and those reflexes may elude definitive statement, but their general outlines are clear enough. In deference to majorities, this approach tells us, judges should practice judicial restraint. In constitutional cases, they do so largely by following the text of the Constitution and the original intent of its framers. Only when judges decide in this fashion can they legitimately overturn a legislative choice by declaring some statute unconstitutional. Due to its emphasis on original intent in the interpretation of constitutional language, this position is sometimes called *originalism* or *interpretivism*. As Arkes's remark suggests, today it is largely the property of conservatives.

As Chapter 1 related, this argument has clear implications for substantive due process. The original meaning of Fifth and Fourteenth Amendment due process, we are continually told, is procedural and nothing else. This means that courts are acting illegitimately when they use due process to strike down substantive government action. Specifically, they are using a judicially concocted doctrine to invalidate laws made by the people's elected representatives. Another originalist argument against substantive due process applies specifically to its *Lochner*-era variant. The liberty protected by Fifth and Fourteenth Amendment due process, some say, simply does not contain freedom of contract; and freedom of contract was central to *Lochner*-era substantive due process. Thus, the old Court also acted illegitimately when it struck down government action on freedom-of-contract grounds.

Chapters 2 and 3 suggested three problems with the originalist position just stated. First, even if the argument is theoretically valid, Chapter 2's data on substantive due process claims accepted and rejected make it clear that the *Lochner* Court was far more majoritarian than is generally realized. Second, Chapter 2 also made it clear that freedom of contract was not an especially important component of *Lochner*-era substantive due process. Finally, Chapter 3 weakened the link between originalism and majoritarianism. Although that chapter was lukewarm about the accuracy of the class legislation hypothesis, the theory obviously has some validity. In situations where it is valid, the old Court was correcting a malfunction of the democratic system rather than frustrating the popular will when it violated originalism by using due process to strike down substantive government action. The animus against class legislation, after all, is an animus against laws that serve partial interests rather than the general good.

Even so, however, the old Court still struck down many laws on substantive due process grounds. And the class legislation hypothesis goes only so far in explaining and justifying those decisions. All that being the case, this chapter focuses on other matters. It begins by briefly examining the claim that substantive due process is illegitimate because freedom of contract is not contained within due process liberty. Then the chapter takes on the main originalist argument: that because due process is entirely procedural, courts should not give it a substantive reading. Employing some recent scholarship, it first attacks this argument's premise—that due process was originally intended to be totally procedural. After that, it considers the attack on *Lochner*-era substantive due process made by the man widely considered its greatest foe—Justice Oliver Wendell Holmes, Jr. Then the chapter maintains that even if the due process clauses were entirely procedural when enacted, that interpretation cannot completely control today. The main reasons are that strict adherence to original intent requires a moral justification, that no such justification can be absolutized, and that therefore other ethical claims sometimes can override originalism. The chapter concludes that at least one of the economic rights protected by the old Court—freedom of occupation—is such a claim.

LIBERTY AND FREEDOM OF CONTRACT

The first claim we consider is the argument that there is something illegitimate about including freedom of contract within the liberty protected against deprivation by the due process clauses. On its face, liberty is a capacious word, one easily broad enough to include freedom of contract. By now, moreover, it has been read as including the right to an abortion. If so nontraditional a right resides within due process liberty, why should freedom of contract not dwell there as well? Almost any argument to the contrary has to rely on the dubious double standard that I attack in Chapter 6.

In any event, the question whether due process liberty contains freedom of contract is mostly beside the point. One reason for this has already been discussed. Quantitatively speaking, as we saw in Chapter 2, freedom-of-contract cases were a minor component of *Lochner*-era substantive due process. To this one might object that because most of them struck down Progressive social legislation, the freedom-of-contract cases have significance out of proportion to their numbers. But even if this is true, the old Court could have reached the same results through an economic right to which no one can deny Fourteenth Amendment protection: the right to property. If the bundle of rights comprising property is construed with any breadth at all, it has to include the right to alienate the "thing" to which that bundle relates. But this is much the same as saying that one's property in *x* includes the freedom to contract about *x*. And *x* might even include one's own labor. The old Court made this basic argument on at least two occasions.

Tyson & Brother v. Banton[2] struck down a New York law regulating the price at which theater tickets could be resold. If ever there were a measure that restricted freedom of contract, one would think, New York's measure was it. But Justice Sutherland's opinion for the majority maintained that the measure deprived the claimant of property. "[T]he right of the owner to fix the price at which his property shall be sold or used," Sutherland declared, "is an inherent attribute of the property itself, and, as such, within the protection of the due process of law clauses of the Fifth and Fourteenth Amendments."[3] After that, Sutherland concluded that the state could not regulate the resale price of theater tickets because the theater business was not affected with a public interest. In at least one of the two subsequent cases striking down state price fixing under this rationale, the Court also seemed to hold that there was a deprivation of property.[4]

Our basic argument—that property in *x* includes the ability to alienate *x*—was stated more throughly a decade before *Tyson*. *Buchanan v. Warley*[5] struck down an ordinance making it unlawful for any black person to occupy a house in any block where white-occupied houses outnumbered black-occupied ones. Early in its unanimous opinion, the Court declared:

> The Fourteenth Amendment protects life, liberty, and property from invasion by the states without due process of law. Property is more than the mere thing which a person owns. It is elementary that it includes the right to acquire, use, and dispose of it. The Constitution protects these essential attributes of property. . . . Property consists of the free use, enjoyment, and disposal of a person's acquisitions without control or diminution save by the law of the land.[6]

Then the Court struck down the ordinance because it restricted both a white person's ability to sell to a black person if he so desired, and a black person's corresponding right to sell to a white person.

WAS DUE PROCESS ORIGINALLY SUBSTANTIVE?

The argument that due process liberty excludes freedom of contract is not made too often today. But as Chapter 1 revealed, commentators continue to maintain that due process is, or should be read as, entirely procedural. One set of arguments for this position maintains that the history of the Fifth and Fourteenth Amendments permits no other result.[7] During the 1990s, however, at least two scholars have challenged this long-accepted standard wisdom.[8] One of them, Robert E. Riggs, first contended that the Fifth Amendment's drafting history reveals nothing about its framers' conception of due process. "Nevertheless," he continued, "a relevant and answerable alternative question can be asked: what might the framers have understood 'due process of law' to mean in 1791?"[9] Specifically, did that clause have substantive content as well as procedural content? "The short answer to that question," Riggs concluded, is: " 'Yes, it probably did.' "

Riggs made several arguments to support his contention that the conception of due process embraced by the Fifth Amendment's framers was partly substantive. Central to most of those arguments is the assertion that the "law of the land" clause in chapter 39 of the Magna Carta was equivalent to due process.[10] As understood and employed over the centuries in England, in the American colonies, and in the states after the Revolution, Riggs maintained at some length, that clause had both substantive and procedural connotations.[11] But did it also check legislative action? Riggs argued that while in England the "law of the land" clause did not restrict Parliament, in the early United States it occasionally constrained the legislature.[12] In particular, he concluded, several late eighteenth-century court decisions applied it in this way.[13]

Unfortunately, all or virtually all of the cases Riggs discussed postdated the Fifth Amendment's adoption. A recent article by James W. Ely, Jr. focuses on Fourteenth Amendment due process and avoids this problem.[14] Ely's aim is to "investigate the evolution of the concept of due process as a restraint on government in American jurisprudence before the Civil War."[15] After some brief general arguments that seem to parallel Riggs's important contentions,[16] Ely discusses a number of pre–Civil War due process cases that certainly appear to be substantive.[17] As one might expect, most of these cases protected property against government action.

The persuasiveness of Ely's and Riggs's arguments is a subject this book happily leaves to legal historians. My aim is sketching those arguments is simply to cast some doubt on the dogma that the framers of the due process clauses intended those clauses to be procedural alone. In order to increase that doubt, I will pause to examine a few of the cases discussed by Ely and Riggs. Despite their differences, these decisions all involve a common substantive theme: government action that takes property from A and gives it to B.[18]

In the first of my four cases, a 1792 South Carolina decision named *Bowman v. Middleton*,[19] the court considered a real property dispute that hinged in part on a 1712 statute that had taken land from one party and conveyed it to a predecessor of one of the disputants. The statute did so without trial by jury or, apparently, any other legal process. In a very brief opinion, the court struck down the statute. The party relying on this law, it said, "could claim no title under the act in question, as it was against common right, as well as against magna charta, to take away the freehold of one man and vest it in another, and that, too, to the prejudice of third persons, without any compensation, or even a trial by the jury of the country, to determine the right in question."[20] Immediately thereafter, the judges declared the statute "ipso facto, void." However, they did not cite any specific provision of the Magna Carta, or of the state or federal constitutions, to support that declaration.

Bowman v. Middleton, then, did not clearly involve either due process or the Magna Carta's law-of-the-land provision and might even be regarded as a takings case. Except for decrying the lack of a jury trial, however, the court obviously condemned the statute on substantive grounds. The substantive principle in question—that the legislature could not vest A's property in B without trial or compensation—received what looks like a separation of powers justification in an 1833 North Carolina case. *Hoke v. Henderson*[21] involved the constitutionality of an 1832 statute that provided for the popular election of court clerks, thus displacing a clerk who owed his position to an earlier law letting judges appoint the clerks. The North Carolina Supreme Court began its inquiry by citing a state constitutional provision forbidding the deprivation of life, liberty, or property, except by the law of the land; and another commanding that the legislative, executive, and judicial powers be kept distinct from each other.[22] Evidently the court saw a connection between these two provisions, for, after declaring decisions about titles between individuals judicial rather than legislative, it used that conclusion to find the 1832 statute unconstitutional because it was not a law of the land.

So prescribing the duties of officers, their qualifications, their fees, their powers, and the consequences of a breach of duty, including punishment and removal, are all political regulations, and fall within the legislative province. But to inflict those punishments, after finding the default, is to adjudge; and to do it, *without default*, is equally so and still more indefensible. The Legislature cannot act in that character; and therefore, although their act has the forms of law, it is not one of those *laws of the land*, by which alone a freeman can be *deprived* of his *property*.[23]

After finding that the displaced clerk's office indeed was property, the court declared the 1832 statute unconstitutional.[24]

At one point in *Hoke v. Henderson*, the North Carolina Supreme Court observed that instead of regulating prospectively the challenged statute was a measure "by which the office, preserved in the law and still regarded as the subject of property, is taken, and merely taken from one man and given to another."[25] That theme loomed larger in *Taylor v. Porter*,[26] an 1843 New York case involving a state statute allowing private parties to construct private roads over another's property, if appropriate damages were paid to the landowner. The New York court opened its inquiry into the statute's constitutionality by posing some questions. "The property of A is taken, without his permission, and transferred to B. Can such a thing be rightfully done? Has the Legislature any power to say it may be done?"[27] After observing that the statute could not be justified as a measure appropriating private property for a *public* use and that no other affirmative power of government seemed to justify it either, the court considered two independent constitutional checks on the legislation.

The first such check was a New York constitutional provision stating that no one can be deprived of rights or privileges secured to the state's citizens, "unless by the law of the land, or the judgment of his peers."[28] After asserting that the words "law of the land" "do not mean a statute passed for the purpose of working the wrong,"[29] the court determined their true definition.

The meaning of the section . . . seems to be, that no member of the State shall be disenfranchised, or deprived of any of his rights or privileges, unless the matter shall be adjudged against him upon trial had according to the course of the common law. It must be ascertained judicially that he has forfeited his privileges, or that some one else has a superior title to the property he possesses, before either of them can be taken from him. It cannot be done by mere legislation.[30]

Much the same argument, which obviously echoes the central point made in *Hoke v. Henderson*, reappeared when the court considered a different independent check on the legislature: the New York Constitution's due process clause.

The words "due process of law" . . . cannot mean less than a prosecution or suit instituted and conducted according to the prescribed forms and solemnities for ascertaining guilt, or determining the title to property. . . . If the Legislature can take the property of A and transfer it to B, they can take A himself, and either shut him up in prison, or put him to death. But none of these things can be done by mere legislation. There must be "due process of law."[31]

These two arguments are not without their procedural components. But their bottom line—that the legislature cannot transfer A's property to B—obviously is substantive. By saying that such transfers require certain judicial procedures, in other words, the court imposed a substantive check on the legislature. This check, I might add, is considerably stronger than the typical obstacle posed by the *Lochner* Court, which usually required that legislation depriving people of property merely pass some test of reasonableness.

The *Taylor* and *Hoke* courts' apparent favoritism toward judicial procedures might strike some readers as strange. Why, they might say, should legislatures be less inclined to respect property rights than courts? The answer, of course, is that majorities and the factions comprising them often use the legislature to redistribute wealth from minority factions to themselves. In other words, some laws taking property from A and giving it to B qualify as class legislation. This theme assumed some importance in an 1831 Tennessee case. *Bank of the State v. Cooper*[32] involved a statute setting up a special court to hear complaints by a particular bank against its officers, their sureties, and customers who had overdrawn their accounts. There was no provision for jury trial and also no appeal from the special court's decision. Among the constitutional challenges to the act was the assertion "[t]hat it is partial in its operation; and for that reason not a " '*law of the land.*' "[33] Each of the three judges writing separate opinions found the law unconstitutional on this basis.[34] Judge Nathan Green's opinion is the most vivid of the bunch.

"By '*law of the land*,' " Green began, "is meant a general and public law, operating equally on every individual in the community."[35] Were things otherwise, he continued, "an edict in the form of a legislative enactment, taking the property of A, and giving it to B, might be regarded as the '*law of the land*,' and not forbidden by the constitution."[36] To demonstrate the absurdity of this proposition, Green provided a short lecture from Political Science 1.

This provision [the law-of-the-land clause] was introduced to secure the citizens against the abuse of power by the government. Of what benefit is it if it impose no restraint upon legislation? Was there not as just ground to apprehend danger from the legislature as from any other quarter? Legislation is always exercised by the majority. Majorities have nothing to fear, for the power is in their hands. *They* need no written constitution, defining and circumscribing the powers of the government. Constitutions are only intended to secure the rights of the minority. They are in danger. The power is against them; and the selfish passions often lead us to forget the right. Does it not seem conclusive then, that this provision was intended to restrain the legislature from enacting any law affecting injuriously the rights of any citizen, unless at the same time the rights of all others in similar circumstances were equally affected by it? If the law be general in its operation, affecting all alike, the minority are safe, because the majority, who make the law, are operated on by it equally with the others.[37]

Because the law at issue in *Cooper* denied the bank's targets both a jury trial and the right to appeal, it plainly failed to meet these criteria. "This law," said Green, "is the same in principle as if a law had been passed in favor of some one merchant, enabling him, by the method therein prescribed, to take judgment against his debtors without the right of appeal."[38]

REVISITING THE HOLMES MYTH

Despite their procedural underpinnings, it is difficult to characterize the four cases just discussed as anything but substantive. Furthermore, they form only a small portion of a larger group discussed by Riggs and Ely. Thus, it seems more or less plausible to say that at the time the Fourteenth Amendment was enacted, due process was thought to have both substantive and procedural components. (Because almost all of these decisions postdated the Fifth Amendment's passage, this conclusion may be less plausible in that connection.) However, the terms "procedural due process" and "substantive due process" did not become popular until well after the *Lochner* era.[39] Thus, it might be more accurate to say that at the time the Fourteenth Amendment was enacted, there was just *due process* and that it had what today we would call substantive and procedural dimensions. Indeed, the previous discussion suggests that these two dimensions may have been intertwined. By saying that certain substantive decisions cannot be made by a legislature and instead require judicial process, our four decisions imposed a significant substantive check on legislative action.

Holmes's *Lochner* Dissent

The conclusion that due process had both substantive and procedural components also gets some support from the man widely regarded as *Lochner*-era substantive due process's most adamant and searching critic: Justice Oliver Wendell Holmes, Jr. As Chapter 2 related,[40] Holmes always gave due process a substantive reading when the issue arose. More importantly, he joined many of the old Court's decisions striking down substantive government action on due process grounds and wrote for the Court in a few others. A few of the cases Holmes joined or wrote were freedom-of-contract decisions.

All that having been said, it remains true that Holmes vigorously dissented from several of the old Court's high-profile decisions striking down government regulation on due process grounds. Among those dissents, one in particular is widely thought to contain an especially telling critique of *Lochner*-era substantive due process. This, of course, is his dissent in *Lochner v. New York*. Lately, however, that dissent has come in for some criticism,[41] as well it should. Of its several flaws, the main vice of this vastly overrated judicial performance is the way it caricatures the position it attacks.

Holmes began his *Lochner* dissent by declaring that "[t]his case is decided upon an economic theory which a large part of the country does not entertain."[42] Perhaps that was so, but it is worth noting that the initial public reaction to the *Lochner* decision was very subdued.[43] More importantly, Holmes does not state why courts are bound to follow public opinion on economic matters—or, for that matter, on noneconomic affairs either. Instead, he followed his opening statement with some posturing. "If it were a question whether I agreed with that [economic] theory I should desire to study it further and long before making up my mind. But I do not conceive that to be my duty, because I strongly believe that my agreement or disagreement has nothing to do with the right of a majority to embody their opinions in law." Given Holmes's personal economic views, this quotation's first sentence is disingenuous in the extreme. As G. Edward White observes, Holmes "repeatedly expressed skepticism about the efficacy of hours and wages legislation, child labor reform, and other policy goals of 'progressives.' "[44] And the quotation's second sentence is belied by the many occasions on which Holmes voted to strike down substantive government action on due process grounds.

Holmes followed these opening remarks by citations to several decisions in which the Court had rejected freedom-of-contract claims or had upheld laws that interfered with the freedom to do as one likes. Had he merely been saying that freedom of contract is not an absolute, he would have been making a sensible, if obvious, point. But Holmes also seemed to accuse the *Lochner* majority of such absolutism. This is the apparent thrust of his famous crack that "[t]he Fourteenth Amendment does not enact Mr. Herbert Spencer's Social Statics." In later dissents, Holmes asserted that freedom of contract had become a "dogma"[45] and that it had "been stretched to its extreme by the decisions."[46] But if all this was true, how was Holmes able to cite so many cases in which the Court had rejected freedom-of-contract claims? If the old Court's conservatives were dogmatic Spencerian extremists, in other words, why had those cases been decided the way they were? It is difficult to escape the conclusion that Holmes wanted to have things both ways. On the one hand, he wanted to portray freedom of contract as a powerful check on legislation because the Court's conservatives were dogmatically committed to it. But he also wanted to maintain that precedent dictated a different result in *Lochner*. These two arguments are difficult to reconcile.

Maybe, however, Holmes merely was accusing the *Lochner* majority of acting in a dogmatically laissez-faire fashion in that particular case. But as the discussion of *Lochner* in Chapters 3 and 4 suggests, this is too sweeping a denunciation of the decision. In those chapters, Howard Gillman portrays the *Lochner* maximum-hours law as a piece of class legislation intended to benefit workers, Bernard Siegan regards it as class legislation favoring big bakeries over small ones, Paul Kens leaves the law's motives and origins in considerable doubt, and I maintain that it probably was not a response to unequal bargaining power. In any event, Holmes had relatively little to say about the substance of that provision. "A reasonable man," he maintained, "might think it a proper measure on the score of health. Men whom I certainly could not pronounce unreasonable would uphold it as a first instalment of a general regulation of the hours of work." These remarks seem to presuppose some test of substantive constitutionality, however weak. And earlier Holmes had articulated such a test. "I think that the word liberty in the Fourteenth Amendment is perverted when it is held to prevent the natural outcome of a dominant opinion, unless it can be said that a rational and fair man necessarily would admit that the statute proposed would infringe fundamental principles as they have been understood by the traditions of our people and our law." Justice Peckham's majority opinion stated the following test: "The act must have a more direct relation, as a means to an end, and the end itself must be appropriate and legitimate, before an act can be held to be valid which interferes with the general right of an individual to be free in his person and in his power to contract in relation to his own labor."[47] Despite Holmes's suggestions that some metaphysical divide separated him from the *Lochner* majority, he and Peckham perhaps were not so far apart after all. From the passages just quoted, it appears that Peckham wanted to apply fairly rigorous rational basis review to laws that restricted freedom of contract, wheras Holmes preferred a weak substantive test.

The Myth of the Modern Court's Economic Neutrality

Even though Holmes's *Lochner* dissent adopted a weak test of substantive neutrality, it also contained a remark suggesting that he did not think any substantive due process review of economic matters appropriate. "[A] constitution," he said, "is not intended to embody a particular economic theory, whether of paternalism and the organic relation of the citizen to the State or of *laissez-faire*. It is made for people of fundamentally differing views."[48] This idea has become a staple of post-1937 substantive due process jurisprudence, particularly in the opinions of

Justices Black and Douglas. "There was a time," Black wrote in a 1963 case upholding a Kansas statute that essentially limited the business of debt adjusting to lawyers, "when the Due Process Clause was used by this Court to strike down laws which were thought unreasonable, that is, unwise or incompatible with some particular economic or social philosophy."[49] Modern justices, however,

> refuse to sit as a superlegislature to weigh the wisdom of legislation, and we emphatically refuse to go back to the time when courts used the Due Process Clause to strike down state laws, regulatory of business and industrial conditions, because they may be unwise, improvident, or out of harmony with a particular school of thought. . . . Whether the legislature takes for its textbook Adam Smith, Herbert Spencer, Lord Keynes, or some other is no concern of ours.[50]

Douglas quoted these lines in a 1973 case rejecting a substantive due process attack on a North Dakota law that basically limited the pharmacy business to licensed pharmacists or to businesses owned by licensed pharmacists.[51] This decision overruled *Liggett Co. v. Baldridge*,[52] which had struck down a similar measure in 1928. According to Douglas, *Liggett* was nothing more than "a derelict in the stream of the law."[53]

The idea we are considering, then, is that of the economically neutral constitution. According to Holmes, a constitution simply is not intended to embody any particular economic theory and instead is made for people of fundamentally differing views. But this statement is pure ideology. The constitution we actually have says, for example, that people cannot be deprived of liberty and property without due process of law, that government cannot take property for a public use without just compensation, and that the states cannot impair the obligation of contracts. These restraints on government may not comprise an economic theory, but they clearly preclude at least some economic arrangements. Then there is Holmes's absurd declaration that constitutions are made for people of fundamentally different views. For one thing, it is difficult to see how people could establish or maintain any constitution at all if their views diverge too fundamentally. On the other hand, are we supposed to assume that tightly knit "consensus societies" do not need a written constitution? Maybe Holmes merely meant that the U.S. Constitution ought to be read as establishing an open society designed to regulate interactions among people with radically diverse life-plans. But then wouldn't the constitution at least embody a *political* theory? In fact, if people with fundamentally different values are really to pursue their different conceptions of the good life, wouldn't the constitution have to embody an economic theory too—and a more or less laissez-faire one at that?

Furthermore, many of those who reject the old Court do so not because it followed an economic theory but because it followed the wrong one.

Consider, for example, the plurality opinion in *Planned Parenthood of Southeastern Pennsylvania v. Casey,*[54] where Justices Kennedy, O'Connor, and Souter considered the Court's 1937 decision in *West Coast Hotel v. Parrish,*[55] which while upholding a minimum-wage law for women had overruled *Adkins v. Children's Hospital.*[56] With the coming of the depression, our three Republican appointees declared, "the lesson that seemed unmistakable to most people by 1937" was "that the interpretation of contractual freedom protected in *Adkins* rested on fundamentally false factual assumptions about the capacity of a relatively unregulated market to satisfy minimal levels of human welfare."[57] "The facts upon which the earlier case had premised a constitutional resolution of social controversy had proved to be untrue, and history's demonstration of their untruth not only justified but required the new choice of constitutional principle that *West Coast Hotel* announced."[58] The trio concluded that "changed circumstances may impose new obligations, and the thoughtful part of the Nation could accept each decision to overrule a prior case as a response to the Court's constitutional duty."[59]

Justices Kennedy, O'Connor, and Souter also said that 1937's changes were not merely "the victories of one doctrinal school over another by dint of numbers."[60] Presumably they did so to avoid the charge that the 1937 Court simply had a different economic theory than its predecessor. But plainly all sorts of economic assumptions undergirded their rejection of the old Court's views. These include the inability of relatively unregulated laissez-faire to satisfy human welfare, the resulting need for more government regulation of social and economic matters, and the desirability of minimum-wage laws as one form of such regulation. Whatever else might be said about these views, they comprise, if not an economic theory, at least a general approach toward economic questions. Furthermore, it is not an approach inexorably dictated by some set of indisputable "facts." Why, for example, is relatively unregulated laissez-faire thought incompatible with human welfare? If the answer is that government regulation is needed to correct for disparities in bargaining power, Chapter 4 argued at length that such claims are less valid than is commonly believed. And just how did the depression prove the desirability of minimum-wage laws? As we saw in the previous chapter, these measures are routinely attacked for reducing the employment opportunities of marginal workers such as middle-age women, young people, and blacks. If "the thoughtful part of the Nation" uncritically embraced the views our three justices attributed to it, how hard and how well could those people have been thinking?

Whatever else might be said about their views, in sum, Justices Kennedy, O'Connor, and Souter were not economically neutral. Instead, they plainly thought that unrestricted laissez-faire is bad and that under modern conditions human welfare demands a considerable degree of government regulation. But maybe the idea of the economically neutral constitution can be made more genuinely neutral. According to Justice Black, the mentors legislatures might follow included Adam Smith and Herbert Spencer. His view, then, was that government should be able to pursue any economic policy it desires, *including a policy of total laissez-faire*, and that courts should not use the due process clauses to second-guess that choice. This particular version of economic neutrality founders not because it assumes in advance that government regulation is good but because its prescriptions are something less than neutral in practice. By this, I do not merely mean that it is implausible to expect the state to voluntarily relinquish power. Nor do I merely mean to say that Black and Douglas were partisan Democrats, that their party was in the saddle for much of the post-1937 period, and that their professions of neutrality minimized the constitutional obstacles to New Deal and post–New Deal government regulation of the economy. Instead, I maintain that the practical effect of their professions was to sanction a particular political/economic theory.

To see why the Black-Douglas position is not neutral in practice, consider the two modern substantive due process decisions just discussed, each of which protected established economic interests against competition. In practice, these cases suggest, the modern Court's asserted neutrality on economic questions has tended to ratify the results of intergroup competition. As Justice Marshall once remarked after disavowing the *Lochner* approach, today "[t]he structure of economic and commercial life is a matter of political compromise, not constitutional principle."[61] Whatever one might think about this position, it hardly is innocent of political or economic theory. Indeed, it sounds like the pluralism or interest-group liberalism described by academic political scientists.[62] If such theories mirror reality, furthermore, the winners of the intergroup struggle will be able to use state power to suppress competition. The result would be a tendency toward corporativism: a fusion of public and private power in which large groups dominate society, government serves their interests, and individuals count for relatively little as individuals.[63] Thus, Black's and Douglas's professions of constitutional neutrality fail on two counts. In their practical results, these positions facilitate a fairly definite and familiar political or economic philosophy. (Indeed, as Arkes has suggested, corporativism may have been the New Deal's main economic philosophy from the very beginning.)[64] Where that philosophy prevails, moreover, legislatures are not completely free to adopt whatever social or economic theory they desire. In particular, they are not completely free to institute laissez-faire policies that would prevent private interests from using government to defeat competitors. This is true even though examples such as Congress's deregulation of the airline and trucking industries and the states' ongoing deregulation of electric utilities suggest that modern government has some ability to institute measures that increase competition.

THE INDEFENSIBILITY OF STRICT INTERPRETIVISM

Holmes's *Lochner* dissent is widely portrayed as a searching critique of *Lochner*-era substantive due process and the judicial mentality that underlay it.[65] In reality, though, it is marked throughout by irrelevance (the public's supposed attitude toward economic laissez-faire), hypocrisy (Holmes's pose as an above-the-battle majoritarian who would never use due process to strike down economic regulations), caricature (his suggestion that the old Court's conservatives were dogmatic about freedom of contract), confusion (his citation of several decisions suggesting the opposite), and simple absurdity (the idea of the economically neutral constitution made for people of fundamentally different views). As a result, Holmes's *Lochner* dissent strikes no telling blows against its target. More important for present purposes, it concedes the main point at issue here: whether due process has a substantive connotation. In technical legal terms, the main difference between Holmes and Peckham was merely the strictness of the review each would apply to laws restricting freedom of contract.

But what if both Holmes and Peckham were wrong to assume that due process has a substantive component? Ely and Riggs to the contrary notwithstanding, that is, what if the original meaning of due process turns out to be entirely procedural when all is said and done? Would that make *Lochner*-era substantive due process—or indeed any form of substantive due process—indefensible? The answer is: not completely so. As we will see, a strict interpretivism that admits of no exceptions cannot stand, and this leaves sufficient space for at least some applications of substantive due process. To make this argument, I will consider the defense of originalism mounted by Robert Bork in his *The Tempting of America*.[66]

Bork's Scheme and Its Justifications

As we saw in Chapter 1, Bork thinks that the Constitution is *law* and that for this reason judges are bound to follow it. To follow a particular constitutional provision, a court obviously must determine what its words mean. To Bork, this meaning is the meaning publicly understood at the time the provision in question was enacted. It is expressed in principles of greater or lesser generality. These principles must be *neutrally derived* (based on the genuine original intent), *neutrally defined* (stated at the level of generality dictated by the text and the historical evidence), and *neutrally applied* (applied equally to different parties). Except for the criterion of neutral application, judges applying these principles are, to the maximum extent possible, following the intent of the Constitution's drafters.

What justifies Bork's adherence to original intent? He admits that the Constitution cannot become law by its own assertion,[67] so he presumably is saying that we should adhere to original intent because that is instrumental to something else. That "something else" seems to be majoritarian democracy.[68] Judges who respect the choices made by the people's elected representatives will not broadly construe due process and other constitutional checks on legislation. And though Bork seems not to make exactly this point, an originalist judge *is* following the popular will when he invalidates government action on such bases. By putting these clauses in the Constitution and refusing to change them, the people authorized the judiciary to strike down lawmaking that offends their original meaning.

But is majoritarianism an absolute? Few would say so, and neither does Bork. He admits that the claims made by existing precedents sometimes override those made by original understanding.[69] The main reason, evidently, is the need to preserve stability and order. For example, he admits that it is too late to overrule the commerce, tax, and spending power decisions underlying the New Deal and the Great Society, because to do so would be "to overturn most of modern government and plunge us into chaos."[70] The details of Bork's attempt to reconcile *stare decisis* and originalism need not concern us here, except to note that under his tests, most forms of substantive due process cannot survive.

> It was never too late to overrule the line of cases represented by *Lochner*, because they were unjustifiable restrictions on governmental power, and allowing additional regulation of economic matters did not produce any great disruption of institutional arrangements. Similarly, it will probably never be too late to overrule the right of privacy cases, including *Roe v. Wade*, because they remain unaccepted and unacceptable to large segments of the body politic, and judicial regulation could at once be replaced by restored legislative regulation of the subject.[71]

Later, however, Bork allowed that *Griswold v. Connecticut*[72] might be allowed to stand, because no state would want to enforce the ban on contraception at issue there.

Opening the Door to Substantive Due Process

Substantive due process, then, might be illegitimate within a moral universe in which democracy and stability are the only values. But is this so if other values of commensurate importance are added to the mix?

These other values, of course, might support some forms of substantive due process. Here the Bork of *The Tempting*[73] would probably object that such values are inherently subjective and thus should not guide judges. At one point in that book, for example, he remarks that a judge who looks beyond original intent in constitutional cases "looks inside himself and nowhere else."[74] Later he observes that moral philosophy has never been able to produce a universally accepted set of values, and that no such set of values finds acceptance in contemporary America.[75] Still later he equates a person's moral positions with her "gratifications."[76]

At this point, one might think that Bork has undercut his own position, since his own methods of judging affirm some values, most notably majoritarianism and the need for stability and continuity. But in fact his skepticism might be thought to support democracy, at least. This is the once-familiar argument that because there is no moral truth, democracy is the least irrational form of government and the one most likely to attract a popular consensus.[77] Bork argues in a somewhat similar fashion at one point in *The Tempting*. When discussing whether judges should impose some scheme of "gratifications" on society, he says that "unless we can rank forms of gratification, the judge must let the majority have its way."[78] "There is no way to decide these questions," he continues, "other than by reference to some system of moral or ethical principles about which people can and do disagree. Because we disagree, we put such issues to a vote and where the Constitution does not speak, the majority morality prevails."[79]

There are few sure things in moral or political philosophy, but the preceding argument almost certainly is bogus. The many contentions of this kind almost invariably take the following form: "There is no moral truth; therefore, you *ought* to respect majority rule, tolerate different value systems, [and the like]." As Bernard Williams once remarked, this "vulgar" form of relativism involves a "logically unhappy attachment of a nonrelative morality of toleration or non-interference to a view of morality as relative."[80] The argument gets its superficial plausibility, I think, by smuggling in a hidden premise: that it is unreasonable and therefore unjustifiable to impose one's values on another or to affirm them against majority will unless those values are rationally justified. In Bork's words, unless we can *authoritatively* rank-order human gratifications, we must let the majority have its way. But if there are no authoritative moral standards, *why not* impose one's will on other people? As Henry B. Veatch once observed, Mussolini used much this argument to "justify" his form of fascism.[81] To this, a liberal might reply: "But if there is no moral truth, what reason have you to oppress me?" The obvious response is that in that event, there is no reason not to.

The previous digression on moral skepticism and its implications began when I maintained that other values besides originalism, majoritarianism, and social stability might legitimately influence judges, and then surmised that Bork might attack this idea on skeptical grounds. The cost of his doing so, it now seems, is to undermine his main argument for majoritarian democracy. If that goes, his judicial method—and his argument against judges' application of such values—seems to fail as well. On the other hand, if Bork were to affirm majoritarianism on some other ground, he would face the problems raised earlier. Because he allowed social stability to trump majoritarianism on occasion, Bork obviously did not make the latter an absolute. But if social stability can do so, what about other values of commensurate importance?

The Importance of Occupational Freedom

If I had to briefly summarize the preceding argument, I would say that because original intent is not self-justifying, it needs a moral justification, and that because any such justification cannot be absolutized, other values legitimately may influence the judiciary. (And if there is no moral truth, how could there be a moral objection to a judge's imposing any values he wishes?) The aim of that argument, in turn, was to undermine originalist attacks on substantive due process. If the values they advance are sufficiently important, therefore, some applications of the doctrine may be legitimate even if the original meaning of due process was entirely procedural. In particular, some applications of *Lochner*-era substantive due process may be legitimate. Of those applications, there is one whose importance is difficult to deny.

Justice McReynolds's classic statement of Fourteenth Amendment liberty in *Meyer v. Nebraska* included "freedom . . . to engage in any of the common occupations of life."[82] That freedom was affirmed by none other than William O. Douglas in a 1954 case:

> The right to work . . . [is] the most precious liberty that man possesses. Man has indeed as much right to work as he has to live, to be free, to own property. The American ideal was stated by Emerson in his essay on *Politics*, "A man has a right to be employed, to be trusted, to be loved, to be revered." It does many men little good to stay alive and free and propertied, if they cannot work. To work means to eat. It also means to live. For many it would be better to work in jail, than to sit idle on the curb. The great values of freedom are in the opportunities afforded man to press to new horizons, to pit his strength against the forces of nature, to match skills with his fellow man.[83]

Douglas's characteristic imprecision makes it unclear whether he is extolling a negative right to choose and ply a particular trade or profession or instead a positive right to a government-provided job. But the quoted passage sits within his dissent from a decision refusing to overturn the temporary suspension of a physician's license to practice medicine. And it gives some reasons why the negative liberty to select one's occupation is important to the individual. People obtain the basic necessities of life through the work they choose. One's job also goes some way toward determining one's income, associations, social status, and access to life's good things. Perhaps most important, a person's work is the principal means through which she develops her capacities and realizes her potential.

The upshot of the preceding discussion is that occupational freedom is as important, if not more important, to much of the population as some liberties that now get considerably more constitutional protection. According to Robert McCloskey, for example, most people "would probably feel that an economic right, such as freedom of occupation, was at least as vital to them as the right to speak their minds."[84] As we will see in the next chapter, furthermore, liberty of occupation should qualify as fundamental under the various tests the modern Supreme Court uses to determine which substantive due process rights get enhanced constitutional protection. As that chapter also argues, individuals deprived of occupational liberty arguably resemble the "discrete and insular minorities" the modern Court has been much concerned to protect.[85]

So far, the criteria we have been examining concern occupational freedom's importance to the individual. But it matters for the general welfare, too. Consider the occupational licensing schemes and other entry restrictions discussed in Chapter 3. Occupational licensing's main justification is the protection of the public against dishonest or incompetent practitioners. This justification speaks with considerable force in cases, such as medicine, in which such people pose significant risks of harm to their patients or clients. Considerations of public health and safety probably go some way toward explaining the many instances in which the old Court upheld constitutional challenges to occupational licensing.[86] But as Chapter 3 revealed, occupational licensing often is less an expression of concern for the public than of existing practitioners' desire to make money by suppressing competition. And as that chapter's discussion of the *Liebmann* and *Liggett* cases also made clear, the same is true where the party denied entry to a line of business is an artificial corporate person. Where entry restrictions prevail, therefore, the public has fewer choices and pays higher prices. As Chapter 3 emphasized, furthermore, most restrictions on entry cannot be justified by their tendency to protect the public against superior corporate power. Indeed, too often they reflect such power. However, the entry restrictions imposed on natural monopolies and "regulated industries" of all kinds, which involve special considerations of their own, are a partial exception to these generalizations.[87]

CONCLUSION

Until the 1960s, liberals could make a double-barreled assault on *Lochner*-era substantive due process. First, they could claim that the doctrine impeded Progressive social legislation crafted to protect powerless individuals against excessive corporate power and the dangers of an industrial society. In addition, they could maintain that substantive due process was an illegitimate assertion of judicial power because the original meaning of the due process clauses was procedural. Once the constitutional right of privacy and modern substantive due process took recognizable shape, liberals no longer could consistently advance this second argument. By now it is largely made by conservatives, some of whom like the old Court's economics but completely reject its conception of due process.

That conception, however, has more to recommend it than is commonly believed. For one thing, the original meaning of due process may not have been entirely procedural after all. (And if due process originally did have substantive content, that content clearly was economic.) The substantive due process decisions of the man thought to be the doctrine's most profound critic, Justice Oliver Wendell Holmes, Jr., never dispute the notion that due process has some substantive content. And his vastly overrated *Lochner* dissent provides few real reasons to reject a substantive reading of due process. Even if the due process clauses originally were 100 percent procedural, furthermore, that history does not necessarily bind us today. The injunction to follow text and history is not self-justifying; it requires a moral argument. But no such argument is an absolute. The result is that some especially important values might trump original intent on occasion. Among them, I think, is the freedom to pursue the trade, profession, or calling of one's choice.

NOTES

1. HADLEY ARKES, THE RETURN OF GEORGE SUTHERLAND: RESTORING A JURISPRUDENCE OF NATURAL RIGHTS 28 (1994).
2. 273 U.S. 418 (1927).
3. *Id.* at 429 (citation omitted).
4. Williams v. Standard Oil Co., 278 U.S. 235, 239 (1929). *See also* Ribnik v. McBride, 277 U.S. 350, 354–59 (1928), where it is unclear whether the claimant was deprived of property, liberty, or both.
5. 245 U.S. 60 (1917).
6. *Id.* at 74 (citation omitted).
7. Robert E. Riggs, *Substantive Due Process in 1791*, 1990 WIS. L. REV. 941, 944 n.20, provides a long list of standard sources making such arguments.
8. For some other scholars who argue that due process traditionally had a substantive component, see *id.* at 945–46 nn.21, 23–24.

9. *Id.* at 999; *see id.* at 947–48, 987.

10. *Id.* at 991–95, 999. The original version of this clause, Riggs says, read as follows: "No freeman shall be taken or [and] imprisoned or disseised or outlawed or exiled or in any way destroyed, nor will we go upon him nor send upon him, except by the lawful judgment of his peers or [and] the law of the land." *Id.* at 949. The brackets appear because the Latin word *vel* may be translated as either "and" or "or." *Id.* at 950.

11. *See id.* at 948–78.

12. *Id.* at 1001–2.

13. *Id.* at 1002. *See id.* at 978–87.

14. James W. Ely, Jr., *The Oxymoron Reconsidered: Myth and Reality in the Origins of Substantive Due Process*, 16 CONSTITUTIONAL COMMENTARY 315 (1999).

15. *Id.* at 319.

16. *See id.* at 320–27.

17. *See id.* at 327–42.

18. *See generally* John V. Orth, *Taking from A and Giving to B: Substantive Due Process and the Case of the Shifting Paradigm*, 14 CONSTITUTIONAL COMMENTARY 337 (1997) (viewing the taking-from-A-and-giving-to-B paradigm as central to the emergence of late-nineteenth-century substantive due process).

19. 1 S.C.L. (1 Bay) 252 (1792).

20. *Id.* at 254.

21. 15 N.C. 1 (1833).

22. *Id.* at 10.

23. *Id.* at 12.

24. *Id.* at 14–15.

25. *Id.* at 11.

26. 4 Hill 140 (N.Y. 1843).

27. *Id.* at 143.

28. *Id.* at 145.

29. *Id.*

30. *Id.* at 146.

31. *Id.* at 147.

32. 10 Tenn. 599 (1831).

33. *Id.* at 601.

34. *Id.* at 623 (editor's note).

35. *Id.* at 605.

36. *Id.* at 606.

37. *Id.*

38. *Id.* at 607.

39. Wayne McCormack, *Economic Substantive Due Process and the Right to Livelihood*, 82 KY. L.J. 397, 404 (1993–1994).

40. *See* Michael J. Phillips, *The Substantive Due Process Decisions of Mr. Justice Holmes*, 36 AM. BUS. L.J. 437 (1999) (containing a longer statement of the arguments made in Chapter 2).

41. *E.g.*, HOWARD GILLMAN, THE CONSTITUTION BESIEGED: THE RISE AND DEMISE OF *LOCHNER* ERA POLICE POWERS JURISPRUDENCE 131 (paperback ed. 1995).

42. Lochner v. New York, 198 U.S. 45, 75 (1905). The full dissent appears in

id. at 74–76. All subsequent quotations from Holmes's dissent appear within those pages.

43. PAUL KENS, JUDICIAL POWER AND REFORM POLITICS: THE ANATOMY OF *LOCHNER V. NEW YORK* 128 (1990).

44. G. EDWARD WHITE, JUSTICE OLIVER WENDELL HOLMES: LAW AND THE INNER SELF 320 (1993).

45. Adkins v. Children's Hosp., 261 U.S. 525, 568 (1923) (Holmes, J., dissenting).

46. Adair v. United States, 208 U.S. 161, 191 (1908) (Holmes, J., dissenting).

47. Lochner v. New York, 198 U.S. 45, 57–58 (1905).

48. *Id.* at 76 (Holmes, J., dissenting).

49. Ferguson v. Skrupa, 372 U.S. 726, 729 (1963).

50. *Id.* at 731–32 (quotations omitted).

51. North Dakota State Bd. of Pharmacy v. Snyder's Drug Stores, Inc., 414 U.S. 156, 165–66 (1973).

52. 278 U.S. 105 (1928).

53. 414 U.S. at 167.

54. 505 U.S. 833 (1992).

55. 300 U.S. 379 (1937).

56. 261 U.S. 525 (1923).

57. *Casey*, 505 U.S. at 861–62.

58. *Id.* at 862.

59. *Id.* at 864.

60. *Id.*

61. City of Cleburne v. Cleburne Living Center, 473 U.S. 432, 471 (1985) (Marshall, J., concurring and dissenting).

62. *See, e.g.*, THEODORE LOWI, THE END OF LIBERALISM: THE SECOND REPUBLIC OF THE UNITED STATES (2d ed. 1979). *See also* Jonathan R. Macey, *Some Causes and Consequences of the Bifurcated Treatment of Economic Rights and "Other" Rights under the United States Constitution*, 9 SOCIAL PHILOSOPHY & POLICY 141 (1992) (making much the same points from the perspective of public choice economics).

63. *See generally* ARTHUR SELWYN MILLER, THE MODERN CORPORATE STATE: PRIVATE GOVERNMENTS AND THE AMERICAN CONSTITUTION (1976).

64. *See* ARKES, *supra* note 1, at 81–118.

65. *E.g.*, MAX LERNER, THE MIND AND FAITH OF JUSTICE HOLMES 146–47 (1943).

66. *See generally* ROBERT H. BORK, THE TEMPTING OF AMERICA: THE POLITICAL SEDUCTION OF THE LAW ch. 7 (1990). For a shorter statement of these ideas, see Robert H. Bork, *The Constitution, Original Intent, and Economic Rights*, 23 SAN DIEGO L. REV. 823 (1986).

67. BORK, *supra* note 66, at 173.

68. *See* Michael J. Phillips, *Review and Commentary*, 28 AM. BUS. L.J. 499, 507–9 (1990) (reviewing *The Tempting*). As this discussion makes clear, Bork's "defense" of majoritarianism relies to a considerable degree on his ethical skepticism.

69. *See* BORK, *supra* note 66, at 155–59.

70. *Id.* at 158.

71. *Id.*

72. 381 U.S. 479 (1965).

73. Bork has since become a traditional moralist of a pronounced sort. *See* ROBERT H. BORK, SLOUCHING TOWARD GOMORRAH (1996).

74. BORK, *supra* note 66, at 242.

75. *Id.* at 254–56.

76. *Id.* at 258.

77. *See, e.g.*, LON L. FULLER, THE LAW IN QUEST OF ITSELF 121 (Beacon paperback ed. 1940) (stating but not accepting this argument).

78. BORK, *supra* note 66, at 258.

79. *Id.* at 259.

80. BERNARD WILLIAMS, MORALITY 20–21 (Canto paperback ed. 1993).

81. HENRY B. VEATCH, RATIONAL MAN: A MODERN INTERPRETATION OF ARISTOTELIAN ETHICS 41 (paperback ed. 1962). Veatch quotes Mussolini as saying that "there is nothing more relativistic than Fascist attitudes and activity." "From the fact that all ideologies are of equal value, that all ideologies are mere fictions, the modern relativist infers that everybody has the right to create for himself his own ideology and to attempt to enforce it with all the energy of which he is capable." Veatch's source for these quotations was HELMUT KUHN, FREEDOM FORGOTTEN AND REMEMBERED 17–18 (1943), which in turn apparently cited pages 374–77 of Mussolini's DIUTURNA.

82. Meyer v. Nebraska, 262 U.S. 390, 399 (1923).

83. Barsky v. Board of Regents, 327 U.S. 442, 472 (1954) (Douglas, J., dissenting).

84. Robert G. McCloskey, *Economic Due Process and the Supreme Court: An Exhumation and Reburial*, 1962 SUP. CT. REV. 34, 46.

85. The term "discrete and insular minorities" comes from Justice Stone's famous footnote in United States v. Carolene Prods. Co., 304 U.S. 144, 152–53 n.4 (1938).

86. *See* Michael J. Phillips, *Entry Restrictions in the* Lochner *Court*, 4 GEO. MASON L. REV. 405, 431–34 (1996).

87. For a brief discussion of those considerations, see *id.* at 409, 411.

Chapter 6

Summing Up and Looking Ahead

Very late in his life, Wittgenstein speculated whether "*all enquiry on our part* is set so as to exempt certain propositions from doubt, if they are ever formulated."[1] The clear inference was that the truth of such propositions is never brought into question: "They lie apart from the route travelled by inquiry."[2] The propositions comprising the consensus wisdom on *Lochner*-era substantive due process may not enjoy quite this degree of acceptance, but they come close. They form part of the toolkit of uncontested truths carried around by educated Americans. Just before I wrote this chapter, an article in a well-known neoconservative monthly forcefully reminded me of how entrenched these ideas remain. *Lochner* and like cases, the author maintained, suggest that "the Supreme Court did not think the New York legislature could regulate economic life at all."[3] That case, he continued, "threatened a wholesale takeover of political authority by the federal courts."[4]

These statements, particularly the first, are demonstrably false, but they continue to be widely believed. The same is true, albeit in lesser degree, for the whole body of beliefs forming the standard picture and the standard critique of *Lochner*-era substantive due process. This chapter begins by restating that picture and that critique and by showing how preceding chapters have undermined them. Then I speculate about why these illusions emerged and continue to persuade. After that, I take aim at another assumption whose acceptance is as widespread as it is unthinking: the notorious "double standard" under which "personal" rights gets considerable constitutional protection and economic rights relatively little. One conclusion from this attack is that, under the tests the Supreme Court uses to determine which rights are fundamental, some economic rights qualify. This leads into the chapter's concluding section, which considers how the nascent return of economic substantive due process might most profitably continue.

EVALUATING THE CONVENTIONAL WISDOM

As Chapter 1 approached the matter, the conventional wisdom about *Lochner*-era substantive due process has both descriptive and evaluative components, with the latter depending to some degree on the former. How accurate are this standard picture and standard critique? We begin with the conventional wisdom's descriptive component.

The Standard Picture

The standard picture of *Lochner*-era substantive due process is easily stated. Above all things, perhaps, it maintains that freedom of contract's insertion within Fifth and Fourteenth Amendment liberty was critical to the doctrine. This is apparent from the twenty or so cases that are thought to exemplify *Lochner*-era substantive due process, many of which were freedom-of-contract decisions. For the most part, these are high-visibility decisions in which the Court struck down social and economic regulations on due process grounds. Like *Lochner* itself, many of these decisions involved employment regulations apparently designed to protect workers against their employers' superior bargaining power. Overall, the standard picture continues, the old Court struck down some 200 laws on substantive due process grounds from the 1890s through the 1930s. Although it does not explicitly say so, the standard picture implies that the 180 cases it does not discuss resemble the twenty that it does. However, this consensus picture concedes that the old Court rejected more substantive due process claims than it granted. It also observes that some justices—notably Holmes and Brandeis—never accepted the dominant paradigms of their time and regularly dissented from decisions striking down substantive government action on due process grounds.

As Chapter 2 revealed, the standard picture of *Lochner*-era substantive due process bears at best a partial resemblance to the real thing. First, its claim that the old Court invalidated some 200 laws on substantive due process grounds simply is wrong. As the barest glance at the source commonly cited for the 200 figure should suggest,[5] the Court struck down 200-odd laws on *personal rights* (mainly Fourteenth Amendment) grounds from the 1890s through the 1930s. This includes, among other things, over thirty cases decided solely on equal protection grounds, nearly thirty procedural due process cases, and over twenty-five incorporation cases of various kinds. Indeed, only some fifty-six decisions struck down substantive government action on genuine substantive due process grounds: that is, only fifty-six did so by applying values native to due process. However, we might add to the list approximately fifty-four cases striking down utility rate orders and other regulations of businesses affected with a public interest. Technically, these decisions probably are best viewed as incorporating the takings clause within Fourteenth Amendment due process. But their practical importance and their apparent conformity to the stereotypes about *Lochner*-era substantive due process arguably justify their inclusion within that doctrine.

Our fifty-six- or 110-odd cases only partially resemble the twenty or so decisions thought to exemplify the *Lochner* era. For one thing, no more than fifteen of them were freedom-of-contract cases. Although they seem to bristle with social significance, furthermore, the "utility regulation" cases rarely get much mention in standard descriptions of the *Lochner* era. Perhaps this is because they arguably are takings cases in substance or because they involve deprivations of property. Of the approximately fifty-six decisions within the core of *Lochner*-era substantive due process, well over half also involve deprivations of property. These include over twenty relatively humdrum decisions involving such subjects as tort liability, tort remedies, taxation, and land use. Our fifty-six "core" decisions also include at least ten that involve liberties other than freedom of contract: specifically, occupational liberty and parental rights over the education and upbringing of children.

As noted earlier, the standard picture concedes that the old Court rejected more substantive due process claims than it granted, but it does not state the degree to which this was true. The omission is critical, for decisions denying a substantive due process attack considerably outnumbered those granting one. For the approximately fifty-four "utility" cases, claims rejected exceeded claims granted by about twenty-five percent. For the approximately fifty-six "core" cases, on the other hand, the ratio of claims rejected to claims granted was between 3.5 to 1 and 3.6 to 1. These ratios were even higher in contexts—such as employment, business regulation, and police power matters generally—thought to exemplify *Lochner*-era substantive due process.

Despite his reputation as the Great Dissenter, finally, Holmes participated in much of *Lochner*-era substantive due process during the thirty years he spent on the Court. So far as I am aware, he never refused to give due process a substantive reading. More importantly, he joined most of the "utilities" cases striking down government action during the years from 1902 to 1932 and something like half of the "core" cases that did so over the period. On a few occasions, he even joined or wrote a freedom-of-contract case striking down government action.

The Standard Critique

The failures of the standard picture weaken the standard evaluative critique of *Lochner*-era substantive due process, which of course is a composite that few people embrace in full. The main body of that critique rests on the perception that the emergence of large corporations late in the nineteenth century created inequalities of bargaining power and conditions of dependency that required government regulation to protect weaker parties. Substantive due process, the critique continues, imperiled such legislation. According to some people, this was due to the conscious efforts of pro-business justices. To others, it was due to their nostalgic and unintelligent attachment to outdated laissez-faire ideas. Either way, *Lochner*-era substantive due process was a significant threat to vitally necessary social legislation. It also was an erroneous and illegitimate reading of the due process clauses—one that offended democracy by letting judges usurp legislative powers. Today the first two arguments tend to be made by liberals, and the last argument by certain conservatives.

Chapter 2's findings have few implications for the argument that *Lochner*-era substantive due process threatened democratic values. However, its various ratios of unsuccessful to successful substantive due process challenges make clear that the old Court deferred to legislatures much more than is generally realized. Those ratios also have implications for the other two arguments against *Lochner*-era substantive due process. They demonstrate that the doctrine was less of a threat to social legislation than most believe. At the very least, they also suggest that the old Court was not entirely a tool of the business class. Another way in which Chapter 2 undermines these last two arguments is through the classes of *Lochner*-era substantive due process cases it identifies. Some, indeed many, of these decisions simply do not involve social legislation designed to protect people against superior corporate power or the hazards of industrialization. Examples include the familial rights cases (*Pierce v. Society of Sisters* and *Meyer v. Nebraska*), some of the tax cases, the land-use cases, and above all, the entry restriction decisions.

Chapters 2, 3, and 4 also attacked the standard critique on various other grounds. The "class legislation" hypothesis, which despite its difficulties has some explanatory power, explicitly argues against the claim that the old Court was business's conscious agent. So does the simplest and most obvious explanation for *Lochner*-era substantive due process: that it expressed the justices' devotion to individual liberty. As Chapter 4 argued at length, furthermore, the whole argument that *Lochner*-era substantive due process ratified superior private power is less compelling than many believe. The conditions under which unequal bargaining power exists are less numerous than the standard critique would have it. Some of the famous cases thought to involve superior bargaining power in fact did not. Indeed, some of those cases involve laws that look suspiciously like class legislation. All these considerations weaken both the agent-of-business theory and the notion that the old Court supported business out of ignorant nostalgia for a departed era of laissez-faire.

Finally, the originalist or interpretivist argument against *Lochner*-era substantive due process is less impressive than its proponents think. Contrary to widespread belief, the original meaning of due process may not be entirely procedural. This is suggested by the fact that even Holmes had no objection to substantive due process as such. (And his vastly overrated *Lochner* dissent provided little independent reason to reject the doctrine.) Even if due process originally was entirely procedural, it is difficult to absolutize the democratic values that usually underlie originalism. For this reason, concerns other than original intent sometimes may legitimately influence judges in constitutional cases. Among them, I think, are at least some economic rights.

EXPLAINING THE CONVENTIONAL WISDOM

According to Melvin Urofsky, the early twentieth-century Progressive agenda involved

> minimum standards to reduce the incidence of child labor; maximum hours for women and children and for men employed in dangerous occupations; payment of wages in cash, to eliminate the abuses of the scrip system and company store; establishment of a minimum wage, first for women and children, and then for men; elimination of employers' common law defenses against liability for job-related accidents; creation of workmen's compensation plans to insure against death and disability in the factory; and laws supporting labor's right to organize and bargain collectively.[6]

As Chapter 2 made clear, except for the minimum wage and a few laws favoring unions, the *Lochner* Court upheld the measures implementing this agenda when they were challenged on substantive due process grounds. From this, one might expect it to receive at least a passing grade on the Progressive report card. Instead, the old Court has regularly been attacked as, either by ignorance or design, a consistent foe of government regulation, a friend of business, and/or an enemy of the disadvantaged. Central to such mischaracterizations is the systematic denial or suppression of evidence that contradicts them. For instance, how often is it observed that the old Court rejected over fifteen substantive due process challenges to workers' compensation laws and other measures regulating recovery for on-the-job injuries?[7]

These observations raise an obvious question. Why has *Lochner*-era substantive due process been so systematically misrepresented for so long? Among the few people who have bothered to address this question, Progressivism is the usual culprit. The Progressives, James W. Ely, Jr. recently remarked, "championed greater governmental intervention in American life and constructed a version of constitutional history serviceable for their purpose."[8] One element in that history, of course, was the idea that Progressive social legislation was motivated solely by the desire to protect dependent individuals against the vicissitudes of industrialization and the depredations of business. Another was the depiction of the *Lochner* Court as a tool of the corporate class. Yet another was the near-deification of Holmes and Brandeis.

An additional component of the Progressive version of constitutional history is one that this book has not previously developed. As Chapters 2 and 5 made clear, the charge that the old Court exceeded its constitutional authority originally came from liberals and Progressives. In their hands, it had a corollary: that in rejecting substantive due process, the Court was returning to its previous posture of judicial deference to government. According to Morton Horwitz, the "constitutional revolution of 1937 was justified not as a powerful break with the old order but as a conservative restoration of neutral constitutional principles that had supposedly been thrown overboard by the *Lochner* Court."[9] This, he made plain, was due largely to "the legitimating needs of the New Deal."[10] Indeed, "[f]or the past fifty years, a symbiotic relationship has existed between constitutional legitimation of the New Deal and delegitimation of the *Lochner* Court."[11]

It is not this book's aim to evaluate this last component of the Progressive story. In arguing for it, though, Horwitz advances what seems to me a dubious accompaniment. Originally, he argues, the Progressive attack on Lochnerism was two-pronged, stressing both the deference/neutrality arguments just stated and the idea that the rise of corporate power forever doomed freedom of contract.[12] However, because "[i]t is more difficult to justify a constitutional revolution on substantive than on procedural grounds," the first argument came to predominate.[13] But as Chapter 1 made clear, the "substantive" critique of *Lochner*-era substantive due process remains very much alive today. Indeed, by now it is all that contemporary liberal critics of *Lochnerism* have left. As creators of modern substantive due process, they hardly are in a position to extol judicial deference and restraint.

No doubt the legitimizing needs of the Progressives go a considerable way toward explaining why *Lochner*-era substantive due process has been so misrepresented for so long. As it stands, however, I wonder whether that explanation renders these people too self-consciously cynical. For that reason, I will try to supplement it with another. I begin with the following statement from Benjamin N. Cardozo, whose topic was the divisions on the Court during the 1920s.

> On the one hand, the right of property . . . was posited as permanent and absolute. Impairment was not to be suffered except within narrow limits of history and precedent. No experiment was to be made along new lines of social betterment. The image was a perfect sphere. The least dent or abrasion was a subtraction from its essence. Given such premises, the conclusion is inevitable. The statute becomes an illegitimate assault upon rights assured to the individual against the encroachments of society. The method of logic or philosophy is at work in all its plenitude. The opposing view, if it is to be accepted, must be reached through other avenues of approach. The right which the assailants of the statute posit as absolute or permanent is conceived of by the supporters of the statute as conditioned by varying circumstances of time and space and environment and degree.[14]

If this passage accurately described the old Court's conservatives, little social legislation would have survived a substantive due process attack during the *Lochner* era. But as we know, most such laws did survive. Furthermore, it is evident from Chapter 2 that the *Lochner* Court did not absolutize property rights and was not invariably hostile to social experiments.

As a longtime New York Court of Appeals Justice at the time he wrote the previous passage, Cardozo had to know that social legislation usually survived a substantive due process challenge. So why did he describe the old Court's conservatives as laissez-faire ideologues? Maybe he viewed this as a Noble Lie that was necessary to advance Progressive ideals, but this seems unlikely of a man so routinely described as saintly. (Or should that description put us on our guard?) But if Cardozo genuinely believed his words, what can account for that belief?

My answer to this question begins with a trite observation: that the Old Court did sometimes strike down government action on substantive due process grounds. That fact alone might be thought to justify Cardozo's portrayal. This would be the case if, for example, such measures were so self-evidently desirable that only the corrupt, the unintelligent, the deluded, or the hopelessly ideological could find fault with them. One might wonder how many of the regulations the old Court struck down really meet this description; for example, even minimum-wage and maximum-price laws remain controversial to this day. However, I will waive this point and repair to another. Some of the measures the old Court struck down on substantive due process grounds, most notably the entry restrictions it invalidated, are not easy to defend. Yet sometimes Progressives and their sympathizers did defend them. Consider, for example, Brandeis's ludicrous suggestions that the special-interest legislation struck down in *New State Ice Co. v. Liebmann* was an experiment, that the legislature enacting it was a laboratory of democracy, and that the industry pressing for its enactment was acting to advance the public good. His position is explicable, I think, only on the assumption that regulation is—or at least is presumptively—a good thing irrespective of its content.

My explanation for the Progressives' extreme portrayals of the old Court, then, is not that it habitually struck down laws regulating social and economic matters but that it did so at all. This of course presupposes that these people had a strong attachment to government regulation. Because some of that regulation was less than self-evidently good, and because the Progressives seemed not to grant or recognize this, we can speculate that their attachment was strong indeed. What might explain that strong attachment? The likeliest possibility, I think, is that the Progressives had an almost-religious faith in the social sciences and in government's ability to improve society through regulations applying social science knowledge. Brandeis's dissent in *New State Ice Co. v. Liebmann* provides an example that is all the more persuasive because of the way his enthusiasm for government experimentation overcomes his doubts about the social sciences. "The economic and social sciences," he admitted, "are largely uncharted seas."[15] "Yet," he continued,

> the advances in the exact sciences and the achievements in invention remind us that the seemingly impossible sometimes happens. There are many men now living who were in the habit of using the age-old expression: "It is as impossible as flying." The discoveries in physical science, the triumphs in invention, attest the value of the process of trial and error. In large measure, these advances have been due to experimentation.[16]

From all this, it naturally followed that the states should be laboratories of democracy and that the Fourteenth Amendment should be construed so as to permit their experiments.

If my surmise is accurate, Cardozo's passage better describes *the Progressives* than it does their foes on the Supreme Court. In other words, it was the Progressives who possessed the "perfect sphere" whose "least dent or abrasion was a subtraction from its essence." That perfect sphere was unfettered government power to regulate social and economic matters, and any substantive due process decision restraining that power was a dent or abrasion subtracting from its essence. Thus, it did not matter that the old Court had upheld most of the social legislation challenged on substantive due process grounds. Because the need for regulation was obvious to any thinking person, furthermore, the relatively few decisions striking it down could only spring from corruption, ignorance, or ideological passion.

THE DUBIOUS DOUBLE STANDARD

One component in the Progressive portrayal of the *Lochner* Court was that, in rejecting substantive due process, the modern Court was returning to a tradition of judicial neutrality and judicial restraint. Although this book does not pursue the subject, Chapter 5 provided some reason to wonder whether the Progressives had their history right. More importantly, the modern Court's commitment to judicial restraint did not endure indefinitely. In fact, it arguably did not endure past a 1938 substantive due process case. *United States v. Carolene Products Co.*[17] upheld the federal Filled Milk Act of 1923, which prohibited the interstate shipment of skimmed milk compounded with any fat or oil other than milk fat. As Geoffrey P. Miller has argued in some detail, the act "was an utterly unprincipled example of special interest legislation."[18] Its main target was canned skimmed milk laced with coconut oil, which was cheaper than canned milk containing milk fat. For that reason, such "filled milk" disadvantaged those segments of the dairy industry that stood to lose from a lower price for milk fat, and these interests were a major force behind the legislation. One of *Carolene Products'* legacies, Miller concluded, was "the unrivaled primacy of interest groups in American politics of the last half-century."[19] But maybe that statement is unfair to the modern Court, for its predecessor did no better. In a highly deferential 1919 Holmes opinion, the old Court rejected a Fourteenth Amendment attack on a state measure that resembled the Filled Milk Act.[20]

The principal legacy of *Carolene Products*, however, lay in another direction entirely. In the due process portion of his opinion, Justice Stone declared that "the existence of facts supporting the legislative judgment is to be presumed, for regulatory legislation affecting ordinary commercial transactions is not to be pronounced unconstitutional unless in light of the facts made known or generally assumed it is of such a character as to preclude the assumption that it rests upon some rational basis within the knowledge and experience of the legislators."[21] This meant that substantive due process review of such legislation was to be weak indeed. Perhaps to dispel the impression that all government action would enjoy a similar presumption of constitutionality, Stone immediately added his famous footnote 4. In it, he said that tougher scrutiny might be applied when the challenged law offended a specific provision of the Constitution; when it restricted the political processes in matters such as voting, speech, political organization, and peaceable assembly; or when it discriminated against particular religious, national, or racial minorities. Then Stone elaborated on the last category by suggesting that "prejudice against discrete and insular minorities may be a special condition, which tends seriously to curtail the operation of those political processes ordinarily to be relied upon to protect minorities, and which may call for a correspondingly more searching judicial inquiry."[22] As Miller observes, today footnote 4 "is widely honored as a cornerstone of constitutional law."[23] This is primarily because it so accurately foretold the future. In Miller's words, "the footnote is seen as paving the way for a two-tiered system of constitutional review in which individual rights are afforded greater protection than so-called economic liberties."[24] In other words, footnote 4 signaled the emergence of the double standard referred to throughout this book.

The Double Standard and "Discrete and Insular Minorities"

Today the double standard is so much a part of the air we breathe that scarcely anyone feels the need to defend it. Perhaps this is fortunate for contemporary liberals, since the defense is not an easy one to make. One problem with the differential treatment of economic and "personal" rights is that the criteria justifying enhanced constitutional protection for the latter sometimes sweep in the former along with them. As detailed in the next section, the most important example concerns the tests the Supreme Court purportedly uses to determine which substantive due process rights are fundamental. But footnote 4's emphasis on the political powerlessness of "discrete and insular minorities" provides another example. As Robert McCloskey observed some years ago, "[I]t is not clear why the thrust of this point should be restricted to ethnic and religious minorities."[25] For all the reasons developed in Chapter 3, the point obviously extends to the people denied the pursuit of a trade by restrictions on entry. "[T]he scattered individuals who are denied access to an occupation by State-enforced barriers are about as impotent a minority as can be imagined." Because they typically have a degree of internal cohesion, even minority racial and religious groups often exert some political influence. But "[n]ot so the isolated economic man who belongs to no identifiable group at all."

The Double Standard and Fundamental Rights

As I suggested in Chapter 5, due process may well be substantive under originalist criteria. In addition, the cases supporting that interpretation of due process almost invariably involve property rights. This suggests that if original intent is our guide, economic rights might be at the core of substantive due process. Were that the case, and were other interpretive strategies denied them, modern liberals essentially would have to use *Lochner* to justify *Roe*. In that unfortunate event, they doubtless would argue that whatever criteria justify enhanced protection for economic rights also justify such protection for so-called personal rights. In the process, they might well complain about an arbitrary "double standard" under which economic rights get considerable constitutional protection and "personal" rights little or none. And they might be right to do so. To see why, we begin with the standard criteria for determinating which due process rights are fundamental and thus get enhanced constitutional protection.

The dominant means of identifying fundamental rights during the 1970s, 1980s, and 1990s has been an approach I call the "tradition of ordered liberty" test. Echoing earlier decisions,[26] Chief Justice Rehnquist recently stated that "the Due Process Clause specially protects those fundamental rights and liberties which are, objectively, deeply rooted in this Nation's history and tradition" and "implicit in the concept of ordered liberty."[27] For the most part, these cases seem to have emphasized the "tradition" component of this test over its "ordered liberty" component. But traditions are not static; as Justice Harlan once remarked, the American tradition "is a living thing," and the balance between liberty and authority established by due process reflects "the traditions from which [the country] developed as well as the traditions from which it broke."[28] Over the course of American history, some rights obviously have waxed in importance over time while others have waned. This raises a question: Should the "tradition of ordered liberty" approach emphasize "old" rights over "new" ones; should it stress "new" rights over "old"; or should it require that, to be fundamental, a right must have enjoyed continuous acceptance over time? Because economic rights were more highly favored before the 1930s than they are today, this question obviously is important for determining the degree of substantive due process protection they deserve.

One recent application of the "tradition of ordered liberty" test emphasized continuity. In *Washington v. Glucksberg*,[29] the Court upheld a state ban on assisted suicide. Considering whether due process liberty includes a right to commit suicide that in turn includes a right to assistance in committing suicide, Chief Justice Rehnquist concluded that "we are confronted with a consistent and almost universal tradition that has long rejected the asserted right, and continues explicitly to reject it today, even for terminally ill, mentally competent adults."[30] Rehnquist's discussion of that tradition, however, definitely emphasized old sources over new.[31] For the most part, those sources were eighteenth- and nineteenth-century state statutes banning suicide or assisted suicide.

Earlier "tradition of ordered liberty" cases went further in emphasizing past expressions of the American tradition over its more recent manifestations. In *Moore v. City of East Cleveland*,[32] which might be read as expanding freedom of choice in marriage and family life to include extended families, Justice Powell emphasized that such relationships, while perhaps on the wane today, have deep roots in the American tradition.

> Ours is by no means a tradition limited to respect for the bonds uniting the members of the nuclear family. The tradition of uncles, aunts, cousins, and especially grandparents sharing a household along with parents and children has roots equally venerable and equally deserving of constitutional recognition. Over the years millions of our citizens have grown up in just such an environment, and most, surely, have profited from it. Even if conditions of modern society have brought about a decline in extended family households, they have not erased the accumulated wisdom of civilization, gained over the centuries and honored throughout our history, that supports a larger conception of the family.[33]

Using some form of enhanced scrutiny, the Court then struck down a Cleveland ordinance limiting occupancy of a dwelling unit to one family and defining the term "family" narrowly.

In *Bowers v. Hardwick*,[34] the question for the Court was whether there is a fundamental due process right to engage in consensual homosexual sodomy. Writing for a 5–4 majority voting to uphold a state sodomy statute, Justice White quickly concluded that no such right exists because the states have traditionally outlawed sodomy and many continue to do so.

> Proscriptions against that conduct [consensual homosexual sodomy] have ancient roots. Sodomy was a criminal offense at common law and was forbidden by the laws of the original 13 States when they ratified the Bill of Rights. In 1868, when the Fourteenth Amendment was ratified, all but 5 of the 37 States in the Union had criminal sodomy laws. In fact, until 1961, all 50 States outlawed sodomy, and today, 24 States and the District of Columbia continue to provide criminal penalties for sodomy performed in private and between consenting adults. Against this background, to claim that a right to engage in such conduct is "deeply rooted in this Nation's history and tradition" or "implicit in the concept of ordered liberty" is, at best, facetious.[35]

However, White did not consider one implication of his statement that half the states continued to ban sodomy during the mid-1980s: While the ban's roots no doubt were deep, the plant they supported had withered considerably.

By so emphasizing the old over the new, White might be thought to have opened the door for economic substantive due process in *Bowers v. Hardwick*.[36] Against this, it can be argued that White's focus on positive law largely negates any such claim, because regulations restricting economic rights have been common events for all of this century. Against a claim that any economic right is fundamental, that is, one could produce hundreds (or thousands) of regulations restricting that right over time. This reply, however, points to a problem with the "tradition of ordered liberty" approach: In its effort to avoid judicial subjectivity, it often tests existing legislation by its conformity to past or existing legislation. This coexists uneasily with the idea that the Constitution's individual rights guarantees are supposed to check legislative activity and that those guarantees become most important precisely when legislatures are malfunctioning most badly.

In any event, the previous argument does not apply to Powell's statement in *Moore*, which did not rely on positive law. That statement's reasoning seems to cover economic rights. "Even if conditions of modern society have brought about more regulation and diminished protection for economic rights," one might say, "they have not erased the accumulated wisdom of civilization, gained over the centuries and honored throughout our history, that supports the intrinsic importance of economic liberty, its contribution to other liberties, and its tendency to promote economic abundance."

The preceding discussion, I think, pushes in two directions. First, it suggests that under what seems to be the dominant test for determining which due process liberties are fundamental, economic rights have some claim to that status. Second, that test is anything but simple to apply. Worse still, efforts to lessen its subjectivity effectively test a positive law's constitutionality by resort to other positive law. However, there is another set of criteria for determining which due process liberties are fundamental. Because those criteria do not resort to positive law and indeed are ethical in nature, they clearly avoid the second problem with the tradition of ordered liberty approach. And because these tests have been most often advanced by the Court's liberals, principally Justices Blackmun and Souter, one would think that they render economic rights nonfundamental as well. In fact, however, they do exactly the opposite.

Our second set of standards is highly libertarian. Perhaps the best example[37] is the opinion of the Court authored by Justices Kennedy, O'Connor, and Souter in a 1992 abortion case.[38] While expatiating on due process liberty early in that opinion, they itemized the areas in which government regulation has attracted stringent review: marriage, procreation, contraception, family relationships, child rearing, and education. "Our cases," they elaborated, "recognize the right of the *individual*, married or single to be free from unwarranted government intrusion into matters so fundamentally affecting a person as the decision whether to bear or beget a child." "These matters," our Republican-appointed plurality continued, "involving the most intimate and personal choices a person may make in a lifetime, choices central to personal dignity and autonomy, are central to the liberty protected by the Fourteenth Amendment." Then came the finale: "At the heart of liberty is the right to define one's own concept of existence, of meaning, of the universe, and of the mystery of human life." A similar remark occurred after the justices began to apply these criteria to a woman's decision to terminate her pregnancy. "The destiny of the woman," they said, "must be shaped to a large extent on her own conception of her spiritual imperatives and her place in society."

It seems, then, that fundamental due process rights involve matters that fundamentally affect a person, are intimate and personal, are central to personal dignity and autonomy, and reflect one's own conception of life's meaning and one's place in society. Except perhaps for the squishy "intimacy" criterion, these standards obviously justify enhanced constitutional protection for some, perhaps many, economic rights. Here, I primarily limit myself to the clearest example: the right to pursue the trade, profession, business, or avocation of one's choice. As we have seen at various points, this right has long been infringed by restrictions on entry to a business or occupation. The modern Court has almost invariably rejected due process challenges to these entry restrictions.[39] The *Lochner* Court, however, sometimes struck them down.[40] Under the libertarian criteria announced by some members of the modern Court, the old Court's conservatives plainly were right to do so.

For most people, the freedom to choose one's life's work is at least as important an expression of "autonomy" as, say, the right to abort a fetus. Indeed, for approximately half the population liberty of occupation almost certainly is more important. It goes without saying that the exercise of this right "fundamentally affects" a person and goes some way toward determining his "place in society." For these reasons, the right just as obviously is "central to personal dignity." In addition, occupational freedom is at least as central to most lives as some other rights cherished by liberals. As Robert McCloskey once remarked, most people probably would feel that liberty of occupation is at least as important to them as the right to speak freely.[41]

How might liberals respond to the preceding argument? One possibility, a possibility perhaps suggested by that word "intimate," is to argue that marriage, procreation, contraception, family relationships, and child rearing deserve greater constitutional protection because they involve the more affective, feeling, nicer side of our nature and hence are of the utmost intrinsic importance. Freedom of occupation, on the other hand, often finds expression in crass, self-seeking business ventures. But this response obviously is vulnerable to charges of elitist arbitrariness. As McCloskey put it, the claim that "personal" rights deserve considerable constitutional protection while economic rights deserve relatively little has "the smell of the lamp about it: it may reflect the tastes of the judges and dons who advance it, rather than the real preferences of the commonality of mortals."[42] More importantly, the claim is utterly at odds with the extreme individualism of our second justification for fundamental rights. The justices making that claim extol autonomy in the strongest terms while simultaneously arguing that certain expressions of autonomy are more important and deserve more constitutional protection than others. But one of the central tenets of modern liberalism, we are continually told, is that government should be neutral among different conceptions of the good life.[43]

The dilemma just posed, I think, derives from liberals' desire to use due process for the advancement of nontraditional liberties that are more or less sexual in nature. Justifying such rights requires a highly libertarian theory, and such a theory also supports economic rights. Conceivably the problem might be solved by invoking John Stuart Mill's well-known test for defining the proper scope of government activity.[44] Mill's "one very simple principle" was that "the sole end for which mankind are warranted, individually or collectively, in interfering with the liberty of action of any of their number, is self-protection." By self-protection Mill clearly meant "harm to others." To elaborate, "the only part of the conduct of anyone, for which he is amenable to society, is that which concerns others. In the part which merely concerns himself, his independence is, of right, absolute." Mill's "simple principle," then, involved a distinction between self-regarding and other-regarding actions. As countless writers have observed, the distinction often is difficult to draw in practice. To the extent that it can be drawn, it might well justify the suppression of many economic rights. But it might also negate much of the Supreme Court's "fundamental rights" jurisprudence. Maybe contraception and some family relationships are sufficiently "private" to be classed as self-regarding, but since when are marriage, procreation, abortion, and child rearing matters of indifference to society at large?

Perhaps the most persuasive argument for the double standard resembles Mill's position in that it stresses the harm economic rights can cause other parties. Here, though, the other party is not society as a whole but the specific people with whom the right-holder deals. This is the familiar argument that, regardless of their intrinsic importance, economic liberties are illusory for the weaker party in a world filled with large corporations that possess superior bargaining power. Laurence Tribe may have had something like this in mind when he argued that "*Lochner*'s downfall did not represent a denigration of economic liberties but a recognition that such liberties were not meaningfully protected by the 'free' market, at least for those who were more its victims than its masters."[45] But as Chapter 4 argued at length, this standard argument packs considerably less punch than is commonly believed even when applied to freedom of contract. More importantly, we saw in Chapter 3 that the argument has no application to entry restrictions. Rather than counteracting superior private power, that is, some of the laws at issue in the Court's entry restriction cases reflected such power. Needless to say, they also restricted freedom of occupation.

THE FUTURE OF ECONOMIC SUBSTANTIVE DUE PROCESS

Contemporary judges almost never pause to justify the double standard. As Chapter 2 demonstrated, however, courts increasingly are acting as if the inconsistency bothers them. I refer to the slow revival of economic substantive due process sketched in that chapter.[46] Actually, this revival appears much less a reaction to the double standard than a pragmatic response to particular governmental abuses. But maybe the loosening of judicial inhibitions brought about by the "personal rights" component of modern substantive due process helped courts act in the economic realm too. In all likelihood, the new economic substantive due process has attained sufficient critical mass to continue. On that assumption, this book concludes by considering in general terms how the doctrine might best evolve. To a surprising degree, I conclude, it should proceed along lines set by the old Court.

The Standards of Review

Although this book is not a critique of modern substantive due process, the previous section revealed some problems with the fundamental rights branch of that doctrine. Perhaps the most obvious is the justices' disagreement about the criteria for determining which rights are fundamental. Only slightly less obvious, if rather more serious, are the vacuity and manipulability of those criteria. Because laws that restrict fundamental rights get full strict scrutiny and laws restricting nonfundamental rights get much less stringent review,[47] modern substantive due process resembles an on-off switch. Consider, for example, the federal court decisions rejecting privacy challenges to state restrictions on the practice of midwifery.[48] Such cases effectively say that while the rights to marry, have children, use contraception, and abort a fetus are fundamental, and laws restricting those rights get the most searching review, a woman's right to choose a midwife rather than an obstetrician is nonfundamental and state restrictions on it only receive rational basis review. The same is true for another substantive due process claim commonly made in these cases: the midwives' occupational freedom challenge.

Lochner-era substantive due process lacked conceptual beauty, but at least it usually avoided problems of the kind just mentioned. The old Court applied a smorgasbord of standards and nonstandards when government action was challenged on due process grounds, but never to my recollection did it require that laws restricting economic rights be "necessary" to achieve a "compelling" government purpose or anything of the kind. In this respect, as in its ratio of successful to unsuccessful substantive due process claims, the supposedly doctrinaire and extremist *Lochner* Court in fact was considerably more moderate than its modern counterpart. The same, however, cannot always be said of the various proposals for reviving economic substantive due process.[49] The view advanced here is that modern courts should imitate the old Court by applying standards of only moderate stringency. Although it is not my aim to specify such tests in detail, the main example before my mind is a some relatively nondeferential form of rational basis review.

One argument for tough substantive due process review of economic regulations was made in the previous section. As we have seen, at least one economic right—liberty of occupation—arguably qualifies as fundamental under the various criteria employed by the modern Court. Due to the various problems they present, however, it is doubtful whether America needs more fundamental substantive due process rights. The other arguments against stringent economic substantive due process review are very familiar. The most important of them, majoritarianism, figured prominently in Chapter 5. In arguing that democratic values do not inevitably trump substantive due process review of government action, I obviously was not denying their considerable importance. Strict economic substantive due process review also would test the courts' economic competence. In applying such review, courts might have to determine, for example, what ends of government are "compelling" and what means are "necessary" to their furtherance. As I have just argued, these sound like decisions we normally leave to legislatures. More important for present purposes, the "means" portion of this test sometimes will involve economic and other social science questions that are intractable in themselves and that most judges lack the skills to resolve in any event.[50] (And on economic questions, at least, the few knowledgeable judges may not agree.) The result is likely to be an incoherent body of decisions. And no doubt there would be many, many such cases. In a society as highly regulated as ours, stricter economic substantive due process review of government action naturally will generate more litigation. Uncertainty in that body of law probably will generate even more. This can only exacerbate the caseload problems faced by the state and federal courts.

The Targets

"[O]nly if we think that government regulation is generally benevolent," Richard Epstein once wrote, will we be unconcerned with checking its power.[51] Epstein's words suggest a more or less utilitarian justification for protecting economic rights that emphasizes the harm their abandonment can cause rather than their intrinsic importance to individuals.[52] The latter approach, of course, dominated this chapter's previous section. What might the former look like? The developing body of modern economic substantive due process cases suggests one possibility. Those cases can be categorized according to the egregiousness of the government behavior they exhibit. Our new justification for economic substantive due process would urge that, in deciding when to intervene, courts emphasize the most egregious categories and the most egregious abuses within each category. This seems consistent with my previous suggestion that modern economic substantive due process review should tend toward leniency without being utterly toothless. The aim is that courts eliminate the worst abuses of government power, without entangling themselves in matters that strain their capacity and their legitimacy.

The least objectionable abuses of government power, perhaps, are those involving government irrationality. Chapter 2's discussion of the punitive damages award in *BMW v. Gore* provides one example. Some land-use regulation cases also qualify.[53] In *Pitoco v. Harrington*[54] for example, the Rhode Island Supreme Court held that a substantive due process claim might lie where a public official denies a building permit for reasons other than those stated in the relevant ordinance. There the plaintiff landowner was denied the permit because he moved heavy construction equipment onto his property after his house had burned down and he tried to rebuild. Apparently this violated a zoning ordinance, but under local law the violation was no reason for denying a building permit. Indeed, one of the individual defendants later conceded as much.

Next up the egregiousness scale are regulations that arguably assist mistreated or economically dependent groups, but do so by making isolated, politically vulnerable economic interests bear the cost. The *Seawall* case that opened this book provides one example, albeit an example that involved the Constitution's takings clause. Another example is furnished by some state cases striking down rent control ordinances.[55] Still another is rendered by two Washington cases striking down state and local laws that attempted to assist lower-income people by requiring that landlords provide tenants with relocation assistance upon the closing of a mobile home park or its conversion to another use.[56] The main point of these cases is that by so acting the government imposed on landowners costs that should more properly have been borne by society as a whole.

Laws like those just described might be described as class legislation, but the economic interests they benefit are at least somewhat broadly based and may have some claim to government's attention. This is not true once we move one step up the objectionability ladder—to laws that benefit fairly discrete private economic interests at the expense of competitors, the public, and/or other interests. As I argued in Chapter 3, it is inaccurate to say that the *Lochner* Court was primarily concerned with laws of this kind. But maybe it ought to have been. Because class legislation of this kind is even more pervasive today, furthermore, maybe *it* should be the main target of a revived economic substantive due process. Imagine, if you will, a Cato Institute–certified Supreme Court taking aim on the Internal Revenue Code. But that pervasiveness also argues against the courts' undertaking the task. If they went after modern class legislation in a serious way, they would scarcely have time for anything else. As Judge Richard Posner observed in a 1992 case, taking economic substantive due process seriously might imperil much of the country's routine legislative product.[57] By now, in other words, much of that product is class legislation.

The decision in which Posner made his observation, however, suggests why it cannot be absolutized. Before the court in that case was an exemption from Multiemployer Pension Plan liability worded so as to exclude exactly one company. The exemption's sponsor was then-Senator Robert Dole.[58] More importantly, one general form of class legislation definitely deserves the attention of a revived economic substantive due process. I refer of course to restrictions on entry, which modern courts usually uphold against substantive due process challenges. As this book has ceaselessly argued, entry restrictions are suspect for two reasons. First, they restrict a right (occupational freedom) of considerable importance to the individual. Second, they often restrict competition. Of course, as the old Court's record suggests,[59] many entry restrictions can be justified. But some almost certainly cannot. Consider, for example, the laws at issue in *Ferguson v. Skrupa*[60] (which upheld a state law restricting the business of debt adjusting to lawyers) and *North Dakota State Board of Pharmacy v. Snyder's Drug Stores*[61] (which sustained a state law aimed at keeping chain stores out of the pharmacy business). Neither case attempted a serious substantive justification for the law it upheld.

This brings us to the most repellant kind of state misbehavior, a phenomenon I call government predation. Over the years, liberals have often argued that with the growth of large corporations private power has come to rival state power.[62] Here, though, this public-private blurring takes a different form—one in which the public organs of government become "privatized." This means that rather than pursuing some conception of the public good, government bodies seek their own self-aggrandizement instead. They do so, furthermore, with the assistance sovereign power provides. Chapter 2 discussed two important examples involving substantive due process. In one, the city of Philadelphia tried to improve its financial position by illicitly acquiring a private parking garage.[63] In another, a local government acquired private property by conditioning the provision of water service on the property's relinquishment.[64] Most readers probably can supply additional examples.

SOME CONCLUDING WORDS

Calls for greater economic activism by the judiciary usually inspire fears that courts will reenact the worst excesses of the *Lochner* era. But as this book has argued at length, those excesses were neither as numerous nor as excessive as advertised. Overall, the old Court rejected considerably more substantive due process challenges than it granted. Some of the latter cases, moreover, are far more defensible than current opinion allows. The major exceptions to these generalizations, perhaps, were the substantive due process decisions striking down minimum-wage laws and price regulations. But while this is not necessarily an argument for judicial intervention, even here the laws in question remain controversial among economists.

Another suggestion that economic substantive due process's revival need not lead to excess comes from *BMW v. Gore*, where the majority consisted of liberals and moderates, and the dissenters tended to be conservatives.[65] This inspires what may seem a strange suggestion: that maybe liberals ought to spearhead that revival. As a group, liberals have displayed few inhibitions about using judicial power to advance what they perceive to be good ends. But it is unlikely that the protection of economic rights will ever strike them as compelling. Thus, were they to embrace economic substantive due process, liberals most likely would deploy it only against the worst abuses of government power. This, of course, is much what I have just urged.

All things considered, though, my (relatively) happy consummation is unlikely. This is because it would force liberals to abandon some pleasing beliefs to which they are deeply attached. For instance, liberals would have to stop casting a blind eye on government's economic irrationality, partiality, and predatoriness. This, in turn, might make them doubt the state's ability to serve as a vehicle for enlightened reform. Such doubts, furthermore, might make liberals question their own importance in the scheme of things. Finally, liberals who embrace economic substantive due process would have to abandon Progressive myths about the old Court, with their standard list of familiar heroes and villains. Worst of all, they would have to admit that the ignorant reactionaries on the old Court knew things about business and government that they and their Progressive forebears were unwilling or unable to grasp.

NOTES

1. Ludwig Wittgenstein, On Certainty para. 88 (1969).
2. *Id.*

3. Peter W. Huber, *Guns, Tobacco, Big Macs—and the Courts*, COMMENTARY, June 1999, at 32, 36.

4. *Id.*

5. This is BENJAMIN F. WRIGHT, THE GROWTH OF AMERICAN CONSTITUTIONAL LAW (Phoenix paperback ed. 1967).

6. MELVIN I. UROFSKY, A MARCH OF LIBERTY: A CONSTITUTIONAL HISTORY OF THE UNITED STATES 543 (1988).

7. *See supra* notes 203–8 and accompanying text in Chapter 2.

8. James W. Ely, Jr., *Melville W. Fuller Reconsidered*, 1988 J. SUP. CT. HIST. 35, 36.

9. MORTON J. HORWITZ, THE TRANSFORMATION OF AMERICAN LAW 1870–1960: THE CRISIS OF LEGAL ORTHODOXY 7 (1992).

10. *Id.*

11. Morton J. Horwitz, *Republicanism and Liberalism in American Constitutional Thought*, 29 WM. & MARY L. REV. 57, 62 (1987).

12. *Id.* at 61.

13. *Id.* at 62–63.

14. BENJAMIN N. CARDOZO, THE GROWTH OF THE LAW 72–73 (1924).

15. *See* New State Ice Co. v. Liebmann, 285 U.S. 262, 310–11 (1932) (Brandeis, J., dissenting).

16. *Id.*

17. 304 U.S. 144 (1938).

18. Geoffrey P. Miller, *The True Story of* Carolene Products, 1987 SUP. CT. REV. 397, 398; *see id.* at 168–96.

19. *Id.* at 399.

20. Hebe Co. v. Shaw, 248 U.S. 297, 303–4 (1919). Because this case did not self-identify as a due process decision, it is not included in Chapter 2's totals.

21. 304 U.S. at 152.

22. *Id.* at 153 n.4.

23. Miller, *supra* note 18, at 166.

24. *Id.* at 165.

25. Robert G. McCloskey, *Economic Due Process and the Supreme Court: An Exhumation and Reburial*, 1962 SUP. CT. REV. 34, 50. The remaining quotations in this paragraph also come from page 50.

26. *E.g.*, Bowers v. Hardwick, 478 U.S. 186, 191–92 (1986); Moore v. City of East Cleveland, 431 U.S. 494, 503 (1977) (plurality opinion). *Cf.* Planned Parenthood of Southeast Pennsylvania v. Casey, 505 U.S. 833, 951–53 (1992) (Rehnquist, C.J., concurring and dissenting); Michael H. v. Gerald D., 491 U.S. 110, 122–23 (1989) (opinion of the Court) (rooted in history and tradition).

27. Washington v. Glucksberg, 521 U.S. 702, 720–21 (1997) (quotations and citations omitted).

28. Poe v. Ullman, 367 U.S. 497, 542–43 (1961) (Harlan, J., dissenting).

29. 521 U.S. 702 (1997).

30. *Id.* at 723.

31. *See id.* at 710–19. The same was true in Michael H. v. Gerald D., 491 U.S. 110 (1989), which upheld a California statute presuming the legitimacy of a child born of a woman who is cohabiting with her husband. There, Justice Scalia, joined for this purpose by three other justices, rejected an alleged natural father's

claim that he had a constitutionally protected liberty interest in his relationship with a child that he fathered with a woman who was married to another man. However, Scalia's opinion seems to conflate two different questions: (1) whether the claimed liberty interest exists and (2) whether such a liberty interest is fundamental.

32. 431 U.S. 494 (1977).

33. *Id.* at 504–5.

34. 478 U.S. 186 (1986).

35. *Id.* at 192–94.

36. In fact, however, he asserted the opposite. According to White, the Court is most vulnerable and comes closest to illegitimacy when it creates constitutional law with few roots in the Constitution's language or design. "That this is so," he continued, "was painfully demonstrated by the face-off between the Executive and the Court in the 1930's, which resulted in the repudiation of much of the substantive gloss that the Court had placed on the Due Process Clauses of the Fifth and Fourteenth Amendments." *Id.* at 194–95. That face-off, however, involved Congress's power under the Commerce, Tax, and Spending powers much more than it did substantive due process.

37. Other examples include: Planned Parenthood of Southeastern Pennsylvania v. Casey, 505 U.S. 833, 926–28 (1992) (Blackmun, J., concurring); Bowers v. Hardwick, 478 U.S. 186, 203–6 (1986) (Blackmun, J., dissenting).

38. Planned Parenthood of Southeastern Pennsylvania v. Casey, 505 U.S. 833 (1992). All the quotations in this paragraph come from *id.* at 851–52. Internal quotations and citations to other cases are omitted.

39. Michael J. Phillips, *Entry Restrictions in the* Lochner *Court*, 4 GEO. MASON L. REV. 405, 417–29 (1996).

40. *Id.* at 429–47. The most notable examples are New State Ice Co. v. Liebmann, 285 U.S. 262 (1932); and Louis K. Liggett Co. v. Baldridge, 278 U.S. 105 (1928).

41. McCloskey, *supra* note 25, at 46.

42. *Id.*

43. *E.g.*, Will Kymlicka, *Liberal Individualism and Liberal Neutrality*, in SHLOMO AVINERI & ANVER DE-SHALIT, COMMUNITARIANISM AND INDIVIDUALISM 165 (paperback ed. 1992).

44. John Stuart Mill, *On Liberty*, in UTILITARIANISM, LIBERTY, AND REPRESENTATIVE GOVERNMENT 95–96 (Everyman's ed. 1951). The following quotations from Mill appear on these pages.

45. LAURENCE A. TRIBE, AMERICAN CONSTITUTIONAL LAW 1374 (2d ed. 1988).

46. *See generally* Michael J. Phillips, *The Slow Return of Economic Substantive Due Process*, 49 SYRACUSE L. REV. 917 (1999).

47. Washington v. Glucksberg, 521 U.S. 702, 719–22 (1997).

48. *E.g.*, Lange-Kessler v. Department of Educ., 109 F.3d 137, 140–41 (2d Cir. 1997); Scammon v. New Jersey Bd. of Medical Exam'rs, 66 F.3d 639, 643–47 (3d Cir. 1995). *See also* Mitchell v. Clayton, 995 F.2d 772, 774–76 (7th Cir. 1993) (acupuncture).

49. *See, e.g.*, BERNARD H. SIEGAN, ECONOMIC LIBERTIES AND THE CONSTITUTION 324 (paperback ed. 1980) (laws restricting economic liberties should be constitutional only if they are substantially related to the achievement of important

government objectives); Ronald J. Krotoszynski, Jr., *Fundamental Property Rights*, 85 GEO. L.J. 555, 559 (1997) (certain property interests should be deemed fundamental, which means that government cannot unduly burden their enjoyment); Richard E. Levy, *Escaping* Lochner's *Shadow: Toward a Coherent Jurisprudence of Economic Rights*, 73 N.C. L. REV. 329, 422–25 (1995) (due process requires that government decisions be sustained by legitimate public purposes of sufficient weight to justify their impact on constitutionally protected interests); Guy Miller Struve, *The Less-Restrictive-Alternative Principle and Economic Due Process*, 80 HARV. L. REV. 1463, 1463 (1967) (economic regulations violate due process if government has a less restrictive alternative).

50. *E.g.*, Robert H. Bork, *The Constitution, Original Intent, and Economic Rights*, 23 SAN DIEGO L. REV. 823, 831 (1986); Antonin Scalia, *Economic Affairs as Human Affairs*, in JAMES A. DORN & HENRY G. MANNE (EDS.), ECONOMIC LIBERTIES AND THE JUDICIARY (1987).

51. Richard A. Epstein, *The Mistakes of 1937*, 11 GEO. MASON L. REV. 5, 20 (1988). On the approach to justifying economic rights sketched in the following sentences, see *id.* at 5–7.

52. *See id.* at 5–7.

53. On the modern economic substantive due process cases involving land-use regulation, see Phillips, *supra* note 46, at 927–34. Most of these cases exhibit a higher degree of government culpability than mere irrationality.

54. 707 A.2d 692, 695–97 (R.I. 1998).

55. *E.g.*, Adamson Cos. v. City of Malibu, 854 F. Supp. 1476, 1484–95 (C.D. Ca. 1994); Kavanu v. Santa Monica Rent Control Bd., 941 P.2d 851, 857, 861, 864–65 (Cal. 1997). *See* Phillips, *supra* note 46, at 945–46.

56. Guimont v. Clarke, 854 P.2d 1, 13–16 (Wash. 1993); Robinson v. City of Seattle, 830 P.2d 318, 330–31 (Wash. 1992) (involving other provisions besides tenant relocation, too). *See* Phillips, *supra* note 46, at 946–47. *See also* Sintra, Inc. v. City of Seattle, 829 P.2d 765, 776–78 (Wash. 1992) (housing preservation ordinance that imposed huge costs on building owner).

57. Central States, Southeast & Southwest Areas Pension Fund v. Lady Baltimore Foods, Inc., 960 F.2d 1339, 1342 (7th Cir. 1992).

58. Robbins v. Lady Baltimore Foods, Inc., 678 F. Supp. 1323, 1328 (N.D. Ill. 1987).

59. *See* Phillips, *supra* note 39, at 429–47 (reviewing the *Lochner* Court's entry restriction decisions, most of which upheld the challenged law).

60. 372 U.S. 726, 728–32 (1963).

61. 414 U.S. 156, 164–67 (1974).

62. *See, e.g.*, Arthur Selwyn Miller, *Toward "Constitutionalizing" the Corporation*, 80 W. VA. L. REV. 187, 200–203 (1978).

63. Parkway Garage, Inc. v. City of Philadelphia, 5 F.3d 685 (3d Cir. 1993).

64. Walz v. Town of Smithton, 46 F.3d 162 (2d Cir. 1995).

65. In that case, Justices Breyer, Souter, O'Connor, and Kennedy joined Justice Stevens's majority opinion, with Justices Scalia, Thomas, and Ginsburg dissenting.

Selected Bibiliography

BOOKS

Arkes, Hadley. *The Return of George Sutherland: Restoring a Jurisprudence of Natural Rights*. Princeton, NJ: Princeton University Press, 1994.

Bond, James E. *I Dissent: The Legacy of Justice James Clark McReynolds*. Fairfax, VA: George Mason University Press, 1992.

Bork, Robert H. *The Tempting of America: The Political Seduction of the Law*. New York: Free Press, 1990.

Currie, David P. *The Constitution in the Supreme Court: The Second Century, 1888–1986*. Chicago: University of Chicago Press, 1990.

Ely, James W., Jr. *The Chief Justiceship of Melville W. Fuller 1888–1910*. Columbia: University of South Carolina Press, 1995.

———. *The Guardian of Every Other Right: A Constitutional History of Property Rights*. 2d ed. New York: Oxford University Press, 1998.

Frankfurter, Felix. *Mr. Justice Holmes and the Supreme Court*. Cambridge, MA: Harvard University Press, 1938.

Gillman, Howard. *The Constitution Besieged: The Rise and Demise of* Lochner *Era Police Powers Jurisprudence*. Durham, NC: Duke University Press, 1993.

Kens, Paul. *Judicial Power and Reform Politics: The Anatomy of* Lochner v. New York. Lawrence: University Press of Kansas, 1990.

McCloskey, Robert G. *The American Supreme Court*. 2d rev'd ed. Chicago: University of Chicago Press, 1994.

Miller, Arthur Selwyn. *The Modern Corporate State: Private Governments and the American Constitution*. Westport, CT: Greenwood Press, 1976.

Paul, Arnold M. *Conservative Crisis and the Rule of Law: Attitudes of Bar and Bench, 1887–1895*. Ithaca, NY: Cornell University Press, 1960.

Siegan, Bernard H. *Economic Liberties and the Constitution*. Chicago: University of Chicago Press, 1980.

Twiss, Benjamin R. *Lawyers and the Constitution: How Laissez-Faire Came to the Supreme Court*. Princeton, NJ: Princeton University Press, 1942.

Urofsky, Melvin I. *A March of Liberty: A Constitutional History of the United States*. New York: Alfred A. Knopf, 1988.

White, G. Edward. *The American Judicial Tradition: Profiles of Leading American Judges*. New York: Oxford University Press, 1976.

Wright, Benjamin F. *The Growth of American Constitutional Law*. Chicago: University of Chicago Press, 1942; Phoenix Books ed., 1967.

ARTICLES

Arkes, Hadley. "Who's the Laissez-Fairest of Them All? The Tradition of Natural Rights in American Law." *Policy Review* 60 (1992): 78–85.

Barnett, Randy E. "Judicial Conservatism v. A Principled Judicial Activism." *Harvard Journal of Law & Public Policy* 10 (1987): 273–94.

Bork, Robert H. "The Constitution, Original Intent, and Economic Rights." *San Diego Law Review* 23 (1986): 823–32.

Brandeis, Louis D. "The Living Law." *Illinois Law Review* 10 (1916): 461–71.

Brown, Ray A. "Due Process of Law, Police Power, and the Supreme Court." *Harvard Law Review* 40 (1927): 943–68.

Bryden, David P. "Brandeis's Facts." *Constitutional Commentary* 1 (1984): 281–326.

Cushman, Barry. "Doctrinal Synergies and Liberal Dilemmas: The Case of the Yellow-Dog Contract." *Supreme Court Review* (1992): 235–93.

Ely, James W., Jr. "Melville W. Fuller Reconsidered." *Journal of Supreme Court History* (1988): 35–49.

———. "The Oxymoron Reconsidered: Myth and Reality in the Origins of Substantive Due Process." *Constitutional Commentary* 16 (1999): 315–45.

———. "The Railroad Question Revisited: *Chicago, Milwaukee & St. Paul Railway v. Minnesota* and Constitutional Limits on State Regulations." *Great Plains Quarterly* 12 (1992): 121–34.

Epstein, Richard A. "The Mistakes of 1937." *George Mason University Law Review* 11(1988): 5–20.

Frankfurter, Felix. "Hours of Labor and Realism in Constitutional Law." *Harvard Law Review* 29 (1916): 353–73.

Gellhorn, Walter. "The Abuse of Occupational Licensing." *University of Chicago Law Review* 44 (1976): 6–27.

Green, Mark, & Nader, Ralph. "Economic Regulation vs. Competition: Uncle Sam the Monopoly Man." *Yale Law Journal* 82 (1973): 871–89.

Hand, Learned. "Due Process of Law and the Eight-Hour Day." *Harvard Law Review* 21 (1908): 495–509.

Horwitz, Morton J. "Republicanism and Liberalism in American Constitutional Thought." *William & Mary Law Review* 29 (1987): 57–74.

Hovenkamp, Herbert. "The Political Economy of Substantive Due Process." *Stanford Law Review* 40 (1988): 379–447.

Kens, Paul. "The Source of a Myth: Police Powers of the States and Laissez-Faire Constitutionalism 1900–1937." *The American Journal of Legal History* 35 (1991): 70–97.

Krotoszynski, Ronald J., Jr. "Fundamental Property Rights." *Georgetown Law Journal* 85 (1997): 555–625.

Landes, Elisabeth M. "The Effect of State Maximum-Hours Laws on the Employment of Women in 1920." *Journal of Political Economy* 88 (1980): 476–95.

Les Benedict, Michael. "Laissez-Faire and Liberty: A Re-evaluation of the Meaning and Origins of Laissez-Faire Constitutionalism." *Law & History Review* 3 (1985): 293–331.

Levy, Leonard W. "Property as a Human Right." *Constitutional Commentary* 5 (1988): 169–84.

Macey, Jonathan R. "Some Causes and Consequences of the Bifurcated Treatment of Economic Rights and 'Other' Rights under the United States Constitution." *Social Philosophy & Policy* 9, no. 1 (1992): 141–70.

McCloskey, Robert G. "Economic Due Process and the Supreme Court: An Exhumation and Reburial." *Supreme Court Review* (1962): 34–62.

Miller, Geoffrey P. "The True Story of *Carolene Products*." *Supreme Court Review* (1987): 397–428.

Note, "Resurrecting Economic Rights: The Doctrine of Economic Due Process Reconsidered." *Harvard Law Review* 103 (1990): 119–39.

Phillips, Michael J. "Another Look at Economic Substantive Due Process." *Wisconsin Law Review* (1987): 265–324.

———. "Entry Restrictions in the *Lochner* Court." *George Mason Law Review* 4 (Spring 1996): 405–55.

———. "How Many Times Was *Lochner*-Era Substantive Due Process Effective?" *Mercer Law Review* 48 (1997): 1049–90.

———. "The Progressiveness of the *Lochner* Court." *Denver University Law Review* 75 (1998): 453–505.

———. "The Slow Return of Economic Substantive Due Process." *Syracuse Law Review* 49 (1999): 917–69.

———. "The Substantive Due Process Decisions of Mr. Justice Holmes." *American Business Law Journal* 36 (1999): 437–77.

Pierce, Richard J., Jr. "Public Utility Regulatory Takings: Should the Judiciary Attempt to Police the Political Institutions?" *Georgetown Law Journal* 77 (1989): 2031–77.

Porter, Mary Cornelia. "That Commerce Shall Be Free: A New Look at the Old Laissez-Faire Court." *Supreme Court Review* (1976): 135–59.

Posner, Richard A. "The Constitution as an Economic Document." *George Washington Law Review* 56 (1987): 4–38.

Post, Robert C. "Defending the Lifeworld: Substantive Due Process in the Taft Court Era." *Boston University Law Review* 78 (1998): 1489–1545.

Pound, Roscoe. "Liberty of Contract." *Yale Law Journal* 18 (1909): 454–87.

Rice, Roger L. "Residential Segregation by Law, 1910–1917." *Journal of Southern History* 34 (1968): 179–99.

Riggs, Robert E. "Substantive Due Process in 1791." *Wisconsin Law Review* (1990): 941–1004.

Scalia, Antonin. "Economic Affairs as Human Affairs." In *Economic Liberties and the Judiciary*, edited by James A. Dorn and Henry G. Manne. Fairfax, VA: George Mason University Press, 1987, 31–37.

Siegel, Stephen A. "*Lochner* Era Jurisprudence and the American Constitutional Tradition." *North Carolina Law Review* 70 (1991): 1–111.

———. "Understanding the *Lochner* Era: Lessons from the Controversy over Railroad and Utility Rate Regulation." *Virginia Law Review* 70 (1984): 187–263.

Urofsky, Melvin I. "Myth and Reality: The Supreme Court and Protective Legislation in the Progressive Era." *Yearbook of the Supreme Court Historical Society* (1983): 53–72.

Warren, Charles. "The Progressiveness of the United States Supreme Court." *Columbia Law Review* 13 (1913): 294–313.

White, G. Edward. "The Canonization of Holmes and Brandeis: Epistemology and Judicial Reputations." *New York University Law Review* 70 (June 1995): 576–621.

Wonnell, Christopher T. "Economic Due Process and the Preservation of Competition." *Hastings Constitutional Law Quarterly* 11 (1983): 91–134.

Table of Cases

Note: This table only contains cases discussed by name in the text.

Index

About the Author

MICHAEL J. PHILLIPS is Professor Emeritus of Business Administration at Indiana University's Kelley School of Business. During his 23 years at Indiana University he wrote more than 40 law journal articles, served as editor-in-chief of the *American Business Law Journal*, and coauthored two business law texts. He is also the author of *Ethics and Manipulation in Advertising: Answering the Flawed Indictment* (Quorum Books, 1997) and *The Dilemmas of Individualism: Status, Liberty, and American Constitutional Law* (Greenwood Press, 1983).